MY HEART IS AN IDIOT

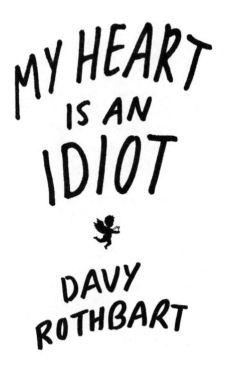

MY HEART IS AN IDIOT

DAVY ROTHBART

FARRAR, STRAUS AND GIROUX   NEW YORK

Farrar, Straus and Giroux
18 West 18th Street, New York 10011

Distributed in Canada by D&M Publishers, Inc.
Printed in the United States of America
First edition, 2012

Lyrics from "Pink Houses" courtesy of John Mellencamp.
Reprinted by permission.

Library of Congress Cataloging-in-Publication Data
Rothbart, Davy.
  My heart is an idiot / Davy Rothbart. — 1st ed.
    p.   cm.
  ISBN 978-0-374-28084-0 (alk. paper)
  1. American wit and humor.   2. Rothbart, Davy.   I. Title.

PN6165 .R68 2012
818'.602—dc23

                                        2012003821

Designed by Abby Kagan

www.fsgbooks.com

1   3   5   7   9   10   8   6   4   2

This book is a memoir. Occasionally, certain aspects—characters, locales, scenes, names of businesses, and bits of dialogue—have been altered, amalgamated, reordered, refashioned, omitted, or even fictionalized to conceal identities and preserve narrative flow. But even as small creative liberties have been taken, all of these stories are grounded in truth. Enjoy!

for the townies

I've come to feel out on the sea
These urgent lives press against me.
—WILL SHEFF

I'm way too deep into the weird life
Broken bottles and a butterfly knife.
—CARSON MELL

Sometimes I hear that song, and I'll start to sing along
And think, Man, I'd love to see that girl again . . .
—ROBERT RITCHIE

CONTENTS

MY HEART IS AN IDIOT

BIGGER AND DEAFER

When I was a kid, I had a friend down the street named Kwame whose older brother was mentally handicapped. This gave Kwame license, he felt, to make fun of other mentally handicapped folks he encountered. If anyone gave him grief for it, he'd say, "Hey, I'm just playin' around—my *brother*'s a retard." Kwame used to dropkick retard jokes right in his brother's face. "He's my brother, I'm allowed to fuck with him," he'd always explain. Of course, if anyone else unleashed the same kind of jokes, they'd get their ass beat quick.

It must've been some adjacent line of reasoning that induced me, growing up, to make fun of my mom for being deaf. She'd lost her hearing through a mysterious illness three years before I was born, and I grew up speaking sign language with her. I picked it up easily, like any kid in a bilingual household, watching my dad and my older brother speak to her in sign. My first word, I've been told, was the middle finger.

I took advantage of my mom's deafness in small ways at first. In the car, she'd be driving, and trying to lecture me about something, but I'd have the radio cranked so loud I couldn't hear her. As long as I kept the bass down, how was she to know that I was nodding along to the Fresh Prince song "I Think I Can Beat

Mike Tyson" and not to her instructions on how to clean out the gutters? She never understood the looks she got from other drivers, who must have been baffled to see a middle-aged mom tooling slowly along in an Aerostar, blasting Def Leppard at rock-concert volume. Funniest, to me, was the time we pulled up alongside a cop and I slipped in my N.W.A tape from the glove box, cued to the song "Fuck tha Police."

Then there were the stunts I pulled in grade school to impress the kids in my neighborhood. My mom would be washing dishes, her back turned to the kitchen, and I'd sneak up behind her, a few kids in tow, and yell at the top of my lungs, "Hey, *BITCH!!* Hey, you fuckin' *BITCH!!*" Then we'd all run, laughing and screaming, out of the room. The whole show lasted ten seconds, but I could've sold admission. Kids I'd never even met from a mile down the road used to knock on our door, heads hung low, talking softly as though they'd come to buy switchblades or porno mags. "Can we see you do the thing where you yell 'Bitch!' at your mom?" they'd say. After I obliged, I'd always invite them to try it themselves, but not even the bravest of them could muster the courage. "That'd just be so *wrong*," they'd say. "That'd be like calling Kwame's brother a retard."

Our house had an unusual feature—a doorbell in the dining room. The room had originally been a screened porch attached to the back of the house, but the previous owners had filled in the walls and added windows to create a one-room addition. What had once been a doorbell at the back door was now a doorbell in the middle of the house—painted over, so my mom had never noticed it. Our family dog, Prince, was trained to fetch my mom anytime someone came to the front door and knocked or rang the doorbell. To the wild entertainment of my brothers and me, we discovered that if we rang the doorbell in the dining room, Prince would start barking furiously and tug my mom by her sleeve to the front door. It was Ding-Dong Ditch from the comfort of our own house! Even my dad got in on the action. We'd watch with barely suppressed glee as my mom opened the door and peeked outside, only to be greeted by an empty front porch. "But there's nobody here," she'd say to Prince, with a confused twinge in her voice. On nights we played the game a bunch of times—okay, most nights—she thought the house was under siege by ghosts. She'd sometimes stand there for a full minute, staring out into the misty dark.

One day halfway through sixth grade, I got into major trouble at school. The music teacher, Mrs. Machida, kept getting upset at me for horsing around with my friends during class. Finally, she ordered me to report to the principal's office. I said, "Okay, fine— you fuckin' *BITCH!*" Wow, who could've known she'd turn magenta and haul me out of the room by the scruff of my neck? I'd grown cavalier with curse words, having called my mom the same thing a thousand times without a flinch.

"We're calling your parents," said the principal, Dr. Joan Burke, searing me with her death stare after Mrs. Machida told the story. I explained to them that my dad was at work and that my mom was deaf. Back then, my mom had no operator-assisted phone—that advance in technology was still years away. When she wanted to make a phone call, whether it was to order a pizza or talk to a friend for an hour, she needed me or one of my brothers to translate for her. "Look," I said to Mrs. Machida and Dr. Burke. "You guys want to talk to my mom, you got to wait till I get home so I can tell her what you're saying."

Tell her what you're saying. I thought about it the whole bus ride home, not sure what exactly I was about to do, but sure I was about to do it. The phone was ringing as I walked in the door.

"Hello?"

"Davy? It's Dr. Burke. Can you put your mother on, please?"

I tracked down my mom and told her the principal of my school was on the phone. "What does she want?" my mom asked me.

I shrugged and flashed a mystified look.

My mom picked up the receiver. "Hello, this is Barbara," she said. She passed it back to me.

Dr. Burke said, "Okay, Davy, you need to tell your mom that there's a serious situation based on your behavior in Mrs. Machida's class today. Does she already know about what happened?"

"Um, naw."

"You need to tell her there's a serious situation we need to discuss with her. Your situation. That *language* was used. Unacceptable language. And that if this kind of behavior occurs again, there will be serious consequences. Suspension or expulsion."

"Okay," I said. "Hold on. Let me tell her all that."

I held the phone low and started signing to my mom, keeping my voice at a whisper so she could still read my lips without Dr. Burke hearing me. "Dr. Burke wants you to know about something that happened today at school." I paused. "It was . . . during recess. Some kids, they . . . they were torturing a butterfly. They were pulling its wings off. And I jumped in the middle of them and I saved the butterfly." Who knows where this shit was coming from? A dream? A demented episode of *3-2-1 Contact*? "The butterfly . . ." I went on, ". . . it was pink. It was from Madagascar. It was the music teacher's pet, Mrs. Machida. She told Dr. Burke, and Dr. Burke thought you should know. But she has to go, she's really late for her dentist's appointment. It's a super-important dentist's appointment." I said to Dr. Burke, "Okay, here's my mom," and passed the phone back to her, praying for the best. But after faithfully translating thousands of calls for her, how could she have guessed that the train had finally jumped the tracks?

"That's a *wonderful* story," my mom said. "Thank you very

much for your call. And please thank the music teacher for passing word along. Take care now. Here's Davy." She handed the phone back to me.

"See you tomorrow, Dr. Burke," I said quickly.

"Wait, what did your mom say about 'wonderful'?"

"She was being sarcastic. I'm in for the whupping of my life."

I hung up in a hurry, my heart booming. The narrow escape should've taught me a lesson. That should've been it—one and done—the kind of trick you retire immediately, and count your blessings for. But it wasn't. It was more like winning big on your first visit to a casino. It was a gateway drug. It was a call to arms. It was an awakening.

I realized, in the days and weeks that followed, that helping my mom with phone calls, which had always been a burdensome chore, could be more like a *Choose Your Own Adventure* book. My mom's friends—weirdly, perhaps, to her—began to make odd suggestions, like that she take my brothers and me to Cedar Point, the amusement park, or that she rent Eddie Murphy's *Delirious*. My dad, calling home before he left work, often requested that my mom pick up a bag of Soft Batch chocolate chip cookies from the store. Anytime an exchange grew dicey, I'd tell my mom that the person on the other end of the line suddenly had to go. "That's so bizarre," my mom said one night after a call had ended abruptly. "Who schedules a dentist appointment at eight p.m. on a Sunday?"

Then, when summer hit, it occurred to me that crossing the wires on my translations was Grapefruit League ball. The truth was, I didn't need a real person on the other end of the line. One afternoon I asked my mom if I could go to my friend Mike Kozura's house to spend the night with a bunch of other friends, and she said no way—Mike lived alone with his dad, and she knew his dad was out of town for two weeks. Protesting her verdict would've been useless, so a couple of hours later, I gave my new tactics a trial run. I was helping my mom mop up some backed-up drain water in the basement, when, out of the blue, I dropped the mop and dashed upstairs, as though the phone was ringing. I took the receiver off the hook and went back down to get her. I told her that my friend Donald Chin's mom was on the line. "She wants to talk to you," I said.

We clomped upstairs, and while the phone started to bark that angry buzz that comes from leaving it off the hook too long, my mom said hello to Mrs. Chin, then passed the phone back to me. For a half minute I nodded my head, pretending to listen, saying things like, "Cool!" "I understand," "Thanks so much," and "That sounds great," and at last explained to my mom that Mrs. Chin wanted her to know that she'd agreed to stay the night at Mike's house to chaperone the party. Mrs. Chin, I told her, had offered to host the sleepover at her house, but some of the kids were afraid of their pet python and boa constrictor. The Chins really had these snakes; my mom had seen them. It had taken me all afternoon to conjure up just the right vivid, walloping fact that would blot out the fictions in its shadow. I handed my mom the phone and she spoke into it, already sold hook, line, and sinker. "Thank you so much," she said, as the phone kept buzzing. "I really appreciate that. You know, I'd invite all the boys over here, but the basement's all flooded and the house is a complete mess." An unexpected low, sinking feeling overcame me as my mom went on, chatting up Mrs. Chin about her other kids, the Chins' family restaurant, and some local school board brouhaha. I felt like Oppenheimer, both thrilled by and afraid of the awesome power of my new, terrible weapon.

All of a sudden, my little brother, Peter, popped into the room. He sized things up for a second—my mom yammering away into the buzzing receiver. "What the hell's going on?" he demanded.

"Mom thinks she's talking to Donald Chin's mom. I had to do it so I could go to Mike Kozura's house tonight. I'll kill you if you tell."

The genius of it made Peter smile. "Then I'm coming, too."

"You can't! It's *my* friends."

"Want me to tell? I'll tell."

My mom, done talking, was passing the phone back to me.

"Okay, fine," I said to Peter. "But this is bullshit." I put the phone to my ear and pretended to talk to Mrs. Chin. Then I told my mom that Mrs. Chin suggested I bring Peter along.

"That's a great idea," my mom said into the empty phone. "I'll drop them off in an hour."

"Wait," I told my mom, before hanging up. "Mrs. Chin wants to know if you can stop on the way and pick up some Soft Batch chocolate chip cookies."

That was the beginning; it was also the beginning of the end. The phone started "ringing" all the time—Mrs. Chin, hosting another sleepover; a teacher asking me to bring twenty bucks to school the next day for a field trip; an elderly neighbor asking if I could help her move boxes when I was supposed to be doing homework (really I was at the arcade playing Gauntlet). The phone was like a magic wand—every day I was creating new, alternate realities for my mom. I'd been acting as her ears my whole life, and she'd learned to trust me and rely on me. Whatever I told her I was hearing through the phone, she took as the golden truth. The only limits seemed to be the boundaries of my imagination.

But it didn't last long. My brother Peter took up the game, too, and we began to fight viciously about each other's technique—we each felt that the other was being too clumsy and over-the-top, and that we'd get found out and our fantastic potion would be gone. Soon enough, our older brother got into the act, and at that point we all kind of went nuts, abusing the phone trick like a stolen credit card you try and max out before it goes dead.

It went dead on my watch. My mom was on the phone, thinking she was talking to my dad, who was visiting his sister in

Atlanta. My dad, as I wove it, was trying to convince her to buy me this elastic net from a sports catalog that you could pitch a baseball into, and have the net fling it back to you. "It just doesn't make sense," she kept saying to the buzzing receiver. "Honey, it costs *seventy-nine dollars*. He can go to the schoolyard and pitch into the backstop. We just don't have the money." But my dad was insistent. He beseeched her to make the purchase. After all, he pointed out in my favor, hadn't I worked my butt off in school the past year? Hadn't I worked hard around the house? I deserved a special reward, right? Hadn't I . . . hadn't I . . . *saved a pink butterfly from cruel hands of evil*?

It was at that exact moment that my dad—my real dad—walked in the front door, home from his trip two days early. The look on my mom's face was a look of such profound shock and confusion—think Socrates at the San Dimas Mall—that I immediately began to cry. All my feelings of betrayal and shame poured out of me and I spent the next hour and a half in tears, lined up next to my brothers on the floor of the dining room like three broken jailbirds hauled back in after an escape attempt gone rotten. My mom was furious—and maybe at the same time a bit dazzled by the extent of our chutzpah and ingenuity. She slammed us and stretched us until every invented phone call had been dragged out into the light. I even came clean about Mrs. Machida and Dr. Burke. My mom kept putting her head in both hands and moaning, though sometimes it seemed like she was laughing, too.

"You guys are all in more trouble than you've ever known," she said at last. "You're obviously grounded for the rest of the year. And there'll be more to it than that. I might need some time to dream up a punishment harsh enough to fit the crime." She surveyed us. "Is there anything else you need to tell me about? I want to know now. No more surprises."

Peter's sad, weary gaze had come to rest on the doorframe between the dining room and the kitchen, where the painted-over doorbell was tucked. He raised his hand and pointed, too deflated to even sign to her.

"Wait!" my dad cried. "Don't get carried away! You got to leave us something."

So we kept the doorbell a secret, though our joy at ringing it never felt quite the same. The dog barking, and my mom quizzically staring out the front door, only reminded us of our earlier treacheries. The magic was gone.

There's a funny coda to this story. Twenty years have passed, and I've been typing this whole thing at the cabin in the woods where my mom spends her summers these days. I told her I was writing something about what it was like to grow up with a deaf mom, so all day she's been peeking over my shoulder to see what it's all about, and reading passages here and there each time I get up to put on another CD or get another beer. Still, I didn't know how she'd feel when she learned about the doorbell. Would there be something satisfying about the mystery being solved? Or would it be a disappointment? Was there, perhaps, something more powerful and alluring about the mystery itself? She'd always had such a glowing sense of wonder about those phantoms knocking at the door—to reveal the secret just now, a few minutes ago, as she sat close, reading over my shoulder, her eyes focused and glinting, a strange smile on her face, made me feel like an old silent-movie villain crushing a child's toy.

But here's what my mom just told me: "I knew. I knew about the doorbell. I knew it was your game. It was your game, but that's the thing, it was my game, too."

HUMAN SNOWBALL

On February 14, 2000, I took the Greyhound bus from Detroit to Buffalo to visit a girl named Lauren Hill. Not Lauryn Hill the singer, who did that cover of "Killing Me Softly," but another Lauren Hill, who'd gone to my high school, and now, almost ten years later, was about to become my girlfriend, I hoped. I'd seen her at a party when she was home in Michigan over the holidays, and we'd spent the night talking and dancing. Around four in the morning, when the party closed down, we'd kissed for about twelve minutes out on the street, as thick, heavy snowflakes swept around us, melting on our eyebrows and eyelashes. She'd left town the next morning, and in the six weeks since, we'd traded a few soulful letters and had two very brief, awkward phone conversations. As Valentine's Day came near, I didn't know if I should send her flowers, call her, not call her, or what. I thought it might be romantic to just show up at her door and surprise her.

I switched buses in Cleveland, and took a seat next to an ancient-looking black guy who was in a deep sleep. Twenty minutes from Buffalo, when darkness fell, he woke up, offered me a sip of whiskey from his coat pocket, and we started talking. His name was Vernon. He told me that when midnight rolled around, it was going to be his hundred-and-tenth birthday.

"A hundred and ten?" I squealed, unabashedly skeptical.

Happy to prove it, he showed me a public housing ID card from Little Rock, Arkansas, that listed his birth date as 2/15/90.

"Who was president when—"

"Benjamin Harrison," he said quickly, cutting me off before I was even done with my question, as though he'd heard it many times before. I had no clue if this was true, but he winked and popped a set of false teeth from his mouth, and in the short moment they glistened in his hand, it seemed suddenly believable that he was a hundred and ten, and not just, like, eighty-nine. His bottom gums, jutting tall, were shaped like the Prudential "Rock" and were the color of raw fish, pink and red with dark-gray speckles. The skin on his face was pulled taut around his cheekbones and eye sockets, as leathery and soft-looking as one of Satchel Paige's baseball mitts in its display case at Cooperstown.

I found myself telling Vernon all about Lauren Hill and explained how nervous I was to see her—surely he'd have some experience he could draw on to help me out. I told him I thought I was taking a pretty risky gamble by popping up in Buffalo unannounced. Things were either going to be really fucking awesome or really fucking weird, and I figured I'd probably know which within the first couple of minutes I saw her. Vernon, it turned out, was in a vaguely similar situation. After a century-plus of astonishingly robust health, he'd been ailing the past eighteen months, and before he kicked off he wanted to make amends with his great-granddaughter, who he was the closest to out of all of his relatives. But, he admitted, he'd let her down so many times—with the drinking, the drugs, and even stealing her money and kitchen appliances—that she might not be willing to let him past the front door. Twice he used my cell phone to try calling her but nobody answered. So much for sage advice.

We both got quiet and brooded to ourselves as the bus rolled off the freeway ramp and wound its way through empty downtown streets, lined with soot-sprayed mounds of snow and ice. Buffalo in winter is a bleak Hoth-like wasteland, and the only sign of life I saw was a pair of drunks who'd faced off in front of an adult bookstore and begun to fight, staggering like zombies. One of them had a pink stuffed animal and was clubbing the other in the face with it. A steady snow began to fall, and I felt a wave of desperate sorrow crash over me. Whatever blind optimism I'd had about the night and how Lauren Hill might receive me had been lost somewhere along the way (maybe at the rest stop in Erie, Pennsylvania, in the bathroom stall with shit smeared on the walls). The trip, I realized now, was a mistake, but at the same time I knew that the only thing to do was to go ahead with my fucked-up plan anyway and go surprise Lauren, because once you're sitting there and you've got a needle in your hands, what else is there to do but poke your finger and see the blood?

At the Greyhound station, a sort-of friend of mine named Chris Henderson was there to pick me up in a shiny black Ford Explorer with only four hundred miles on the odometer but its front end and passenger side bashed to shit. "You get in a rollover?" I asked him, after hopping in up front.

"Naw, I just boosted this bitch yesterday in Rochester, it was already like this. Who's your friend?"

"This is Vernon. He's gonna ride with us, if that's cool. In a few hours it's gonna be his hundred-and-tenth birthday."

"No shit?" Chris glanced in the rearview and nodded to Vernon, in the backseat. "Fuck if I make it to twenty-five," he said, gunning it out of the lot.

Chris was the kind of guy who always made these sorts of claims, hoping, perhaps, to sound tougher, but really he was a sweetheart with a swashbuckler's twinkle who was rarely in serious danger and probably had decades of fun times ahead of him, if he could stay out of prison. He had pale white skin, a rash of acne on his neck, and his own initials carved into his buzz-cut hair in several places. He looked Canadian and sounded Canadian and was indeed a Canuck—he'd grown up on the meanest street of Hamilton, Ontario, and, as he'd told me more than a few times, he and his older brother had stolen seventy-six cars before finally getting caught when Chris was nineteen. Chris did the time—three years—while his brother skated. Then Chris moved in with an uncle in Charlotte and had gotten a job as an airline reservationist, which was how I'd met him a couple of years before. He had a gregarious nature, and after we'd found ourselves in deep conversation while I was buying tickets over the phone, he'd come to Chicago a few weekends in a row to pursue his dream of becoming a stand-up comic and stayed on my couch. The problem was that he was absolutely sorry as a stand-up comic, just woefully bad. I saw him perform once, at the Improv Olympic at Clark and Addison, and it was one of the hardest, saddest things I've ever had to watch—someone's dream unraveling and being chopped dead with each blast of silence that followed his punch lines. But where I would've been destroyed by this, Chris was over it by the next morning, and freshly chipper. He told me the lesson he'd learned was that he needed to focus on his strengths, and he knew himself to be an ace car thief. Before long, he'd moved to Buffalo and was working at his older brother's "mechanic" shop. When I called and told him I was coming to town, and explained why, he told me he actually knew Lauren Hill, because for a while he'd been a regular at Freighter's, the bar where she worked, though he doubted she knew him by name, and anyway, he said, he wasn't allowed in there anymore because he'd left twice without paying when he'd realized at the end of the night that he'd left his cash at home. "I'll tell you one thing," he said. "That girl's beautiful. Every guy who wanders into that damn bar, they leave in love with her."

Vernon had asked if he could roll with us for a bit while he kept trying to reach his great-granddaughter. If nothing else, he suggested, we could drop him off later at the YMCA and he'd track her down the next morning. He sat quietly in the backseat, looking out the window, while we cruised toward the east side of town, running every sixth light, Chris catching me up on some of his recent escapades, half-shouting to make himself heard over the blare of a modern-rock station out of Niagara Falls, Ontario, that slipped in and out of range. "Hey, check this out," he said. He reached beneath the driver's seat and passed me a fat roll of New York Lottery scratch tickets. "You can win like ten grand!" he cried. "Scratch some off if you want."

"Where'd you get these, man?"

"Get this—they were in the car when I got it! Just sitting in the backseat! I already scratched off some winners, like forty bucks' worth." He passed me a tin Buffalo Sabres lighter from his coat pocket, its sharp bottom edge gummed with shavings from the tickets he'd scratched. "Go on," he said, "make us some money."

I tore off a long band of tickets and handed them back to Vernon, along with a quarter from the center console, and Chris cranked up the volume until the windows shook and piloted us through his frozen, desolate town toward Lauren Hill's apartment, singing along to the radio, while me and Vernon scratched away: *"You make me come. / You make me complete. / You make me completely miserable."* I looked up and saw him grinning at me and nodding his head, as if to ask, "Doesn't this song fucking rock?" I grinned and nodded back, because yes, in a crazy way it kind of did. A barely perceptible but definitely perceptible drip of hopefulness had started to seep back into the night.

No one was home at Lauren's place; in fact, the lights were out in all six apartments in her building even though it was only seven thirty.

Chris cracked his window and flicked a pile of my losing scratch tickets through like cigarette butts. "She's probably at the bar," he said. "She works every night, and she's there hangin' out even when she ain't workin'. We'll go find her." He whipped the Explorer around the corner and we fishtailed a bit in the gathering snow.

A mile down, five tiny side streets spilled together at a jagged-shaped intersection, and from its farthest corners, two squat and battered bars glared across at each other like warring crabs, panels of wood nailed over the windows and painted to match the outside walls, and one neon beer sign hanging over each door—Yuengling and Budweiser—as though they were the names of the bars.

Chris pulled over and pointed to the bar with the Yuengling sign. "That's Freighter's," he said. "See if she's in there. And if she is, see if you can call off the dogs so I can get in there, too—we'll all have a drink."

I jumped out and took a few steps, then had a thought and went back to the truck and asked Vernon if he wanted to come in with me. I was nervous to see Lauren, and afraid she would find something creepy and stalker-like about me taking a Greyhound bus a few hundred miles to make an uninvited appearance on Valentine's Day. If I rolled in there with Vernon, it seemed to me, his presence might help defuse any initial tension.

Vernon was a little unsteady on his feet, from either the whiskey he'd been sipping or the quilt of fresh snow lining the street paired with his ludicrously advanced age, so I held him by the arm as we crossed the intersection. A plume of merriment rose in my chest that was six parts the gentle glow of heading into any bar on a cold, snowy night and four parts the wonderful, unpredictable madness of having a hundred-and-ten-year-old man I'd just met on the Greyhound bus as my wingman. I heaved open the heavy door to Freighter's, letting out a blast of noise and hot, smoky air, and once Vernon shuffled past, I followed him in.

Inside, it was so dark and hot and loud it took me a few seconds to get my bearings. People shouted over the deafening thump of a jukebox and the thunderous rattle of empty bottles being tossed into a metal drum. Directly overhead, two hockey games roared from a pair of giant TVs. It smelled like someone had puked on a campfire. All of which is to say, just the way I liked it, and just like the 8-Ball Saloon back in Michigan where Lauren had worked before moving to Buffalo for school.

A hulking, tattooed guy on a stool was asking me and Vernon for our IDs. I flashed him mine, while Vernon pulled out the same fraying ID card he'd showed me earlier. The doorman plucked it from his hand, inspected it, and passed it back, shaking his head. "Nope," he shouted over the din. "I need a driver's license or state ID." At first I laughed, thinking he was just fucking with us, but then I saw he was serious.

I leaned to his ear and protested, "But he's a hundred and ten years old! Look at the guy!"

The doorman shook his head and pointed at the exit. It was useless to try to reason with him over the din, and I figured once I found Lauren, she'd help me get Vernon and Chris in.

"Wait in the truck," I shouted in Vernon's ear. "I'll come get you guys in a few minutes."

He nodded and slipped out into the cold. I took a few steps further in. The place was packed, mostly older, rugged-looking dudes—factory workers, construction workers, bikers, and their equally rugged-looking girlfriends—with a sprinkling of younger indie kids and punk rockers mixed in. All of a sudden I caught sight of Lauren Hill behind the bar and my heart twisted like a wet rag—she had her back turned to me and was getting her shoulders thoroughly massaged by a tall, skinny, dark-haired guy in a sleeveless shirt, dozens of tattoos slathered on his arms. My first thought was to immediately leave, but I also knew that would be silly—this was surely just some guy who worked with her, not a true threat. The guy finished his little rubdown and they both turned back to the bar. Lauren's beauty made my stomach lurch. She had long straight hair, dyed black, big, expressive eyes, and an enormous, bright smile. I made my way over, feeling stupid for having spent the last eight hours on buses without the foresight to dream up a single witty or romantic thing to say when I greeted her.

I edged between a few guys at the bar and pulled a ten-dollar bill from my back pocket. When Lauren came close, I called out, "Can I get a Bell's Amber?"—a local Michigan brew that wasn't served in Buffalo—my spontaneous, wilted stab at a joke. Even Chris Henderson could've conjured up something funnier.

She looked at me and the smile drained off her face. "Davy? Oh my God, what the hell are you doing here?" There was no way to hug across the bar; instead, Lauren offered what seemed to me a slightly awkward and tepid two-handed high five.

I slapped her hands and said, "I came here to surprise you," feeling suddenly lost in space.

"Oh, that's so awesome," she said, sounding possibly genuine. "But what are you doing in Buffalo?"

"No, I came to Buffalo because I wanted to see you." I shrugged and heard the next words tumble out of my mouth, even as I instantly regretted them. "Happy Valentine's Day!"

Just then, a barback rushing past with a tub full of empty glasses crashed into her, knocking her a couple of feet to the side. Now she was within shouting range of a few guys further along the bar, and they started barking out their drink orders. She leaned back toward me and hollered, "I'm sorry, Monday nights are always like this, and we're short a guy. Can you come back later? It'll be less insane."

"Sure, no problem," I said, putting both hands up idiotically for another slap of hands, but she'd already turned and was cranking the caps off a row of Yuengling bottles. I slowly lowered my hands, waited another fifteen seconds or so until she happened to glance my way, and gave her a little wave. She flashed a polite smile in return, and I whirled and slunk out the door, utterly defeated, making a promise to myself not to come back later in the night unless she called my phone in the next few hours and begged me to. It was just past eight o'clock. I'd give her till midnight.

"Should we come inside?" Chris asked as I climbed in the backseat; Vernon had made it back to the car and was up riding shotgun.

"It's kind of busy in there. Let's get some grub and come back later."

"Well, how'd it go?" asked Vernon, once we were moving again.

"Not too bad. I don't know. Not too good, either." I told them what had gone down. They both tried to reassure me that Lauren was probably really excited I was in town, but that it's always hard when someone pops in to see you and you're busy at work. I granted them that, but it still seemed like she could've maybe flipped me the keys to her apartment, in case I wanted to take a nap or chill out and watch a movie until she got home. Or really done anything to give me the sense that she was happy I'd rolled in.

"Don't worry, man," Vernon said. "Trust me, it'll be cool." This from the guy who was now using Chris's cell phone—and had been the whole time I was in the bar—to try to reach his great-granddaughter, to no avail. He was hoping we could stop by her house, which was on the west side of town, about a twenty-minute drive.

"I'm down," I said. "Chris?"

"Rock 'n' roll," said Chris. "We can take the Kensington." He pumped up the Green Day song on the radio, zoomed through side streets to the on-ramp for an expressway, and looped the Explorer back toward the lights of downtown, slapping the steering wheel along to the music. Vernon tore off a few scratch tickets for himself, passed me the rest of the roll, and we both went to work.

Each losing ticket I scratched out socked me a little blow to the heart. I couldn't help but feel that trying to find the right girl was like trying to get rich playing the lottery—both were games for suckers. And why didn't scratch cards just have a single box that told you if you'd won or not? Why the slow build, all the teasing hoopla of Tic-Tac-Toe game boards and Wheels of Fortune? You kept thinking you were getting close and then, once again: Loser. All of the unanswered questions made my head hurt: Had I blown things by coming to Buffalo and putting unfair pressure on Lauren Hill? Should I have simply come on any day other than Valentine's Day? Had she meant all of the things she'd said in her letters? Some of it? None of it? And what would be the best way to salvage the night when I went back to the bar? (Because, face it, I was headed back there later whether she called me or not.) A small heap of losing tickets gathered at my feet.

"Holy shit!" cried Vernon from up front. "I think we got a winner!"

"How much?" said Chris, suddenly alert, punching the radio off.

"Wait a second. Did I win? Yeah, I did. Ten bucks!"

"Not bad." Chris nodded enthusiastically. "That's yours to keep," he told Vernon. "You guys just keep on scratching."

"You bet your goddamn ass," said Vernon, still believing a bigger payday was near.

His minor stroke of glory made me glad, but to me, winning ten bucks instead of ten grand was like getting a drunken kiss on the corner of the mouth from a stranger at the bar that you'll never see again. What I really wanted was to spend the night in Lauren Hill's arms, kissing her and holding her tight; to wake up with her at dawn, make love once or twice, and walk hand in hand through the woodsy park I'd glimpsed by her apartment, which by morning, I imagined—if it kept snowing the way it was now—would be transformed into a place of quiet and exquisite majesty. That was my wish. Anything less I'd just as soon chuck out the window.

From the outside, Vernon's great-granddaughter's house looked like a haunted mansion out of *Scooby-Doo*. It sat on a wide section of an abandoned half-acre lot overgrown with weeds, brambles, and the remaining debris from houses that had been leveled on either side. Across the street, TVs flickered dimly from the windows of a low-rise housing project, and at the end of the block a closed-down liquor store with both doors missing gaped like a sea cave, open to the elements. As we pulled up in front, Vernon looked back at me and said, "Hey, would you come inside with me?" It was my turn to be wingman.

I followed him up the front walk and up three stairs to the porch, and he lifted the enormous, rusted horseshoe knocker on the front door and let it land with a heavy thud. We waited. I watched snowflakes touch down on the Explorer's windshield and instantly melt. The knocker squeaked as he lifted it again, but then, from somewhere deep in the house, came a woman's voice, "I hear you, I'm coming."

Her footsteps padded near and Vernon edged back until he was practically hiding behind me. "Who's there?" the woman called.

I looked over to Vernon, waiting for him to respond. He had the look of a dog who'd strewn trash through the kitchen and knew he was about to be punished. "It's your granddaddy," he said at last, weakly.

"Who?"

"Vernon Wallace." He kicked the porch concrete. "Your great-granddaddy."

The door opened a couple of inches and a woman's face

appeared, eyebrows raised, hair wrapped in a towel above her head. She was in maybe her early fifties. Through a pair of oversized glasses, she took a long look at Vernon, sighed, shook her head, and said, "Granddaddy, what're you doing up here in the wintertime?" As he cleared his throat and began to respond, she said, "Hold on, let me get my coat." The door closed and for a half minute Vernon painted hieroglyphics with the toe of his old shoe in a pyramid of drifting snow, looking suddenly frail and ancient. Exhaust panted from the Explorer's tailpipe out on the street, and I could make out the hard-rock bass line rattling its windows but didn't recognize the song.

After a moment, the door opened again and the woman stepped out and joined us on the front porch, hair still tucked up in a towel. Over a matching pink sweatsuit she wore a puffy, oversized, black winter coat, and her feet, sockless, were stuffed into a pair of unlaced low-top Nikes. She gave Vernon a big, friendly hug and said, "I love you, Granddaddy, it's good to see you," and then turned to me and said, "Hi there, I'm Darla Kenney," and once I'd introduced myself she said, "Well, it's good to meet you, I appreciate you bringing Vernon by." She turned back to face him and crossed her arms. "What you been drinking tonight, Granddaddy?"

He flinched slightly but didn't respond.

"Listen," she said, "I love you, but I ain't got no money. You know my whole situation. You're gonna have to stay with your friend here, 'cause I can't just invite you in."

Vernon nodded deeply, unable to meet her gaze. "I was just hoping we could spend time together," he said, growing sorrowful.

"We can!" she said. "But not tonight. I got all kinds of shit to deal with tonight. I can't even get the damn car started. You got to learn to call people ahead of time so they know you coming." She softened. "How long you gonna stay in town for?"

Vernon shrugged. "A week or two?"

"Okay, then. Look, you give me a call tomorrow, or the next day, and we'll go for a drive, we'll play cards at Calvin's. He know you're in town?"

Vernon shook his head.

Darla looked past us, to the Explorer out on the street, its motor revving, Chris Henderson behind the wheel, slapping his hands on the dash and crooning to himself. "That your friend?" she asked me.

"Yeah. That's Chris."

Darla tugged her coat closed and fought with the zipper. "Hey, listen," she said. "I got cables. Think I can get a jump?"

Ten minutes later, Chris was shouting instructions to me, banging under the hood of Darla Kenney's '84 Lincoln Continental with a wrench while I pounded the gas and jammed the ignition. Is there any sound more full of frustration and futility than a car that won't start when you turn the key? Click-click-click-click-click. All I could think of was Lauren Hill's dismayed expression in the bar when she'd first seen me.

"Okay, cut it!" Chris shouted. I felt his weight on the engine block as he bobbed deep within. A ping and a clatter. "Now try."

Click-click-click-click.

"Cut it!"

I heard Chris disconnecting the jumper cables, and then he dropped the hood with a magnificent crash. "I'll tell you what's happening, ma'am," he said to Darla, who stood in the street, looking on, still in her unlaced sneakers and coat with a towel on her head. "Your battery cable's a little frizzy, down by the starter relay. We get this in the shop, it's nothing—ten minutes, you're on your way. Tonight, though, no tools? Ain't gonna be easy." He passed her the jumper cables and put a consoling hand on her shoulder. "I'm really sorry. Usually I can get anything moving." I was touched by his level of kindness—if this was how sweetly he treated a woman he'd just met, it was hard to imagine there was anything he wouldn't do for his friends.

I climbed from the car and joined Chris and Darla. Vernon was sitting in the Explorer, keeping warm up front, scratching off lottery tickets.

"Well, it was nice of you to try," said Darla. She looked back and forth between us. "How do you guys know my granddaddy, anyhow?"

I wasn't sure how to answer—I felt it might incriminate Vernon (and me) if I explained that we'd bonded over a flask of whiskey on the Greyhound bus. Instead, I gave her a less comprehensive version of the truth. "Well, we met on a Greyhound bus once; we were row-mates." The word "once"—tossed in there—made it seem like this was years ago.

But Darla saw through it. "Oh, okay, when was that?"

"Well. Tonight."

She weighed this for a second. "Is he staying with you guys?"

"I don't know," I said. "I think he was saying something about the Y." The way my awesome surprise had gone over with Lauren Hill, I'd probably end up in the next bunk.

"I stay with my brother," Chris piped up. "But we got a cot at the garage, right around the corner. It's heated. I mean, that's where we work. Shit, he can stay in my room and I'll stay on the cot."

"We're not gonna leave him on the street," I said. I meant to be reassuring, but realized a second later that my words could be taken as an accusation.

Darla toyed with the clamps of the jumper cables in her hands; the metal jaws, squeaking open and shut, looked like angry, puppet-sized gators shit-talking back and forth. As little as she seemed to want to deal with Vernon, she also seemed aware that he was her responsibility as much as anyone else's, and she wasn't ready to ditch him with two white kids he'd met an hour before. "Here's the thing," she said. "He can't stay at my house, and I got no money to give him right now. But I've got a tenant that owes me four hundred fifty dollars—I was gonna stop there tonight anyhow. We get some of that money together, I'll give my granddaddy half and put him up a week at the Front Park Inn."

Me and Chris nodded. "That'll work," I said. Fuck the Y—maybe at the Front Park Inn there'd be an extra bed for me.

Darla went to the Lincoln, heaved open the back door, and tossed the jumper cables on the floor behind the driver's seat. She turned back toward us. "Can I get a ride over to this house with you guys? It's really close, like ten, fifteen blocks from here. Larchmont, just the other side of Lake Drive."

"Ain't no thing," said Chris.

I asked Darla if she wanted to get dressed first, at least pull on some socks, but she was already climbing into the backseat of Chris's Explorer and sliding over to make room for me. "We're just going and coming right back," she said. "Come on, hop in."

The snow kept falling. On the way to her tenant's house, Darla filled me in on a few things while Chris blasted music up front. It both irritated and charmed me that he kept the radio going max-force no matter who was in the car with him. Even when he'd stayed with me in Chicago all those weekends, every time we were in my truck he'd reach over and crank the volume. Vernon rode shotgun, dozing, the dwindling spool of lottery tickets in his lap.

Darla had four children, she told me. She'd had the same job—quality control at a metal-stamping plant—for almost thirty years, and as she was careful with her money, she'd been able to buy homes for each of her children in nearby West Buffalo neighborhoods. "Nothing fancy," she said, "but a roof over their heads." One daughter had split up with her husband two years before and moved to Tampa, Florida. Darla rented out one half of their house to a friend from work, and the ex had stayed on in the other half, though Darla had begun to charge him three hundred bucks a month in rent, which was more than fair, she said, and less than what she could get from somebody else. But her daughter's ex, whose name was Anthony, and who was, overall, a decent, hardworking man, had fallen behind—he still owed her for January, and now half of February. It was time for her to pay a visit, Darla said.

She coached Chris through a few turns. We crossed a big four-lane road, and beyond the neighborhood deteriorated, making Darla's street look regal by comparison. Every third house was shuttered or burnt out. On a side street I glimpsed four guys loading furniture out of a squat apartment building into a U-Haul trailer. "Okay," said Darla, "take this right and it's the first one on the right."

We pulled up in front of a tiny, ramshackle house with cardboard taped over a missing window and its gutters hanging off, dangling to the ground. Still, the dusting of snow softened its features, and there were hopeful signs of upkeep—Christmas lights draped over a hedge by the side door, and a pair of well-stocked bird feeders, swinging from low branches in the front yard, which had attracted a gang of sickly but grateful-looking squirrels.

"I'll be back in a couple minutes," said Darla, stepping gingerly down to the snow-filled street. She closed her door, picked her way across the lawn to the side of the house, knocked a few times, and disappeared inside.

Chris's cell phone rang and he answered it and had a quick, angry spat with his older brother. He'd explained to me that he'd been in hot water with his brother all month. His brother had a rule that anytime Chris boosted a car he was supposed to get it immediately to their shop to be dismantled (or at least stripped of its VIN number) and resold. Chris admitted that he had a habit of keeping stolen cars for a while and driving around in them to impress girls. A couple of weeks before, another guy who worked with them had landed a cherry-red PT Cruiser in Pittsburgh, and Chris had whipped it around Buffalo over Super Bowl week-end while his brother was out of town. His brother found out, of course, and had been hounding him about it ever since. Now he seemed to be giving Chris grief for driving the Explorer; I could hear his brother on the other end of the phone, shouting at him to bring it back to base. "Fuck that motherfucker!" Chris shouted, hanging up and slamming his phone on the dash. "Who the fuck does he think he is?" To me, there was something ecstatically rich, appealing, and sonorous in someone who acted so gangsta but sounded so Canadian; at the same time, I could see in the rearview mirror that Chris's eyes had gone teary, and I felt a guilty and despairing tug of responsibility for dragging him around town and sticking him deeper into his brother's dog-house.

The shouting roused Vernon from his mini-nap, and without missing a beat he resumed his dedicated work scratching off the squares of each lottery ticket. A heaviness had settled over him, as though he understood that he'd become a burden on his great-granddaughter and other people in his life. He inspected a ticket after scratching it off, sighed greatly, and let it slip from his fingers. We were like some sad-sack version of the Three Musketeers—loveless, homeless, and, if Chris didn't patch things up with his brother, soon jobless.

In the front yard of the house next door, a band of ragtag little kids wrestled in the snow and hurled snowballs at parked cars and each other, shouting, "I'ma blast you, nigga!" The oldest of them, a boy around ten, was trying to rally the rest of them through the early stages of building a snowman. I powered my window down a few inches so I could hear his pitch. "Start with a giant snowball," he said breathlessly, as he worked on packing one together, then placed it on the ground. "Then we keep rolling this thing, and rolling it, and rolling it, until it's as big as a house, and then we'll have the biggest snowman in all of Buffalo!" The other kids dove in to help him, and they slid around the yard, accumulating more snow, then breaking off chunks accidentally as they pushed in opposite directions. Everyone shouted instructions at everyone else: "Roll it that way!" "Get those Doritos off it!" "You're fucking it up!"

Lauren Hill had been about the same age—nine or ten—when her dad was killed by a drunk driver. She'd told me the story in the most recent letter she'd sent me—her mom had appeared at the park where Lauren was playing with her friends and pulled her away and told her the news. Even though that had happened in summertime, I couldn't help but picture a fifth-grade Lauren Hill building a snowman with her neighborhood pals, her mom galloping up, crazed and wild-eyed, and dragging her away to a sucky, dadless future in a grim apartment complex near the Detroit airport, populated by creepy neighbors and a steady stream of her mom's low-life live-in boyfriends. When you first got involved with any girl who'd been punctured by that kind of sadness, I'd learned, you had to be extra-cautious about flooding them with goodness and light. A gentle and steady kindness appealed to them, but too much love straight out of the gate was uncomfortable, even painful, and impossible to handle. I felt like a fucking idiot for coming to Buffalo and freaking Lauren out.

"Hey, Vernon," I said, leaning between the front seats. "Did you ever get married?"

"Yes I did. Wanda May. Fifty years we were married." He paused, passing a scratch-off to Chris. "I think this one wins a free ticket." Then, to me, with a sudden touch of melancholy, "She died in 1964."

"Damn. That's way before I was born."

Vernon slipped his whiskey bottle out, touched it to his lips, and peeked back at me. "You want some advice?" he said.

"Definitely."

"You should marry this girl you came to see. Marry her right away. Tomorrow, if you want. You don't know how much time you get with someone, so you might as well start right away."

"The problem is, it's not up to me. She gets a say."

"It's more up to you than you think."

I let that sink in, watching the kids in the neighbors' yard. Their snowman's round trunk had quickly swelled from the size of a soccer ball to the size of a dorm fridge. It took all of them, pushing and shouldering it together, to keep it rolling across the lawn. Finally they ran out of juice and came to a stop, slumping against their massive boulder of snow, tall as the oldest boy. There seemed to be two opinions about what to do next. The boy in charge wanted to go down the street and recruit his older cousin and some of his cousin's friends to keep pushing. But one tiny girl pointed out that the snowman had already gotten too big to add a middle and a top. Also, she suspected that if the boy's cousin and his friends glimpsed the half-built snowman, all they'd want to do is destroy it. "We made it, we should get to knock it down," she said.

Vernon passed his bottle to Chris, who took a long gulp and passed it back to me. I drained the last of the whiskey down, and watched as the kids gave their big, round heap of snow a pair of stick arms, then collaborated on the face—two deep holes for eyes, a Dorito for a nose, and, strangely, no mouth.

By now, Chris and Vernon were watching them, too. "You want some more advice?" Vernon asked.

"Yes, I do."

"Okay. Don't outlive your wife."

The oldest kid pulled off his red winter hat and plopped it on top of the snowman's rounded head, just above the face, and at last the whole crew of munchkins stood back to silently admire their handiwork, reverential and proud as Boy Scouts at the raising of a flag. It was surely the saddest, fattest, strangest, and most beautiful snowman I'd ever seen.

After a few long moments, there was the sound of voices, as Vernon's great-granddaughter Darla banged her way through the side door of the house she owned. The towel on her head had been replaced by a black baseball cap, and she was trailed by two others in heavy winter coats with their hoods pulled up. Her appearance seemed to somehow release the kids in the neighbors' yard from their spell. The oldest boy let out a mighty cry and charged the snowman—he plowed into its shoulder, driving loose its left arm and a wedge of its face, before crashing to the ground. The other kids followed, flailing with arms and feet, and even using the snowman's own arms to beat its torso quickly to powdery rubble.

Darla and her two companions crossed the yard toward us.

Vernon turned to me and Chris. "That's how long I was married, feels like," he said, eyes blazing. "As long as that snowman was alive."

We took on two new passengers—Anthony, the ex-husband of Darla's daughter who owed Darla all the back rent, and his shy, pregnant girlfriend, Kandy. They squeezed in back with me and Darla and we circled around the block and headed back the way we'd come. Our next destination was a Chinese restaurant where Anthony worked as a dishwasher, on the east end of town, not far from Lauren Hill's bar. Anthony told us that his car was dead, too; apparently, one of the few operational vehicles in all of Buffalo was Chris's Explorer, which he'd driven off the lot of a body shop in Rochester the night before.

Anthony and Darla continued a conversation they must have started in the house. Anthony—dark-skinned, small and compact, with a thin mustache, roughly forty years old—spoke softly but had a thoughtful, commanding presence. He was explaining why he hadn't quit his job, even though he hadn't been paid in a month. "Here's the thing about Mr. Liu," he said. "Last winter, business got so slow, sometimes there was no customers in there, he could've sent me home. But he knows I got bills, and I'm scheduled to work, so he gave me the hours and found shit for me to do. You know, shovel the parking lot, clean out the walk-in cooler. Sometimes he paid me just to sit on a stool in back and watch basketball. Now that he's in a pinch, business down again, how'm I just gonna walk out on him?"

"What if he goes out of business?" Darla asked. "He gonna pay you those paychecks?"

"That's what *I'm* saying," said Kandy. She sat on the far side of the backseat, deeply ensconced in the hood of her jacket; it was hard for me to get a good look at her, but she seemed no older than me or Chris, and was maybe seven months pregnant.

"We talked about that," said Anthony. "First of all, we ain't goin' out of business. It's slow every winter, Mr. Liu just had some extra costs this winter. Second of all, he do go out of business? Mr. Liu told me he's gonna sell the building and all the equipment an' shit, and he'll have plenty enough to pay me what he owe."

The general plan, it seemed, was for Anthony to ask his boss for at least a portion of his paycheck so he could turn the money over to Darla, who might then have enough to support Vernon during his visit and buy him a ticket home to Little Rock. My own plan, less noble, perhaps, was to scarf down some shrimp lo mein and ask Chris for a ride back to Freighter's. I wondered if bringing Lauren a carton of Chinese food would be a sweet gesture or just seem demented. I felt I'd lost all bearing on how to reel in her heart, and thinking about seeing Lauren again made my insides feel panicked and cramped—I was mad at her for forcing me to wrestle with so much doubt, and mad at myself for being so in love with her. I should've been shooting pool all night with the old bikers at her bar, with short breaks to make out with Lauren in the kitchen. Instead she'd cast me out into the night. At least my misery had a truckful of company.

Chris had been quiet since the phone call with his brother, but now he dropped the music a few notches, glanced back at Kandy, and said, "You having a girl or a boy?"

"A boy," she peeped.

"What you gonna name it?"

"Floyd."

"That was her granddaddy's name," Anthony offered.

Chris nodded. "I like that name. Question is, he gonna take after his mom or his dad?"

"Not his dad, I hope," Anthony said cryptically.

"Well, I'll tell you what," said Vernon. "I'm sick of these scratch tickets." Over the seat, he handed back what remained of the roll. "You guys have at it. I'm too old for this shit." His night, like mine, was not going the way he'd hoped. He reached for the radio, turned the volume back up, and sank into his seat, eyes out the window.

This was a song I knew: "What It's Like" by Everlast. Chris slid us back onto the Kensington Expressway, and the swirling snow gusted this way and that, rocking the SUV like a baby plane in turbulence. I closed my eyes and let myself sway.

> *Then you really might know what it's like.*
> *Yeah, then you really might know what it's like . . . to have*
>   *to lose.*

Mr. Liu's Chinese restaurant anchored a shambling commercial strip between a Popeye's fried-chicken joint and a defunct video store. It was called the Golden Panda, though just the right letters had burned out on the neon sign in its front window to leave *The Golden an*, which reminded me of an old favorite bit from *Sesame Street*. "Look!" I cried, rallying from the waist-deep darkness I'd slipped into, "it's the Golden An!" Everyone stared at me flatly. "You know, from *Sesame Street*?"

"Wait a second," said Chris. "I know this fucking place. My brother loves this place. He always gets takeout here. It's so fucking *nasty* but he loves it." He looked at Anthony in the rearview mirror. "I mean, no offense."

Vernon and Kandy hung back in the Explorer while me, Chris, and Darla followed Anthony inside. The place had an odd, foul, but unidentifiable smell. It had just closed for the night, and a pretty Chinese girl in her late teens was blowing out red candles on each table that I supposed had been set out for Valentine's Day, and loading an enormous tray with dirty dishes. "Hey, Anthony," she said, tired but friendly. "If you came for dinner, you better let my mom know, she's shutting down the kitchen right now." She flipped a switch for the overhead fluorescents, and as they flickered on, the restaurant's interior grew more drab and dingy.

Anthony asked the girl if her dad was still around, and the girl told him he was. "Hey, Mary, these are my friends," he said, and told us he'd be back in a minute.

"Hi, Anthony's friends," she said. "You can have a seat if you want."

"Oh," said Anthony. "Did you hear back yet?"

"Not yet," said the girl. "The admissions office, they were supposed to call or e-mail everybody last week, but they never called me. So that's not a good sign. That reminds me, I need to check my e-mail."

"Well, look, if it don't work out, you just keep on trying." Anthony pushed his way through a blue silk curtain at the back of the dining area and disappeared down a hallway.

The three of us found a table that the girl had already cleared and sat down. Darla lowered her voice and said, "That's a fine young man right there. You know, that baby, Floyd, that's not even his baby. But he's gonna raise it and take care of that baby like it is." She shook her head. "I still call him my son. And that baby will be my grandson." Then, in a near-whisper, "I hate putting the squeeze on him, but that ain't right he ain't getting paid." She eyed Mary, the owner's daughter, and said, under her breath, "This ain't the plantation. This is Buffalo!"

"I'm sure the guy'll give him some cash," I said.

As if on cue, a sudden, jarring eruption of shouting rose from deep in back. It was Anthony's voice, but the only word I could make out was "motherfucker." Soon a second voice joined the fray—Mr. Liu, no doubt, shouting back. And then a woman's voice jumped in, yelling in Chinese, shrill as a tea kettle, followed by the sound of pots and pans clattering to the floor. Mary set down her tray and rushed through the blue curtains, and Darla said, "Oh no," and leapt up and dashed after her.

Chris gave me a dismal look and sank his head to the table. "Today's retarded," he said, sounding truly pained, his voice cracking a bit. "You know what sucks?"

"Yeah," I said, as the shouting in back increased. "That old man out there, Vernon, he thinks I should marry Lauren Hill tomorrow, but I don't think she wants anything to do with me, and you know, she's probably fucking this dude at her work."

"Yeah, that does suck," said Chris. "And I'll tell you what else sucks. I am really, really, incredibly fucking hungry. I was banking on getting dinner out of this."

"Maybe it'll all boil over back there and mellow out," I suggested, and again, Anthony's timing was splendid—he came ripping through the curtain just then, shouting and cursing, Darla at his heels, tugging at his sleeve and begging him to chill out.

"Get your fucking hands off me!" he said. "Fuck that motherfucker. I'll kill that slant-eyed faggot." He stopped in his tracks, turned, and screamed full force, "Fuck you, Mr. Liu! Suck my fucking dick, you little bitch!" From in back somewhere, Mr. Liu was shouting back in Chinese. Anthony kicked over a chair, and said, "Come get some of this! You want some? Come out here and get some!" Darla grabbed his shoulders and steered him toward the front door. "Fuck this place," Anthony said, deeply aggrieved, shoving her arm away. He fought his way outside.

"Come on," said Darla to me and Chris, holding the door open. "Time to go."

Back in the Explorer, Anthony was still shouting. We sat in the lot, trying to calm him down. Kandy seemed inappropriately entertained, a strange smile on her face as she pleaded with him to explain what had happened.

"That fucker," he said, jaw clenched, breathing hard through flared nostrils. "I told him he better pay me, not the whole month he owes me, just like two weeks, and he's, like"—here Anthony mocked Mr. Liu's Chinese accent—"'I no have your money. Give me more time.' And I said, 'Fuck that. Pay me.' So then he's, like, 'I can't afford you no more. I hafta let you go.'" Anthony rubbed his face. With great anger, sadness, and shame, he said, "I didn't come all the way down here tonight to get my ass fired." He had tears in his eyes.

I saw that Darla, beside him, had tears in her eyes, too. She put her arm around Anthony and soothed him. "Okay, it'll be all right. It'll all be all right."

I caught Chris's gaze in the rearview mirror. Even his eyes were wet. Strangely enough, I realized, mine were, too. I thought of the kids we'd seen building the snowman—how blissfully carefree they'd seemed—and felt a mournful gulf open up inside me. Whatever lumps those kids were taking as they sprouted in their bleak, tundra-like ghetto had nothing on the disappointments and humiliations of adulthood.

Kandy took Anthony's hand and said, "Listen, baby. You need to take a few deep breaths. I got to show you something."

"Five fucking years," said Anthony. "You know how many times I coulda gone somewhere else? My cousin in Syracuse, he's roofing now, twenty bucks an hour. That job coulda been mine." He blasted the back of the front passenger seat with his fist and Vernon bolted upright. "Sorry, Vernon," said Anthony. He looked at the empty front room of the Golden Panda. "Five years. Chinese people don't know shit about loyalty."

"I'm sure you guys can work it out," said Kandy. Her odd smile broadened. "Vernon, come on, will you just tell 'em?"

Vernon turned the radio off and looked around, gathering our attention, wide-eyed and mysterious. Then he melted into a smile, held up a scratched-out lottery ticket, and said, "We just won two thousand dollars."

Darla immediately screamed and slapped her hands to her cheeks in astonishment. Chris's eyes bugged out of his head. Anthony turned to his girlfriend, Kandy: "Say what?"

Kandy laughed. "It's true! I scratched it off!"

Vernon handed the ticket to Chris. "Really, how it is, *you* won two thousand dollars. We were just the first ones to find out."

Everyone grew suddenly quiet, watching Chris as he brought the ticket close to check it out. He nodded slowly, gave a low whistle, and flipped it over to read the fine print on back. "Looks like . . . redeem anywhere," he said softly, to himself. "They just print you a check right there. Damn. Two grand." He twisted around, looked back at all of us, and laughed. "Shit, this ain't a funeral," he said. "If I won, we all won. What the fuck, we're splittin' this fucker!"

Wild, joyous whoops of celebration filled the SUV, and all at the same time Vernon, Darla, Anthony, and Kandy hugged Chris and rubbed his shaved head. Everyone began shaking back and forth and the whole Explorer rocked side to side.

"Chris," I said. "You are a great American."

He was giggling, giddy at this sudden turn of events and all of the combined adulation. "Fuck you, dude. I'm Canadian!" Then he sobered up. "Okay, when I say we're splitting it, what I mean is, I get half, and the rest of you split the other half."

Everyone settled down a little, doing the math in their heads, and then murmured agreeably—this seemed like a more-than-fair arrangement, without asking Chris to be unreasonably generous.

Chris went on, peering back toward the restaurant, where Mr. Liu's daughter, Mary, had emerged to gather the last of the dishes. "Look, Anthony," he said, "I know the last thing you wanna do right now is go back in there. But, yo, I got an idea. And I *need* some fried wontons."

A minute later, there were nine people clustered in the cramped, pungent kitchen of the Golden Panda—me, Chris, Old Man Vernon, Darla, Anthony, and Kandy, along with Mr. Liu, his wife, and their daughter Mary, who sat on a milk crate, pecking away at a laptop. Mr. Liu had small, round glasses and graying hair, and wore an apron over a dirty white T-shirt and baggy, brightly patterned swim trunks. He was bent over an industrial-sized sink, wiping it out with a blue sponge, still tense, it seemed, from his confrontation with Anthony, who stood behind Vernon, glowering at the floor.

I could guess that Chris was aiming to broker a truce between the two of them, but didn't see the tack he planned on taking even as he dove right in. "Mr. Liu," he said. "I have been a customer of your fine establishment here for a couple of years. My brother, Shawn, he's been coming here for longer than that. I love the food you have here. It's kind of nasty sometimes, but it's good nasty. It's filling. I especially like the pork fried rice. And I like how you give fortune cookies even on to-go orders."

"Thank you," said Mr. Liu, with a heavy accent, standing straight. "I see you in here before. I think I know your brother." His wife, tiny and anxious, wearing a Buffalo Bills hoodie and a hairnet, said a few rapid words in Chinese to Mary, and Mary gave a one-word response without looking up.

"I recently came into some money," Chris went on. "And knowing me, I'll spend it, it'll be gone, and that'll be that." He took a breath. "I've got an idea, though. It'll be a good thing for me, and maybe it'll help you, too. Here's what I'm thinking—I want to come here tomorrow and give you . . . let's say . . . eight hundred bucks, cash money."

Mr. Liu crossed his arms, not quite sure where Chris was going with this.

"I'm thinking I give you eight hundred up front," said Chris, "and me and my brother eat here free for the rest of the year." He explained that they wouldn't take advantage of the arrangement—they'd only come by once or twice a week. Basically, Chris said, he was offering to pay in advance for a year's worth of meals. But he had a few conditions. "I want you to hire Anthony back. He's been loyal to you, you gotta be loyal to him. And you gotta pay him at least half of what you owe him right now in back wages."

Mr. Liu and Anthony glanced up toward each other without actually letting their eyes meet. Mr. Liu said to Chris, "I want Anthony to work. But not enough customers."

"Well, for one thing," Chris said, "you guys need to have delivery. A Chinese place without delivery, that's like a dog with no dick. That's why my brother always sends me down here to pick up. In snowstorms and shit. I hate that shit. You have delivery, you'll double your sales. Anthony can wash dishes and go on runs, both. You need a delivery car, I can even help you find one, for a good price."

Mr. Liu spoke to his wife in Chinese, translating Chris's appeal. She responded at great length, gesturing at Anthony, Mary, and Chris. I couldn't help but marvel at Chris's command of the situation. My image of him as a failed comic and petty criminal could barely accommodate the ease and confidence he now seemed to possess. At last Mrs. Liu fell silent, and Mr. Liu turned and said to Anthony, "Okay. You want to work here?"

Without unclenching his jaw, still staring down, burning holes in the tile, Anthony nodded.

"Good," said Chris. "Now hug it out, you two. Seriously. Go on. It's part of the deal."

Shyly, like two bludgeoned boxers embracing at the end of twelve rounds, Anthony and Mr. Liu edged near each other and slumped close in a kind of half-hug, patting each other quickly on the back, but not without an evident bit of emotion.

Darla started clapping, and I found myself joining in, unexpectedly stirred; soon Kandy, Vernon, and even Mrs. Liu were clapping, too. Chris was beaming. "That's good," he said. "That's perfect." I had goose bumps. My only sorrow was that Lauren wasn't there to witness the moment.

Chris laughed, growing comfortable in his role as peacemaker. "Now, before we hit the bar to celebrate—and drinks are on me tonight—there's just one more part of the deal."

Mr. Liu eyed him nervously.

"If it's not too inconvenient," Chris said, "I was hoping we could all dig in to some grub. Golden Panda leftovers, I don't care. I could eat a horse, this guy's been on a bus the last twenty-four hours"—he pointed at Vernon—"and this girl's eating for two," with a sideways nod toward Kandy. "What do you say?"

"No problem," said Mr. Liu.

All of a sudden, his daughter Mary shrieked and leapt to her feet like she'd been stung on the butt by a bee. She let out some rapid birdsong to her parents in Chinese and Mr. Liu took the laptop from her hands and inspected the screen while Mrs. Liu threw her arms around Mary and began to sob into her shoulder. Mary looked at Anthony, tearing up herself, and cried, "I got in! I got in! Medaille College e-mailed me! Anthony, I got in!"

A half hour later, well fed, all nine of us were crammed into Chris's Explorer, speeding toward Freighter's. I sat up front in the passenger seat; behind me sat old Vernon Wallace, his great-granddaughter Darla, and Anthony and Kandy. Squashed way in back, and squealing like kindergarteners with every pothole we bounced over, were Mr. Liu and his wife and daughter. Chris was driving, phone clamped between his ear and his shoulder, talking to his older brother. "Shawn, just meet us there. It's good news, I'm saying, though. I'll tell you over a beer and a couple shots."

I could hear Chris's brother chewing him out on the other end, calling him a moron, a loser, and a punk. All of the merriment and gladness quickly drained from Chris's face. "Yes, Shawn. Okay. Okay, Shawn. Yes, I understand." He closed his phone and tossed it up on the dash, shaking his head and biting at a thumbnail. In the back, full of jolly banter, no one else had caught the exchange.

"Fuck that dude," I said to Chris. "Shake it off."

"It's not that easy," he said, hurt and sinking. He mashed on the gas pedal and we veered right, back tires sliding out a little, and bolted through a light that had just turned red. A few blocks down, the five-way intersection with Lauren's bar came into sight. I felt supremely nervous, but fortified by the size of my brand-new posse.

Chris clouded over with a look of fierce intensity. He reached for his phone again, dialed his brother, and propped the phone to his ear, battle-ready. Then, without warning, a siren whooped in the night, and a blinding strobe of red and blue lights filled the SUV. "Yo, man," said Anthony, "you just blew right past that stop sign." I twisted around and saw, through the back window, a cop car right on our tail, flashers twirling giddily, high beams punching the air, one-two, one-two.

"No fucking way!" Chris cried, as the phone slipped from his shoulder to the center console and tumbled to the floor at my feet. "What the fuck do we do?" He kept rolling forward, while everyone in back began shouting instructions in both English and Chinese. I was pretty sure that only Vernon and me knew that the truck was stolen. A forlorn tide rose in my chest.

I could hear Shawn's voice on the phone, saying Chris's name.

I plucked it up and said, "He's gotta call you back," and folded the phone closed.

"Okay," said Chris frantically. "Here's what we're gonna do. I'm gonna pull over up here, and then all of us, we're just gonna scatter in every direction. Just fuckin' haul ass into the alleyways, all these side streets, into the bushes. They can't get more than one or two of us."

"Are you crazy, boy?" said Darla. "You think my granddaddy's gonna take off running? You think *I* am? I ain't got nothing to hide from. Cops can't fuck with me."

From the way back, Mary said, "You know, there's always policemen at the restaurant. I know a ton of 'em. I got my friend out of a speeding ticket once."

"I'm not worried about a damn ticket," Chris said.

"Well," said Mary, "if we are gonna run, could somebody please pop the hatch door? I think we'll lose some valuable seconds if me and my mom and dad all have to climb over the seat."

Anthony sat forward and got close to Chris's ear. "Nobody's running," he said. "Chris—listen to me—you got warrants?"

"No."

"Is this shit hot?"

Chris nodded. "Burning."

"Okay. Listen, just pull over and talk to the guy. Just act like it's nothing. Play it cool, like everything's cool. I'm telling you, I've seen dudes talk their way outta way worse."

"I'm not going down tonight," said Chris. He was so deeply spooked, it made me remember the time I'd suggested he incorporate his time in prison into his stand-up routines and he'd told me with a grave, distant stare that there was nothing funny about being in prison.

"That's right," said Anthony. "You're not going down. Now pull over and talk to this man."

Chris pulled to the curb and turned off the radio. He reached slowly for his shoulder belt and clanked it into its buckle.

"The guy's coming!" Mary called from in back.

I watched the cop's cautious approach. He wielded a powerful flashlight and shined it at each of our windows, but they were so fogged up from all the bodies in the car, I doubted he could see much. He took position just behind Chris's window and tapped on the glass with gloved fingers.

Chris lowered the window. "Hello there, sir, good evening," he said, laying on a healthy dose of Canadian politeness.

"License and registration." I couldn't see the cop's face, but he sounded young, which to me seemed like a bad thing. Seasoned cops, I'd found, were more likely to play things fast and loose; rookies went by the book.

"Here's my license," said Chris, passing over his New York State ID. "As far as the registration, I don't have any. I just bought this thing yesterday at an auction in Rochester. I know I shouldn't be driving it around till I get over to the DMV, that's my bad." Fat snowflakes spiraled in through his window and tumbled along the dash.

"You know you ran a light back there?"

"Yes sir. I believe I ran a stop sign just now, too. I was talking to my brother on the phone and I got distracted. That's my bad. I'm really sorry about that."

Chris was handling things as well as he possibly could, I thought. But once the cop checked the plates, we'd be doomed. If I bailed and ran, it occurred to me, maybe the cop would chase after me and Chris could peel away. My heart jangled, and my fingers crawled to the door handle, ready to make a move.

"You been doing any drinking tonight?" asked the cop.

"Not really, sir," said Chris. He ejected a barklike laugh. "Planning to, though. We're just going up there to Freighter's." He hitched his thumb toward me. "Even got a designated driver."

The cop bent his head down and poked his flashlight at me. He had dark, close-cropped hair, and was maybe in his mid-thirties. I dropped my hand from the door handle. Then he leaned through Chris's window a shade more and played his light over our bizarre array of passengers—four generations of black folk in the backseat, and a Chinese family in the trunk. His face crinkled up in utter bafflement. Either we were human traffickers with a payload of Asians or a tour bus covering the last leg of the Underground Railroad.

I heard Mr. Liu's daughter call out from the back, "Officer Ralston?"

He ducked his head further into the Explorer. "Who's that?"

"Mary. From the Golden Panda."

"Oh!" said the cop. "Mary! Hey, is that your dad?"

"Yeah. Guess what? I got into Medaille College! We're all going out to celebrate. These are our employees and some of our regulars. You might know some of them."

"But you're not old enough to drink."

"Don't tell the bouncer!" Mary giggled, playfully—even masterfully—redirecting the conversation. "I'm just gonna have a glass of wine."

The cop said, "All right, then," and withdrew his head from inside the truck. He handed Chris back his license. "I'll tell you what," he told Chris. "No more driving with your head up your— you know. Especially when the roads are this bad. You all take care." He doused his flashlight and headed back to his cruiser.

Chris zipped his window up. "Wait for it," he said tersely. "Wait for it."

The cop's flashers went dark, and a moment later his squad car swished past, hung a left at the next side street, and disappeared. Chris turned to look at all of us and broke out into relieved, maniacal laughter. "Holy shit!" he said. "What just happened? This is a magical night!"

Even as everyone began cheering and dancing around in their seats, slapping each other on the back, a cold ball pitted itself in my stomach. It was time to go see Lauren Hill. I prayed our magical night had one more trick up its sleeve.

"Fuck no, you can't bring all these people in here," the massive bouncer at Freighter's told me, shouting over the music. He eased from his perch and barged forward, using his bulk to crowd us back toward the door. He pointed at Vernon. "That dude didn't have an ID earlier. And this little fucker right here"—he jabbed Chris in the chest—"he's eighty-sixed for life." He took a look at Mary. "She's underage, I'll put money on that, but she's kind of cute; she wants to stay, we can probably work something out. Get the rest of these clowns out of my face. Try Cole's, across the street. They'll serve anybody."

I said in his ear, "I'm Lauren Hill's boyfriend. And these are my friends."

"Darrell is Lauren Hill's boyfriend," said the bouncer. "Get your Rainbow Coalition the fuck outta here."

Darrell? Who the *fuck* was Darrell? "Just let me go find Lauren," I pleaded.

"Knock yourself out," said the bouncer. "But these people got to wait outside."

I hustled everyone back through the door, into the freezing night. "Just give me two minutes," I said. "I'll be right back."

I rushed in, my neck hot, blood crashing through my veins. In the three or four hours I'd been away, the Freighter's crowd had gone from tipsy to riotously drunk. Two old bikers had their shirts off and were holding a tough-man contest, affectionately slugging each other in the gut. A pair of young punk rockers dry-humped in a booth. People were screaming along to a song on the jukebox and hooting at hockey highlights on the TVs. At a table in the middle of the room, a man in a winter coat dumped a humongous boot-shaped glass of beer over his own head. I was desperate to be that drunk.

The crowd tossed and turned me like a piece of driftwood, until finally I reached the bar and stood a few feet from Lauren

Hill, staring at the back of her neck and her bare shoulders as she mixed a row of drinks at the rear counter. I felt like a vampire, dying to taste her skin. Lauren turned toward me, and the whole scene seemed to grind into slow motion and go mute. I waited for the moment of truth—the expression on her face when she saw that I was back. She set the drinks down in front of the guys next to me, and as she looked up she saw me, and smiled, a jolting, radiant, zillion-watt smile. The room's roar slammed back in and the world returned to normal speed. "There you are," she shouted. "What do you want to drink?"

"I made some friends," I shouted back. "Can you help me get 'em in?"

"Just tell Greg I said it was cool."

"I think you better come with me."

She looked around. The other bartender had left and she was now the only person serving drinks, but there seemed to be a momentary lull. "Okay," she said. "Really quick." She ducked under the bar and followed me through the raucous crowd to the front door.

"Come outside for a second," I said. I blasted the door open and we spilled out onto the sidewalk, where a stocky, young white guy in a powder-blue FUBU sweatshirt and Timberland boots was talking to Chris and Mr. Liu while the rest of the crew looked on.

"All the food we want, all year long?" the guy said.

"My guests," said Mr. Liu.

"Rock on!" The guy wrapped his arm over Chris's shoulders, pulled him close, and rubbed his head with his knuckles. "I love you, ya little fuckhead," he said, laughing. "You are just full of surprises." This, I realized, had to be Chris's older brother Shawn. Chris scrapped his way loose and looked up at me with a magnificent gleam.

"Davy! Let's get our drink on," Chris hollered. "They gonna let us in or what?"

"Yes sir," I said. "But wait, you guys, everyone come here, I want you to meet someone. This is Lauren Hill." The whole group gathered close, joining us in a tight little huddle. "Lauren," I said, "these are my new friends." I went around the circle, introducing her to each of them, and as I introduced them, they each gave her a friendly hello. "This is Mr. and Mrs. Liu, they own the Golden Panda on Randall Avenue. And Mary, their daughter, she just found out she got into college tonight! This is Anthony, and this is Kandy—they're having a baby soon." I patted Kandy's stomach. "That's little Floyd in there. And this is my Canadian friend Chris I was telling you about, a man of many talents. And, Shawn, right?"

He nodded. "That's right. You're Davy?"

"Yup." I explained to Lauren that Shawn was Chris's older brother.

"And evil boss," said Shawn with a grin.

"But how'd you meet all these people?" Lauren said, a bit dazzled.

"Hold on." I continued around the circle. "This is Darla Kenney. She lives over on the West Side, in Front Park. And here's her grandfather, actually her great-grandfather, Vernon Wallace. Hey, wait a second, what time is it?"

Shawn glanced at his cell phone. "Ten to midnight."

"In ten minutes," I told Lauren, "it's gonna be Vernon's hundred-and-tenth birthday!"

"No way!" she said.

"It's true!" said Darla.

Lauren looked at me with wide, whirling eyes, really taking me in, as beautiful a girl as I'd ever seen in my life. "You were only gone a couple hours," she said. "This is crazy. This is awesome." She shivered.

"Let's go inside and have a drink," I said.

"Let's drink!" Chris echoed.

Lauren reached for the door, glowing. "Okay, all of you come on in, I'll pour a round of birthday shots. Let me tell Greg what's up." Then she paused, giving Chris an odd look. She seemed to recall his status on the Freighter's blacklist. "Except you," she said, pointing at him. "I'm sorry, but . . . you just can't skip out on a tab. Not three or four times. Not here. Not in Buffalo."

"I just, sometimes I leave my wallet at home," Chris sputtered.

"I'm sorry," said Lauren.

"Wait," said Anthony. "What if we pay off everything he owes? Can he be forgiven then?"

Lauren thought about this. "Not forgiven. But if he pays every dollar he owes, plus a twenty-*five*-percent tip, then he's allowed back in."

"Done," said Shawn.

"All right, then," Lauren said. She hauled open the door and grasped my hand and led me through. My heart thrummed.

For a moment she leaned close to Greg the bouncer and explained the situation. At last he nodded and Lauren waved everyone past, into the mad melee inside. She squeezed my hand as we swept across the room to the bar and whispered in my ear, so close I could feel her hot breath, "Thank you for being here." The universe had finally, improbably—almost unbelievably— become perfectly aligned.

Our whole crew stood in a crushed knot against the bar. Lauren ducked under and popped up on the far side. "What'll it be?" she shouted, spreading out a constellation of shot glasses.

"It's Vernon's night," said Chris.

Vernon peered around, the tallest of us, soaking it all in, like an ancient willow admiring an orchard of saplings. "Knob Creek!" he declared.

Lauren found the bottle and poured nine Knob Creeks, plus a shot of Dr Pepper for Mrs. Liu, who asked for root beer instead, and, at Kandy's request, a shot of Molson Ice. As Lauren passed them out, I saw Greg, the bouncer, waddling quickly in our direction. I had the gut-shot feeling that everything was about to go from wildly festive to ferociously violent in the next several seconds. But instead, Greg howled, "Let me get in on that!"

Lauren saw the confusion in my face. "Greg loves to be a badass," she said, "but he's just a big softie. He goes to those Renaissance fairs. He swings swords around and wears dresses!"

"They're called kilts!" Greg bellowed, grumpy and happy at the same time. Lauren handed him a shot of whiskey; in his massive paw it looked the size of a thimble.

Lauren slipped under the bar again and pressed herself against me. We all raised our glasses, mashed tightly together, and looked around at each other, everyone's face filled with a golden glow. Darla and Vernon had their arms around each other, as did Anthony and Kandy, and Chris and Shawn Henderson, and Mr. Liu, Mrs. Liu, and Mary. I put my arm around Lauren's waist and pulled her close.

Later in the night, much later, I ended up telling Lauren that I loved her, and she told me she loved me, too. And the next afternoon, when we woke up, hung over but in fine spirits, we went for the walk I'd fantasized about, through a city transformed by almost two feet of snow. Every tree, every bush, every fire hydrant, and every garbage can was laced with soft, gentle beauty, like we'd crossed through a portal into some distant, magic land. In a few weeks, of course, Lauren Hill was no longer with me, she was with that dude named Darrell, the other bartender at Freighter's, and Mr. Liu's restaurant, I learned, went out of business just a few months after that. Vernon made it to late summer, Darla told me later, then he simply lay down on a park bench in Little Rock and died. But don't you see, none of that mattered, none of that mattered, none of that mattered. Because you can take away Lauren Hill, you can take away the love we had for each other, but you can't take away the feeling I had that night at midnight, as I squeezed her hand and looked around at my new, glorious tangle of friends, letting my eyes briefly catch their eyes and linger on each of their faces, the whiskey in each shot glass sparkling like a supernova. If there's ever been a happier moment in my life, I can't remember it.

"To Vernon!" I cried at last.

"To Vernon!" they shouted in chorus.

The Knob Creek went down like a furious, molten potion. I turned and looked down at Lauren. She was smiling up at me, sweet, soulful, and open.

"Happy Valentine's Day," I said.

"Happy Valentine's Day," she said.

And we kissed.

WHAT ARE YOU WEARING?

Late one cold wet November night a few years ago, maybe three a.m., I was sitting on my bed in a Motel 6 just south of Austin, Texas, brushing my teeth and watching the closing moments of a college basketball game on ESPN2 that had been played earlier that night but was being rebroadcast and whose outcome was still a mystery to me, when the phone on the night table beside me jangled to life.

Who could possibly be calling? Nobody knew I was there; I'd arrived only an hour earlier. It had to be the old Pakistani guy down in the motel office, I figured, or else my little brother, Peter, who I was traveling with; he'd gone out walking down the I-35 service road, looking for better reception on his cellie so he could call his girlfriend. After the third ring, I picked up. "Hello?"

There was a silence, then a woman's voice, half whispering. "Hey there."

"Um . . . hi."

"What are you doing?" she asked. This sure wasn't Peter, and it wasn't that desk clerk, either. I felt the hairs on my forearms prickle upwards.

"Well," I said, "I'm watching the Providence-Niagara game. I think it might go into overtime. Who *is* this, by the way?"

"I'm Nicole." I could hear the push of her breath on the other end of the line, as though her mouth was pressed close to the receiver. I went to the window and peered through the curtains—the parking lot was dark and still. Was this someone's idea of a joke? Maybe so, but I was just bored and lonely enough to play along.

"Hi, Nicole. My name's Davy."

"I like that name," she said.

"Yeah, it's a . . . uh, it's a good name. Listen, where are you?"

A pause. "I'm in your motel." The room seemed to slowly whirl backward, like a carnival ride catching speed. "What are you wearing?" she whispered.

"Well," I said, "I've got on gray mesh basketball shorts with, let's see, three thin white stripes down each side, and a Bell's Pizza T-shirt." I was quiet for a second, then rushed to fill the silence. "It's blue. I used to deliver for Bell's Pizza. We made these shirts for our rec-league basketball team. Hey, I've got a question for you. Can I ask you a question? What are *you* wearing?"

"Nuh-thing," she breathed.

There was a stirring in my gray mesh basketball shorts with the three thin white stripes down each side. Nicole explained that she'd hit the bars all night with her friends, and that now they were drunk and passed out and she was bored. "Pretend you're here with me," she said. "I want to tell you what we would do."

I'd never had phone sex before. Not that I was opposed to it—it was just one of those things that never came up. I guess it had always seemed sort of strange and silly to me. Real sex was so much more appealing. And in times when that was hard to come by, well, the Internet's tawdrier recesses offered workable substitutes.

"If you were here," Nicole said, "I'd lick your lips. I'd lick you everywhere." She moaned a little. "I'm fucking myself right now. Tell me what you're doing."

"Umm, touching my privates?" I started touching my privates.

"I'm sucking your dick right now. Oh yeah, I'm sucking you *good*. I want you to fuck my mouth like you're fucking my pussy."

Nicole's dirty talk was both ridiculous and oddly arousing. But a part of me wondered if this was all being recorded, if out in the parking lot, staked out in the back of an ice cream truck that had been pimped into a mobile surveillance unit, friends of mine were listening in, wide-eyed and gleeful, headphones clamped to their ears, having a laugh at my expense. It was hard to be serious. "Nicole," I said, "I'm grabbing on to your titties! I'm kissing you with reckless abandon! I'm pumping in and out of you, like, well . . . well, like an oil derrick! Or a piston? I'm the sword, baby, and you're the scabbard!"

Eventually, I grew less bashful and got into it for real, and a few minutes later we came to a happy ending. Soon after, we said good night. The basketball game on the TV had ended long before, and I had no idea who'd won.

At seven thirty the next morning, the phone rang again, jarring me awake; my brother, too. He lifted his head from the pillow and said, "Who the fuck is calling?"

It was Nicole. "Girl," I said, "I'm sleeping. Don't you know what time it is?" I was about to hang up, but then, remembering our little moment of shared bliss a few hours before, I softened. "Look, here's my cell number. Call me later, okay?"

A few months earlier, I'd published a book and hit the road with Peter for an eight-month cross-country tour. At each event, I read from my book and Peter played guitar and sang. We burned from one city to the next in an old Dodge conversion van we'd bought on eBay. Mostly, we crashed on sofas and floors at friends' houses or stayed with folks we'd met that night at our show, though sometimes we'd take turns driving through till dawn while the other slept in the backseat, which folded down into a bed. It was actually so comfortable, a lot of nights I chose to sleep out in the van rather than on a stranger's sagging couch. Once a month or so, dusted from the road, we'd splurge on some raggedy hotel, like that Motel 6 on the outskirts of Austin. The night Nicole found me, Peter and I had been on the road for six months; we were about a hundred shows into the tour.

Three nights later, in Oklahoma City, I was getting ready for bed out in the van when my cell phone rang. PRIVATE CALLER, it said. It was Nicole. She was still whispering. "What's up with the whispering?" I asked. She said her roommates were sleeping in the next room. We chatted for a few minutes, then got into the phone sex again. She told me she was tonguing my balls. This time I went Shakespeare: "Oh baby, wherefore art thy labia?" Afterward, she was about to hang up, but I said, "Nicole, that's so impersonal. If the fantasy is that we're having sex, I don't want to just zip up my pants the second we're done and leave. Can't we just talk for a bit? You know, cuddle?"

I was curious about Nicole. Now that we'd had sex a couple of times, I wanted to know what she was all about—I wanted to know where she worked; I wanted to know what she was into (besides having phone sex with strangers); I wanted to know what kind of person calls hotel rooms to have phone sex with strangers. She told me she'd studied psychology at the University of North Texas and that now she worked as a nurse at an old-age home in Waco; she'd just been down in Austin visiting friends. She also told me that her mother had passed away recently and that she'd been having a tough time with it—they'd been especially close.

The next few times we talked, she was still whispering, which was starting to seem a little suspicious. She claimed her boyfriend was studying just outside her bedroom door. It was hard to place, but something about her whisper sounded almost . . . husky. I got a little freaked out—was this a *guy* I'd been talking to?

"Nicole, what the fuck?" I said. "Just talk out loud for a second so I can hear your real voice." She refused. Still, she *seemed* like a girl—there'd been a few times when I thought I'd heard her real voice, times when she laughed, times when she moaned. So I went ahead and had phone sex with her anyway. It wasn't as good as the real thing, but it was better than getting myself off all alone. Her company was growing on me.

Houston, Baton Rouge, New Orleans, Tampa—Nicole and I skittered across the South; it was like *Badlands* for the new millennium (less killing, more "anytime minutes"). Every few nights, I'd be out in the van after a show, making my bed in the backseat, when Nicole would call, and we'd get hot and heavy. I was still wary that this was all some crazy prank by my friends and that our calls were being recorded, so during phone sex I kept things tongue-in-cheek, as though hamming it up for an audience. Nicole would be talking dirty, telling me how she wanted to squeeze my dick with her pussy, and I'd just start riffing on some goofy shit: there was NASCAR-themed pillow talk ("Straddle my throttle, Nicole. Take me to the checkered flag!"), and then sometimes I'd do it up in a stiff, upper-crust British accent ("Oh, God save the queen, I'm coming, I'm coming, tea and crumpets for all!"), and then other times, I performed in the voice of a black comedian making fun of the way white people talk, overpronouncing each word ("Oh yes, baby, golly gee, keep licking my penis, that just feels absolutely stupendous!"). Only irony could distance me from the sad truth of what I was really doing: jacking off in the back of my van in a Taco Bell parking lot in Jefferson City, Missouri, while talking on my headset to someone who was possibly a man.

My brother gave me shit for it. "I can't believe you still talk to that *dude*," he said.

"It's not a dude," I said.

Over the phone, Nicole had more of the resigned spirit of a woman who'd had a lot of attention from guys in high school but then, knocked around by life, had let herself go. She described herself as "pretty enough," and said guys often hit on her at the bar, but I knew this was no guarantee that if we ever met in person I'd be attracted to her. Ultimately, it seemed to me, phone sex was really about the power of the imagination, and in that case I could imagine her to be whoever I wanted. After I'd first seen, years before, the video for Fiona Apple's song "Criminal," Fiona Apple had become the girl who best represented my physical ideal. On those late nights in the back of the van, it wasn't hard to imagine Nicole as Fiona Apple's double.

Our relationship deepened. My phone had a special ring for PRIVATE CALLER, and since Nicole was the only one who rang like that, I could tell when she was calling. I started looking forward to her calls. She finally gave me her number so I could call her, too. I dropped the funny guises and just talked to her genuinely— sometimes we'd talk for half an hour before phone sex. Some nights, she'd tell me stories about work and share favorite memories of her mom. Other nights, out in my van after a long night in Phoenix or Des Moines, I'd be lonely, drunk, and depressed, and tell her about my problems. Nicole was a great listener, willing to indulge each tangent of every story she was told. She was as curious about my life as I was about hers. In a fucked-up way, this was the closest I'd had to a real girlfriend in years. Living on the road, a new city every day, she was one of the few constants in my life, and I both came to depend on her and, in our shared fantasies, dependably came on her. And the more we got to know each other, the more the sex improved. Nicole was insatiable. She started calling me every day, a half hour before my reading, when she knew I'd be out in the van getting my notes ready. "Hey, Davy," she'd breathe, "how 'bout a quickie?"

In December the book tour ended, and I resumed a more regular kind of life—staying put in Michigan, playing basketball twice a week at the rec center, sleeping in my own bed. For the most part, I stopped answering Nicole's calls. I was busy with work, and I had more interest in local girls I could meet for a drink and try to make out with than in someone across the country I could only hook up with by phone. But I also felt bad that I'd left Nicole in the lurch, and on occasion I'd still have a late-night phone tryst with her. We were like those couples who break up but still end up sleeping together every once in a while. Then, one day, her number was no longer in service. Nicole was gone.

One night the following winter, the old Dodge van broke down on the freeway near my house, and as I waited for a tow and the bitter cold edged in, I started playing that game I play when I'm feeling lonely, the one where I review all of my prior relationships, marveling that so many sweet, smart, pretty girls have come into my life and that I've found a way to fuck things up with every one of them. This game usually ends with me calling two or three of my exes and leaving miserable voice mails on their cell phones or their machines at home. Inevitably, one of their new beaus calls back to say, "Hey, man, I heard your message. Emilie's down in Chile for two weeks, but you sounded really down . . . I just wanted to call and make sure you were doing all right."

That night, marooned on the shoulder of I-94, big rigs howling past, I thought of Nicole. We'd had kind of a nice connection, hadn't we? All the funny and mournful stories she'd told me about working at the nursing home flooded my mind, along with her reminiscences of her mom, and I got the urge to track her down and meet her, find out who the fuck she was. I knew she might be four hundred pounds, or my grandma's age, or a guy, but there was also a possibility that she was, well, hot. So I tried her old number. A moment later, I heard her familiar whisper. "Hi, Davy," she said. "Been a while."

"I know! I can't believe I reached you! I've tried you every few months but I always get that lady's voice saying your number's out of service. Listen," I said, "this is gonna sound crazy, but okay, I've been doing some thinking, and what I think is, I think we should meet. We should meet up." There was a long pause, the kind of silence you hear when the TV's showing footage of a plane crash or a natural disaster and the anchorman's at a loss for words. "Look," I said, "I just want to meet you in person. I'll come down to Austin or Waco or wherever you're living. It's fucking freezing here, anyway."

Another long pause. Then she sucked in a deep breath and said, "You sure you're ready to meet the real me?"

Ten days later, I flew to Austin. I rented a car and dropped my bags at the same Motel 6 where Nicole had first found me. She suggested we get together at an Applebee's off I-35 at the far north end of town. I pulled into the parking lot at eight; this was one of those grim, anonymous commercial strips where Americans carry out their ordinary lives that appear on MSNBC after, say, a sniper shooting, or a child abduction. I went inside. Nicole knew what I looked like—I'd directed her to my picture online— but I had no idea who to be looking for other than somebody sitting alone. A weary hostess greeted me: "Table for one?"

"Actually, I'm looking for a friend." I walked past her into the restaurant. The place was mostly empty; on a jumbo-sized TV, the Pro Bowl was on. At a table in the back, gazing at me with an odd smile while sipping a Coke, was a woman who was at least eighty-eight years old. *No fucking way.* I almost bolted right then. But I'd come fifteen hundred miles to meet the real Nicole, even if the real Nicole had stumbled off the set of *Cocoon.* I ambled over and stood above her table. "Nicole?"

"There's no radishes in my soup!" the lady cried. "I asked for radishes!"

It wasn't Nicole. "Let me check on that for you, ma'am," I said, and wheeled away.

At another table, sitting by himself and halfheartedly watching the game, was a skinny Eminem-looking kid in a white Spurs hoodie who couldn't have been out of high school. I went over to him, squeamish and cringing.

"Yeah?" he said.

"Hi. I'm Davy."

"Okaaa-aay." He looked at me sideways.

Not Nicole. I felt dizzy with relief, and asked him, so as not to seem like a total weirdo, "How's your meal, sir?"

"I haven't ordered yet."

"That's great! You need anything, I'm shift supervisor, just let me know."

Then I saw her, perched on a red stool at the bar, toying with her cell phone—a curvy Latina girl maybe twenty-four years old. No J.Lo, but perhaps a young Rosie Perez. *Nice!* I felt a little tingle. This was the kind of girl I'd move to Texas for. I wondered if in eighty minutes we'd be having actual sex back at the Motel 6.

I moved close, and she turned to me with a smile.

"Nicole?"

"No," she said.

"Oh," I said.

What the fuck? Had she stood me up? I rushed back out toward the parking lot in such an anxious daze, I almost crashed into a guy on his way in. Out in the lot, there wasn't a soul in sight. It came to me: Nicole wasn't coming at all—she'd sent me on this wild goose chase as payback for disappearing on her when the tour had ended. I spun dismally in place and saw, to my surprise, that the guy I'd almost run into on my way out was still standing in the doorway, halfway in, halfway out. He was black, with a shaved head, maybe thirty years old, about my height but a bit more stout. We gazed at each other for a long couple of beats. Then slowly, shyly, he raised his hand and gave a little wave.

Nicole's real name was Aaron. We went inside and sat in a booth far from everyone. He ordered a Long Island iced tea; I ordered two whiskeys. The world seemed to rattle and buzz. Each steamy moment Nicole and I had shared over the phone flickered through my mind like a porno on fast-forward. But now, in each frame, I had to replace Fiona Apple with this—HOLY FUCK!—this *guy*. Honestly, I couldn't do it. What kind of deranged motherfucker even pulled stunts like this? My neck got hot, and I thought about just getting the fuck outta Dodge, but after a minute, the drinks and Aaron's bashful, slumping presence cooled me down.

Aaron began to explain things. He'd been doing the Nicole voice since he was thirteen, he told me. His first calls were to a guy at his high school who he had a crush on. Over the years, he'd had dozens of relationships with the same general trajectory as ours: heated phone sex gradually evolving into a deeper friendship, then, after three weeks or three years, an inevitable flameout.

But how had he come to find *me* that night at the Motel 6? Was he staying in another room and saw my TV on?

"No, I was at home," Aaron said, his voice soft and effeminate. "There's five Motel 6's in Austin; I have all their phone numbers memorized." These motels were somewhat unique, he said. Calls don't go through the front desk; they're handled by an automated system that asks for a room number. Many nights, after the clubs had closed, he'd be bored and drunk and start dialing random rooms. If a girl answered, he'd hang up—Aaron was gay; he didn't want to talk to girls. If a guy answered and he sounded nice, "Nicole" would start whispering.

He had dated—by phone—cops, businessmen, students, even a butcher and a baker (truly, but no candlestick maker). "I always want to be able to reach someone when I'm in the mood," he said. "So I like to have two or three things going at any one time."

"You mean all that time you were cheating on me?" I said in mock horror. "*Whispering* to other guys?"

He laughed—a squeaky girlish laugh. I could see how I'd mistaken him over the phone as female.

Aaron revealed more: I wasn't a very adventurous phone-sex partner. Spanking, domination—sometimes his calls veered into these territories. As Nicole, he'd led guys into the shower and had them pee on themselves. Once he'd arranged to have a guy fuck his wife while he listened, without the wife knowing. All of this information was dispensed with the sheepish amusement and reluctant pride of a criminal reflecting on his work at the end of a spree.

Did he think Nicole's phone buddies knew she was a guy? Some knew, he figured, but chose to ignore it. Others had no clue. A few guys had become so obsessed with Nicole that they'd proposed marriage. One even promised to leave his wife for her. "That's when I have to tell them who I am," Aaron said. "I feel bad for deceiving them for so long. It can be really heart-wrenching, because I might have feelings for them, too, but I have to tell 'em, 'Look, I'm a guy.'" There'd been shock, anger, promises of a beating. A lawyer he'd been screwing over the phone for a year called him a fucking faggot, slammed down the phone, and then, hours later, called back, confessed he'd had fantasies about guys, and asked to meet up. They ended up having sex at

Aaron's apartment. A half dozen times, he said, he'd hooked up with guys he'd met as Nicole. All of them claimed to be straight, only curious.

I still couldn't understand the allure of all this. Aaron was a handsome guy, fit, with kind eyes. I knew from months of calls that he was a sweet soul and bighearted. Why didn't he find himself a boyfriend?

"I had a bona fide boyfriend once," he said. "A few years ago. I was so in love. But then he took off." Aaron looked down. "It's hard in the gay community. People are not faithful. It's hard to find someone who wants to be committed and serious."

That sounded like a cop-out to me; plenty of my gay friends had managed to find long-term partners.

"Maybe I'm in the wrong scene," Aaron said. "Guys at the clubs, they don't want what I want." Over the phone, he could get to know someone as a person first. It wasn't all about looks. "Sometimes," he said, "you can express yourself better with a stranger."

I asked about his mom—had she known he was gay? "We never had 'the conversation,'" he said, "but I think she suspected. Didn't matter. She loved me no matter what."

"She passed away last year?"

Aaron paused. "Nineteen ninety-nine."

"Oh, my bad," I said. "For some reason I thought it was more recent."

"Yeah," he said, "I lie about that. I always want to talk about her with people, but I think they'll think I'm weird if they know it's been so many years and I can't get over it."

"Wow." I ordered us another round of drinks.

Aaron drifted from one story about his mom into another, and gradually his double life as Nicole began to make sense to me. Here was a guy still grieving over the loss of his mother, crushed from a broken relationship, and surrounded by death at his job—no wonder getting involved with people felt harrowing.

As Nicole, it seemed, he managed to get his rocks off and find meaningful human contact without risking true intimacy. I could only applaud his innovation, though it struck me as incredibly lonely.

The Pro Bowl had ended, and Applebee's was clearing out. The junior hip-hopper I'd mistaken earlier for Nicole walked past our table, glanced at me, and muttered, "Your food here sucks."

I paid the bill, and me and Aaron made our way out to the parking lot. A gloomy mist had settled in; the wet pavement had a dull shine. "You know," I told him, standing by his car to say goodbye, "I feel like I lost Nicole but gained Aaron, and it's a trade up."

Aaron flashed a forlorn smile.

"How 'bout a hug?" I suggested.

We hugged. He smelled of musky cologne, salt, and beer, like a football stadium after the stands empty out.

"See ya around," Aaron said, though he knew I'd soon be flying back to Detroit.

"Yeah. See you around."

We got in our cars and rolled out of the lot, both headed for the I-35 South ramp. On the freeway, we drove side by side for a half minute with the fellowship of two truckers. I tapped the radio on; a sorrowful trumpeter blurted low notes. I saw Aaron playing with his phone, and then my phone buzzed—he'd sent me a text: Wanna try a guy?

I looked across at him, shook my head sadly, and held up my hands—*Sorry, man, no can do.*

Aaron gave a little tight-mouthed nod and lifted his hand— the same understated wave as when we'd first spotted each other outside of Applebee's. Then he zoomed ahead, and a mile later, at a split in the highway, peeled away. I watched his taillights until at last they disappeared into the foggy, aching Texas night.

THE 8TH OF NOVEMBER

One night, about ten years ago, a woman handed me an old, weathered journal she'd discovered on a wet street in Washington, D.C.—I make a magazine called *Found* which compiles these kinds of personal notes and letters that folks have plucked up off the ground. The journal, written by a soldier in Vietnam named Jim Thompson, chronicled his year of brutal combat as a member of the 173rd Airborne. In the fall of 1965, Jim had fought in one of Vietnam's bloodiest battles, known as Hill 65—a battle recalled in the Big & Rich song "8th of November." In his journal, Jim described the initial ambush: *"Chunks of flesh rained down on me."* Hours later, when both sides ran out of bullets, they fought with knives and entrenching tools. Out of twenty men in Jim's unit, only he and three others survived.

I was absorbed by Jim's journal, its honesty, introspection, gallows humor, and insight. This kind of plainspoken, on-the-ground account of life in battle belonged in libraries, I felt, not in a puddle, and though I'd never tried to return a *Found* item before, I resolved to do what I could to track Jim down and reunite him with his journal. I had no idea if he was even still alive, but after visiting a few veterans' organizations around D.C., I caught a tip that I could likely find Jim pulling the graveyard shift at the Last

Firebase—a wooden hutch a hundred yards from the Vietnam Wall that was part POW/MIA vigil and part trinket stand. I biked down a couple of nights later, around midnight.

Inside the Last Firebase stood a man in his mid-fifties, wearing old glasses and a brown leather coat, reading a newspaper by the light of a Coleman lantern, while a talk show's steady banter sounded from a portable radio on the counter beside him. I held up the journal. "Excuse me, are you Jim Thompson?" I asked.

"Hey, I've been looking for that!" he said with astonished glee. "Where on Earth did you find that thing?"

After being consumed with his journal for months, it was thrilling to meet Jim face-to-face. He had big ears, a sparkle in his eyes, and a creased, hangdog demeanor. I'd imagined that someone who'd experienced so many horrible things would be distant and sullen, but Jim was the opposite: a whirlwind of laughter and mischievous energy. In a rich New England accent, a fountain of likable, grandiose stories poured out of him. He had large opinions about everything, and a fondness for outsized pronouncements—his favorite diner was not just a favorite diner, it was "perhaps the greatest diner in the D.C. Metro area, the country, and maybe even the world!"

Jim lived in a tiny ramshackle rooming house in Alexandria, Virginia. On Sundays I started watching football at his place. In his room, he'd stacked three ancient TVs totem-pole style so he could watch two games at once, plus the news. Every few minutes the picture on one set or another conked out, and he'd blast the side of the TV with his open palm to fix it. I'd sit on a folding chair while Jim paced the room, talking, laughing, and adding his own commentary to the games. After a rookie running back scampered into the end zone for a score, Jim would declare him a future Hall of Famer. "Mark my words," he'd shout. "He'll be the greatest rusher in the history of Redskins football, and maybe even the NFL!"

Two families of recent Ethiopian immigrants occupied the houses on each side of Jim's, and he was an enthusiastic neighbor—he patched flat bicycle tires, tinkered on troubled engines, helped the grown-ups navigate the local bus system and fill out government paperwork, and gathered the kids for hours-long football games that sprawled across all three front lawns. The kids called him *Eessuma*, which meant "Uncle" in their native Oromo. Jim, meanwhile, coined an affectionate nickname for me— Sadsack—a moniker I earned for my inability to throw a spiral, and from confessing to him that the only fight I'd ever been in was in sixth grade, when I'd brawled with a third-grader over a bag of Doritos and ended up with a bloody nose. Jim was in the habit of referring to himself in the third person, which inspired me to do the same. He'd emerge from underneath the hood of his old '63 Mustang and announce, "I got it runnin' again—Jim Thompson may be the greatest Ford mechanic in the Beltway!" "That's great," I'd say. "Then he can give Sadsack a ride to work."

Beneath Jim's exuberance, though, was a weary sadness. As our friendship deepened, he began to share more of his past with me. In Vietnam, he'd seen his best friends killed, and he'd killed a couple dozen people himself—with his M16 and even with his hands. After he'd finished his tour of duty and returned home, he'd slowly deteriorated from post-traumatic stress disorder. For fifteen years, he told me, he'd roamed the western U.S. with violent gangs of other veterans, drinking and doing drugs ("self-medicating," in Jim's parlance), and terrorizing town after town. Finally, he'd landed in a VA hospital's psych ward for two years, where he'd been a rare success story: he'd emerged restored, able to piece together a life for himself. Still, there were signs that his experiences in the war continued to wrap him in shadows. One of Jim's housemates, an old drifter named Chuck, asked me once, "Why do you think a guy as charming and intelligent as Jim is living in this dump with a bunch of weirdos like me? Should be married, a family and all. Working somewhere. But he's damaged. He's wounded. He can't form connections, man. It's too difficult for him. You'll see."

In early November, as the NFL season reached its midpoint, Jim suddenly vanished. I kept stopping by his house and looking for him at his post near the Wall, but he seemed to have disappeared. I ran into Chuck on the street. "Every November, brother," he told me. "Jim takes off. That Hill 65 time of year, he can't be around nobody." Eventually, a couple of weeks later, Jim returned, but he seemed changed, as though he'd been to the darkest of places. The glint in his eyes had been snuffed out, and his wild mile-a-minute stories were replaced by a brooding silence. Sometimes when I came over to watch football, he wouldn't answer the door, even when I pounded and yelled, "Let me in, Jimmy, I know you're home!" Finally, during a Thanksgiving visit from his daughter and granddaughter, Jim began to emerge from his funk. "That was probably the best turkey I've ever had," he told me over the phone. "Maybe the best turkey *anyone* has ever had."

Jim may have a self-isolating streak, but a decade later, we're still tight. When I moved to Chicago, he took an Amtrak train out to visit for a week; we played pool every night and went to punk rock shows. We've traveled together to Colorado and New Mexico, and I even visited his hometown of North Conway, New Hampshire, and saw the house he grew up in. Each November he retreats deep within himself, and for a couple of weeks his phone goes straight to voice mail. I get anxious. And then, after a period of troubling silence, there's a message from him: "Hey, Sadsack, it's Jim. Learn how to fight yet?"

A couple of years ago, Jim moved to northern Michigan, a few hours from my home in Ann Arbor, and last fall, as November rolled around, I decided that for the first time I'd impose myself on his annual fugue. I drove up I-75 on a bright, cold autumn afternoon, and as evening fell, I wound my way through small towns, already buttoned up for winter's approach. Flags set out for Veteran's Day swished from front porches and hardware-store awnings.

It was dark by the time I reached Jim's trailer deep in the woods. At his door, six-pack in hand, I was about to knock, when from inside I heard a single thunderous bang. My heart froze. I peered through his front window and saw Jim standing in his dark living room, bathed in eerie blue light from a tower of beat-up television sets, a cigarette hanging from his bottom lip. The picture on the top TV was slipping, and Jim delivered another mighty blow to its fake-wood casing. The picture straightened out. Jim took a couple steps back. The sound of the TVs was muffled, but on each set flashed a different network's evening news, separate but syncopated images of American soldiers in Iraq and Afghanistan. The light from the TVs washed over Jim's face and reflected off his wide, hollowed eyes. I felt frozen in place, haunted, oddly transfixed, and for almost five minutes I watched Jim watch TV, standing ten feet from me on the other side of the glass. Then at last he mashed out his cigarette in an ashtray atop the top TV, and somehow that broke the spell. I turned and knocked on his door. "Jimmy, let me in!" I cried. "Sadsack is here. Sadsack brought the beer."

A part of me was worried that he'd view my visit as an intrusion. But when he opened the door, a smile slowly crept across his face. "Welcome," he said, throwing an arm over my shoulder. "Come in, come in. Pop a couple of those. Looks like the finest beer in the history of the world!"

NINETY-NINE BOTTLES OF PEE ON THE WALL

The first time I peed in a bottle was in the spring of 2006, at a folk concert in Ann Arbor—my brother Peter's album release party. I was tending bar in the back of a small art space while Peter played for a packed house of friends, family, and local fans, crammed side by side in metal folding chairs. It's hard to serve drinks without drinking plenty yourself, and by the middle of the show, I desperately had to take a leak. Peter was singing his most earnest, heartfelt tune, and the place was so full, there was no way I could've made it to the bathroom without creating a disturbance.

An empty Orange Mango Nantucket Nectars juice bottle in a bin on the floor called to me. Hidden by the bar, I twisted the cap off, popped my zipper, and as slowly and gently as I could, whizzed into the bottle, all the while standing straight and nodding my head to the music. You know how tinkling against the side of the toilet bowl keeps the sound down? I discovered that peeing against the inside of the bottle did the same. The bottle filled just past the top of the label. I was surprised at how hot my pee felt through the glass. I screwed the cap tightly back on, dropped the bottle in a trash can, and just like that the crisis was averted, a swift and easy victimless act.

Of course, like speeding or shoplifting, once you see how simple it is to get away with something, there's nothing to stop you from doing it all the time. On our months-long tours, where each night I'd read *Found* notes and stories and Peter would play guitar and sing a few songs, I often preferred sleeping outside in the back of our van while my brother crashed on the couches of friends or hospitable strangers. For me, the problem had always been what to do when I woke up in the van after a night of drinking and really had to pee. What had been an empty street at three a.m. could be alive and bustling at a quarter after seven. Now I began to plan ahead, and before I went to sleep, I'd make sure an empty Nantucket Nectars or Odwalla bottle was handy (wide-mouth bottles required less docking precision). At dawn, crouching in the van behind tinted glass, head pressed to the ceiling, I'd fill a bottle—sometimes two, a couple hours apart— and crash right out again. Before we got on the highway to head for the next town, I'd stop at a gas station or a park and slip the bottles into a garbage can, surreptitiously, like condom wrappers at your girlfriend's parents' house, or a vandal's spent cans of spray paint.

Here and there, I began to pee in bottles even under less urgent circumstances. Sometimes, before our *Found* shows, if there was no bathroom backstage, I'd huddle in the corner and fill an empty water bottle with pee, rather than wade through the crowd, already in their seats waiting for the show to start. The more you do something—even something a bit weird and aberrant—the more normal it becomes to you. Nudists know this, as do bulimics, self-cutters, compulsive hand-washers, scratch-off lottery addicts, and people who masturbate while driving on the interstate. Peter walked in on me a few times backstage, caught me peeing into a bottle, and hissed, "That's fucking sick, dude," and I always thought he was the one being unreasonable.

Still, for every bottle I peed in while we were on tour, I took sixty run-of-the-mill leaks in a rest-stop urinal or behind a tree on the side of a country road. Mostly, the bottles were a last resort. And once I got home, I might never have peed in a bottle again if I hadn't fallen off my friend Mike Kozura's roof while helping him change out the storm windows for screens. My right ankle was completely shattered, and for a couple of months I was laid up in my bedroom—a hot, sweaty attic lair—feeling like Martin Sheen at the beginning of *Apocalypse Now*, but with only five-eighths the madness.

The staircase to my room was incredibly narrow and steep, and to descend it to take a leak required ten minutes of precarious maneuvering. Instead, I began to pee almost exclusively in bottles. I became an expert at it. I knew, for instance, before I peed how much pee was going to come out of me—I could select the right half-filled bottle and fill it right to the top and be done with it, sending it to pasture on the floor behind the TV stand. Not that I meant to start a collection, but there was no easy way to dispose of them. My housemates were happy to bring a pizza upstairs when I ordered for delivery, but wouldn't have been as gracious, I didn't think, about carrying out my sloshing portable urinals. And with my useless, throbbing ankle, the thought of fighting my way downstairs and out to the driveway to dump them in the garbage bins felt overwhelming. The funny thing was, years before, I'd heard a story from a friend about a roommate he'd once had who was so lazy, he'd pee in an empty milk jug in his basement bedroom rather than walk upstairs and use the john. At the time, I'd thought that sounded completely nasty, but now my own pee-filled bottles had outgrown their nest behind the TV and began to line the shelves of the towering bookcase at the foot of my bed. I peed in all kinds of bottles, and developed favorite brands—Odwalla, Naked, SoBe, Fuze, and those small, round, glass bottles of apple juice called Martinelli's, which, dangerously, looked like they contained apple juice even when filled with pee. I began to hoard empty bottles to have on reserve. When my housemates had parties, I'd creep down from the attic at five a.m. after everyone had cleared out and crawl back upstairs with abandoned forty-ounce screw-top bottles of Miller High Life and St. Ides tucked in my armpits.

July Fourth arrived. From my window, I watched little kids running around freely in the park across the street, waving sparklers, peeing wherever they chose, and I cradled my swollen, misshapen ankle, heartsick—the girl I'd been dating on and off for several years and loved dearly, Sarah Locke, had decided to move to Oakland to live with her new boyfriend, an animator and budding art star she'd met on MySpace named Ghostshrimp.

Sarah was a tiny, beautiful punk rock girl who'd grown up on a Sioux reservation in Michigan's Upper Peninsula. She made me soup when I was sick, "answered" bananas like they were a telephone—"Hello? I can't hear you. Hello?"—and helped me put together each issue of *Found* magazine in my basement. I'd never been involved with someone so closely or for so long. The night before she left, she stopped by my house to say bye and sat at the foot of my bed. We'd already talked through it all plenty of times, and by now the agony had subsided, and we were full of a love for each other that seemed larger than Ghostshrimp and the brokenness of the present. Sarah marveled at the collection of pee-filled bottles I'd amassed. "It's absolutely incredible," she said. "I've never seen anything like that." She sniffed the air. "I can't believe they don't smell." I was ashamed, but also sort of proud, and fascinated with them myself. The range of pee color, in itself, was striking—dark, hornet gold, to pale yellow, to nearly clear. "There must be fifty bottles here," said Sarah.

"There's more behind the TV stand," I confessed.

Sarah said, "Let's count." We tallied them up. There were ninety-nine. Sarah began to sing, *"Ninety-nine bottles of pee on your wall, ninety-nine bottles of pee . . ."* She trailed off. "I can't believe I'm leaving you," she said.

I picked up the song, and continued on, sadly: *"Take one down, pass it around, ninety-eight bottles of pee . . ."*

Sarah was gone, and all I had was my pee bottles and a ruptured ankle that buzzed with excruciating pain if I brushed it against anything. I was as hobbled as the dude in *Misery*, but without a number one fan. Besides the sheer effort involved, it seemed to me that to simply bag up all the bottles, a dozen at a time, and crutch my way to the street to toss them out would be squandering a unique and bizarre opportunity. It's not every day you end up with an arsenal of ninety-nine bottles of pee, and though I wasn't sure what exactly I might do with this kind of unusual stockpile, my instincts told me I'd somehow find a use for them, as part of a prank or a practical joke, perhaps, or some darker form of mischief.

Stuck in my tiny sweatbox room all summer, I spent hours at a time online, exploring the Internet's odd, dark reaches and fanciful buttes. I researched how far flying squirrels and flying fish can actually fly, then watched clips of the kidnapped journalist Daniel Pearl's beheading. I absorbed every beat of each national news story, first on the *New York Times* site and then on the sites of the local papers where the incident had gone down, enjoying the battles waged in the comments sections, which were often unrelated to the topic at hand, like a discussion—after an article about an armored-truck heist on KCStar.com—of the Royals' relief-pitching woes. Before long, I was clicking on obscure links sent to me by relatives I barely knew, and reading mass e-mails I would've deleted in an instant in the days before my reverse jackknife off Mike Kozura's roof.

An e-mail landed in my in-box—"The Times Square Literary Agency Announces 'Great American Novel' Writing Contest!"—and I read it carefully through. It looked pretty standard: send us a copy of your book and a sixty-dollar reading fee, and if the stars line up right you'll win a cash prize, along with the promise of agency representation. This particular entreaty had a few weirdly shaped cornices, though. For one, even though the contest was sponsored by the Times Square Literary Agency, the address for submissions was on Mission Street in San Francisco. Also, an awards ceremony was to take place in New York City in just six weeks, hardly enough time to collect all the entries and give a panel of judges an adequate chance to read through them. And another thing seemed strange—the e-mail specified that any book was eligible, fiction or nonfiction, no matter when it had been written or whether it had been published or not. But despite its whiff of fishiness, I forwarded it to a couple of high-school kids I'd met on tour who were aspiring writers, and also to my dad, who'd just self-published a book of autobiographical vignettes called *Brooklyn Boy*. Then I dropped it into one of my e-mail folders and moved on, probably to watch eighties rap videos on YouTube—"Iesha" by Another Bad Creation was a current favorite.

The next night, another e-mail caught my attention—"The Golden Gate Literary Agency Announces 'The Next Heming-way' Writing Contest!" The details were identical to those in the previous e-mail, with the same address for submissions, but for this contest the entry fee was eighty-five bucks instead of sixty. I clicked around the Web and discovered a half dozen other "literary agencies" of questionable provenance, all listing the same office address, responsible for a handful of dubious writing contests, including the Golden Typewriter Awards, the Guggen-heimer Writers' Circle Awards, and the O'Henry Awards (different from the esteemed, legit O. Henry Prize). Sketchy, no doubt, but I simply deleted the e-mail and hauled myself up to put *Black Knight* in the DVD player and pee into a tall, empty Evian bottle that one of my housemates had left behind in the kitchen.

Then, two days later, blooping into my in-box—"Times Square

Literary Agency Announces New Contest Categories!" The e-mail explained that their Great American Novel writing contest was expanding from six categories (Mystery, Romance, Science Fiction) to eighteen, and that they were awarding six prizes in each category instead of just one. The more I poked around, the more I got the sense that someone was blasting out thousands of e-mails, sounding the call for these shady contests, then sitting back and watching the checks roll in. It was clever, in a sense, maybe ingenious, but over the years I'd always drawn a sharp distinction between hustlers and scam artists. Hustlers: me and the other eleven sad sacks scalping tickets outside a Chicago Blackhawks game in mid-January, freezing our fucking asses off, and heading home with a hundred bucks in our pockets, if we were lucky; or the kid in Albuquerque, say, who used to sell me nickel bags of weed outside the Laundromat at Central and San Mateo. Scam artists: the guys outside Soldier Field before the Rolling Stones concert dealing counterfeits, which are handsome enough to fool the untrained eye but don't scan at the gate and get turned away; the dude who takes a twenty from you, presses a Ziploc bag of oregano into your hands, and darts off. Hustlers get you what you want at a price you're willing to pay; the "hustle" is convincing you that you want what we've got. Scammers abuse your trust and hang you out to dry—they're the ones who make things tough for your everyday honest hustler, and among hustlers, no one is more despised.

I read back through all three of the contest e-mails. It became crystal clear that some piece-of-shit scam artist was preying on aspiring writers just hoping for a wisp of recognition. I considered this an added insult—nobody deserves to be swindled, but it took a particular kind of cruelty to bilk sweet, earnest, well-meaning writers, especially the ones who'd worked hard enough to actually finish a book and were now struggling to get it out there and read by people. Still, the world's full of hostile scams, as I well knew from the dozen hours a day I was spending online, and in the Internet's Wild West, I was no sheriff, just a lonely homesteader trying to get by. The question was: What was I going to do about it?

About a week after Sarah left, my dad stopped by my house. A year before, at the age of seventy-one, he'd retired from the University of Michigan Health Service, where for almost three decades he'd managed the janitorial staff and overseen building repairs. He now reveled in his new freedoms, reading books he'd always meant to read, taking theater classes, and writing plays and stories. We'd had a party for him at a local mom-and-pop shop called Nicola's Books when *Brooklyn Boy* had come back from the printer's.

But in retirement, money was tight, and I often got texts from friends who'd seen my dad hustling tickets outside U of M football, basketball, and hockey games, and concerts at Hill Auditorium. I was sitting on my front porch when he pulled up in his '81 Ford Fairmont, muffler hanging by a rusty tendril, clattering along the pavement, sending up a geyser of pink sparks. He waved and cut the engine and the Fairmont went into its customary death rattle and coughed up a cloud of green smoke. "Check it out!" he said, crossing the street to my house, a wide U.S. Postal Service flat-rate box in his hands. "I got your e-mail. I'm sending *Brooklyn Boy* to that contest you told me about!"

Oh fuck. He gave me a hug and sat next to me. I said to him, "Don't do it, Dad. It's my bad. I shouldn't have sent you that thing. It's a scam."

"No it's not. I went to the worldwide website." He told me he was sending in four copies of his book, entering four separate contests—the Great American Novel, the Next Hemingway, the Golden Typewriter, and the Tom Wolfe Memorial Challenge. He'd written a check for $265.

We haggled about it for twenty minutes. Here was my dad, seventy-two years old, who couldn't afford to get his tailpipe fixed and was on his way to scalp tickets at the Ann Arbor Summer

Festival for the gospel group Sweet Honey in the Rock, about to flush a couple hundred bucks down the shitter. But he couldn't understand why I wasn't being more supportive. "Maybe they'll like *Brooklyn Boy*," he said forlornly. "You told me it was good."

"Dude, I'm telling you, it's just some fucking scam."

"How do you know?"

"I don't know. I just know. I mean, Tom Wolfe's still alive! Why would they have a *Memorial* Challenge? Look, I'll see if I can figure out a little more about it, just give me a few days."

"Today's the deadline," he said. "I'm sending this in. I want people to read my book. Finding an agent's the first step to getting a real publisher." He turned the package over in his hands, addressed to the Times Square Literary Agency in San Francisco. "I better go. Sweet Honey in the Rock's an early-arriving crowd."

I watched my dad drive away, then crutched back into the house and crawled up the stairs to my room. In a fever, I slapped and Googled my way through dozens of websites, trying to peel back the curtain on the Times Square Literary Agency's sleazy Wizard of Oz. It only took about half an hour to find him—his name was Lon Hackney, an appropriate name for a failed writer, which is what he seemed to be. A film-biz veteran, he'd written a somewhat prescient book in the nineties about Hollywood's overreliance on stars to deliver blockbusters at the box office, which was largely ignored. Since then, he'd freelanced for a series of dodgy Internet news sites like the Bong Smokers' Review, published a couple more books through a vanity press, and then, a few years before, had created a series of nationwide music and film conferences which he dubbed "The Future Is Now," where turnout had been dismal, according to a couple of disgruntled accounts I tracked down from those who'd paid to become sponsors. The writing contests appeared to be his latest concoction—meant, perhaps, to exact revenge on a publishing world he'd found impenetrable, but actually victimizing writers like himself. I could hardly think of a more cynical, mean-spirited swindle. To be fair, I knew it was possible that I was only jumping to conclusions. In a couple of online interviews, he spoke earnestly about the role of independent literary agents in helping new authors gain exposure. Reading between the lines, though, I could smell the bullshit.

Night had fallen. I looked up from my laptop, and in the darkness of my room, quietly humming, stood more than a hundred bottles of pee, proudly at attention, like soldiers ready to be shipped off to battle. In an odd, deranged trance, I tucked four bottles into a plastic grocery bag, put the bag inside my backpack, strapped it on, and scooted awkwardly downstairs, keeping my swollen ankle raised high. I pulled myself across the floor of the kitchen and down to the dank basement where I have my *Found* office. It's a true fact that at the University of Michigan I lived in the same exact dorm room on Prescott Hall in East Quad that had been inhabited thirty years before by a student named Theodore Kaczynski, who became the Unabomber. No doubt I was channeling a bit of old Kaczynski's rage and maniacal righteousness as I composed a six-page handwritten letter to Lon Hackney, lambasting him for being such a fraud. I signed it, "A Concerned Citizen." Finally, I cracked the folds on a USPS flat-rate box, placed the bottles of pee inside, and stuffed it with Styrofoam packing peanuts to keep the bottles in place and make sure they didn't pop open in transit. I folded my letter and squeezed it into the box.

Before I sealed it up, though, I second-guessed myself. I remembered a story I'd heard from a scalping pal of mine in Chicago who went by the name of Lobster. Lobster had told me about something this dude called Thirty-fifth Street Frankie—who I'd met a few times—had once felt compelled to do. Some guy owed Frankie eight grand—maybe for tickets, maybe a gambling debt, who knows—and he kept laughing it off whenever Frankie levied a threat. At last, Frankie hired four giant Southside thugs (friends of his, probably) to take care of the matter. One night when the guy came home from the bar, they grabbed him outside of his apartment, tied his hands behind his back, blind-folded him, shoved him into the trunk of a Lincoln, drove him up to Wisconsin, and left the car deep in the woods for two days. Then they drove him back to Chicago and dropped him off in the same alley they'd snatched him from, still tied up and wear-ing the blindfold but without a scratch. All they said, before roaring off in the Lincoln, was, "Hey, buddy, fly right."

"Can you imagine?" Lobster had said to me. "Two days in the trunk of a car, literally shitting yourself, not sure if you're going to live, and the whole time wondering who you wronged. And the message wasn't 'Pay Frankie,' it was 'Fly right.' He might've guessed it was Frankie, but he probably had debts all over town. Frankie got his money the next week."

I had no idea how true Lobster's story was, but something about it was inspiring. Down in my basement, reading over my long, chicken-scratched letter to Lon, I realized there would be something splendidly ominous in sending him the bottles of pee without any note of ordinary, petty complaint. Most likely, he'd just shrug off my criticisms and tear the note up. Instead, why not let him be haunted, like the dude in the trunk of the Lin-coln, led to a deeper reflection of who might be angry with him, and why? I ripped up my Kaczynski letter and with a black ballpoint pen carved a new note, tracing the words fifty times over: "FLY RIGHT."

The next day, I drove forty minutes south on M-23 and mailed the box from a post office in Toledo, Ohio.

That was only the first shot fired. As August edged in and the dog days of summer wore on, I packaged up fresh pee bottles every two or three days and cruised around Lower Michigan, northern Ohio, and northern Indiana, left foot on the pedals, right foot up on the dash in a bag of ice, scouting post offices and mailing packages. I preferred post offices with an automated scale in the lobby so I could pay the flat-rate postage and drop my box through the parcel slot without coming face-to-face with any postal clerks. Then I'd crutch it back to the van and blast tunes on my triumphant drive home, flush with adrenaline, like George McFly in *Back to the Future* after finally punching out his nemesis, Biff. I may have been a brokenhearted writer blowing $9.85 to mail his own urine to California, but I felt like a fucking cowboy, a vigilante, rolling into town on my steed to dole out my own brand of frontier justice. I never fully lost track of just how psychotic all of this would've seemed to anyone else, so as with most weird, fucked-up things you find yourself doing in life, I kept these outings a secret. But to me, at the time, it all made sense. It even seemed courageous and noble. I was just trying to make America right again.

In response, seemingly, the e-mails from Lon Hackney's phony contests intensified. "Great American Novel Deadline Extended!" "Reserve Your Gold-Area Booth For The Golden Typewriter Awards Gala!" "Tom Wolfe Memorial Challenge Now Accepting Submissions in 12 Languages!" I'd lie in bed sweating, gulping mouthfuls of Advil to keep my ankle from throbbing, and growing more and more incensed at Hackney's bold, unapologetic deceits. At last, I'd haul myself to the basement and compose short, blunt grenades of condemnation, writing with my left hand to disguise my scrawl: "STOP IT LON," "NO MORE CONTESTS," "GET RICH? DIE TRYING." One night, sealing pee bottles into one of the flat-rate boxes, I cut my hand on its sharp, gummed edge, and went ahead and smeared blood all over my note before tucking it inside. I was half Travis Bickle, half Jimmy Stewart from *Rear Window*—laid up, certain I was witness to a troubling crime, but unable to do much about it or get anyone to pay attention.

One weekend in late August, just to get outside, I crutched

across Wheeler Park to a house party on Main Street and drank a pint of Maker's by myself, watching young punk drifters twirl fire in the yard. Wasted, I called Sarah in the East Bay. "Oh my God, are you okay?" she said. "Your voice sounds really weird. Not just drunk, but weird. Are you crying?" I tried to explain my battles with Lon Hackney, but I'd drunkenly conflated Hackney with Sarah's new boyfriend, Ghostshrimp, and I kept saying one name when I meant to say the other. In a certain sense, they'd merged in my mind, even when I was sober—not only was Hackney robbing from the poor to give to himself, it sometimes seemed to me, he'd stolen my girl, too. "I can't talk to you when you're like this," said Sarah. "I'm hanging up now."

I made it home, dragged myself up to my room, opened a bottle of water, and took a long, mighty swig—but it wasn't water, it was my own goddamn pee. Even through my rigorous drunkenness, the taste was horrendously, mind-meltingly sour. I gagged and spit out what I could into the trash can, accidentally leaning my weight onto my useless right foot. A bolt of hot pain lanced up my leg and I crashed to the floor, crying to myself, full of sorrow and self-pity. I desperately had to get the taste of pee out of my mouth, but the only thing within reach was a small carton of blue Play-Doh that I'd bought as a gift for my nephew. In utter defeat, I clawed loose a couple of doughy chunks and chewed on them until I passed out.

Late one night, a new page appeared on the Times Square Literary Agency website, an overview of a conference Lon Hackney had put together in San Francisco the previous summer called "The Future Is Now"—apparently he'd been recycling the name from previous scams. This new conference featured an awards ceremony where authors were invited to read from their work (and rent vendors' booths for a hefty fee). Twenty thousand people had attended the day-long event in Golden Gate Park, Hackney boasted. He'd posted a dozen pictures, perhaps to try to legitimize the festival in the minds of any doubters—especially, I figured, his pee-bottle provocateur. In the photos, folks read from self-published books in front of a tiny bandshell to a half dozen people seated in folding chairs, while joggers, roller-bladers, tourists, and young mothers with strollers sidled past without a glance. Twenty or thirty folding tables had been erected haphazardly across a concrete plaza, and authors hovered behind them with stacks of their own books, lonely as Yankee Stadium ice cream vendors during an April snow squall. Yellow, blue, and green balloons clung to trees in sad clumps, draped with wet streamers, and amid the gloom, a woman dressed as a clown, wearing a blue Afro wig and face paint, stood picking her nose. If Hackney's intent in posting the pictures had been to lend cred-ibility and glamour to his writing contests and their associated events, he'd failed miserably.

I noticed in one photo a young, pretty woman seated behind a table stacked with books, which I presumed she'd written, holding up a copy, and smiling wanly. Her name was visible on the book's cover—Ondrea Wales—and after a quick Google search, I found my way to her website. She'd written three teen novels for a major publisher, and in her author photo looked confident and bright. I dropped her an e-mail: Investigating Lon Hackney and "Future Is Now" conferences. Please call. My phone rang the next night—Ondrea.

"It was one of the most humiliating days of my life," she told me. "I'd been hearing from so many people that these days pub-lishers don't have the resources they used to, that if you want your book to get out there, you have to do it yourself. I paid five hundred dollars for that table, and sold two books the whole day. It was a disaster." Ondrea told me that she was the only one there who hadn't self-published their book or put it out through a van-ity press. The most embarrassing moment of her day was when an editor from another publishing house had wandered by and stopped to chat. "She was aghast that I was out there—she thought my publisher had set it up. I confessed that I'd set it up myself, and she just kind of smiled at me like I was a crazy person and walked away. I felt duped. I felt lied to. The whole thing had been misrepresented to me in every way."

She got a little upset, just thinking back on it all, but her voice was sweet, even silky, and as we talked on, I gazed at Ondrea's author photo on her website, aware of the beginnings of a crush, the tips of my fingers tingling. I asked her if she felt so out of place simply because she was an established author surrounded by self-published folks, and she said no, that wasn't it. "It's not that I didn't belong there because I thought I was better than the other authors," she said. "It's because *nobody* belonged there. The awards gala was a joke. *Everybody* was disappointed." A conference aimed toward self-published authors could still be dignified and inspiring, she said, but this one lacked even the slightest semblance of anybody's effort or care. No press, no promotion. People had come from all over the country, only to get up on stage and read for ten minutes to a crowd of three. Twenty thousand people? There might've been twenty thousand people in Golden Gate Park that day, she said, but there were never more than a couple dozen at the bandshell. Ondrea lived in New York City, and she'd flown to San Francisco to participate. One guy she'd met, a children's book writer, had traveled all the way from Belgium. "He was really disconsolate," Ondrea said. "But he—and all of us—tried to put on a brave face, at least till we got home. Who wants to admit that they've been scammed?"

We talked for another forty-five minutes, the longest conversation I'd had with anyone since Sarah had left for California. Ondrea was likable, upbeat, thoughtful, and perceptive, and apparently a fairly successful writer with a healthy dose of talent— the kind of girl I often fantasized about meeting. I thought of Lon Hackney, that piece of shit, and my swollen ankle pulsed and throbbed. It was one thing to gyp my dad for a couple hundred bucks, it was another to put sweet, darling Ondrea Wales through a day of hellish awkwardness and shame.

"How'd you get interested in all of this, anyway?" asked Ondrea, a flirtatious note of curiosity creeping into her voice. I told her my dad had been suckered in, and explained that I'd been sending hate mail to Lon Hackney, without mentioning any specifics.

"I met Lon," she said.

My ears perked up. "Yeah? What was he like?" I hadn't been able to find any pictures of him online, I told her.

"He was—and look, I don't have anything against fat people—but he was a fat, sweaty slob."

I laughed nervously. My bedroom was as hot as a sauna, and I was sticky with sweat; I hadn't showered in a week and hadn't shaved in two. "Really?" I squeaked.

"Yeah," said Ondrea. "He could tell I was on to him, and he avoided me the whole day."

"He's got to be stopped," I said. "Listen. Ondrea. I'm gonna stop him."

"Yes, Davy!" she cooed. "My hero."

I flew to San Francisco. It was November, and I could walk again, sort of, but only short distances and with great pain. My mission was twofold—visit Sarah and beg her to come home with me to Michigan, and confront Lon Hackney and dump a bottle of pee on his head. That was my actual plan—to dump pee on his head, and let him know that I was doing it in the name of all the writers he'd ever fucked over.

I'd thought I would surprise Sarah, but when I called to tell her I was in the Bay Area for a week, she told me she was camping with Ghostshrimp in the Redwoods and wouldn't be back for five days. While I waited for her to return, I turned my focus to stalking Lon Hackney. His office was just a few blocks from my friend Eli's apartment in the Lower Mission, where I was staying. I shuffled my way over around three in the morning after a long night with Eli at the Peacock Bar, just to scout things out.

The headquarters of the Times Square Literary Agency (and Lon's entire trick deck of business ventures) were housed, I discovered, in a single dingy office among a block of six others above a liquor store and a tanning salon. A flight of exposed concrete steps led upstairs from the parking lot to an outdoor T-shaped corridor, with a row of office doors on either side, numbered with faded stickers from a hardware store. I found Suite #4. After all those months of sending flat-rate boxes to the address on Mission Street, it was a rush to actually be there, outside the door where my pee bottles had been delivered. The shades were drawn, and for all I knew nobody had been there in months, though a handwritten label remained affixed to the mail slot that said: LH LITERARY SERVICES/FUTURE IS NOW—Lon's umbrella groups. The mail slot's inside duct kept me from spying into the room, but I was able to peek down at the floor, where a mid-sized pile of manila envelopes and bubble-wrapped packages lay spread on the worn carpet, like a Christmas haul prepped by elves from Staples. I could read a few of the return addresses—Guymon, Oklahoma; Key West, Florida; Regina, Saskatchewan—enough to confirm the reach of Lon's operation. It was late, I'd had plenty to drink, and I had to pee, but had no bottle to piss in. I looked around to make sure I was alone, unzipped, and peed straight onto the door of Lon's office—one of the most enormously pleasing whizzes I'd ever taken. Then I headed back to Eli's place.

Over the next few days, I visited Lon's offices a dozen times, hoping to cross paths with him. In a plastic bag, I carried three bottles of pee in Vitamin Water bottles in case we met face-to-face. I tried to imagine how he might respond as I doused him— would he run? Would he fight? But as the days passed with no sign of him, I began to fear that his office visits were few and far between. Maybe he'd glimpsed me from the parking lot, lingering outside his office door, and had known to stay away. Mail accumulated on the floor of his office. My pee bottles were too big to fit through the mail slot, but one night I left one wedged between the knob of his office door and the door jamb, and another balanced atop it. It was one thing for him to receive pee bottles in the mail—deranged threats shipped from the Midwest—but it gave me an evil thrill to picture him arriving at his office and finding my bottles waiting for him, creepy as tarantulas, announcing my arrival in California.

When I showed up the next morning, I saw that the bottles were gone, and my heart flim-flammed at the idea that he'd returned to his post, and was in there, on the other side of the door. But his office was dark, and through the mail slot, I saw that all the packages were still heaped on the floor. Most likely, the bottles had been chucked out by the old Bangladeshi woman who owned the building and ran the liquor store below, or her teenage grandson, who halfheartedly swept the parking lot every day at dawn and at dusk. I'd asked them one afternoon about Lon, telling them he was an old friend I was trying to get in touch with, but they'd noticed me skulking about gimpily the past few days and seemed to sense my darker intentions. After conferring in Bengali, the grandson turned back to me and said, "Sorry, boss, we don't see him much. But I got you a case of those Orange Mango Nantucket Nectars you were asking about."

Sarah returned from her camping trip and called me, and we made plans to hang out the next day. "What do you want to do?" she said. "Go to bookstores? See a movie? You ever been to the Cartoon Art Museum?"

"I need your help," I told her. "It's a stakeout."

Sarah brought disguises—a tiger mask for her, glasses-with-giant-nose-and-bushy-mustache for me. We sat for hours on a pair of overturned buckets in the alleyway beside the liquor store, within sight of the cement steps from the parking lot to the offices upstairs. Anytime someone disappeared up the steps, Sarah raced over, tiptoed after them, then emerged a minute later, shaking her head: "Not our guy." We played Go Fish, worked on Word Search puzzles from a gigantic book, filled out Mad Libs, and munched wasabi nuts, while I drank mango juice and a half pint of R & R whiskey, and Sarah sipped a jug of chocolate milk through a tiny straw. I was still in love with her, and told her so plenty of times over the course of the afternoon, and she found ways to politely deflect my advances without making me feel too crummy. She even tolerated me squeezing her knee, kissing her ears, and resting my head on her shoulder. "Come back to Michigan," I said, my voice crackling with emotion. "Let's just try this one more time. Come home, Sarah."

She jumped to her feet. "Did you see that? The mailman! He'll know something." She dashed across the alley and up the stairs. I waited, hunched on my bucket, swirled in the hot shrieks and honks of rush-hour traffic. When she came back, she told me what the mailman had said: he'd met Lon once or twice but almost never saw him in the office. Often, packages arrived that were too big to fit through the mail slot, and he'd leave them for Lon with the accountants in Suite #6. "I knocked on their door," Sarah said. "I thought they might know when he'd be back. But they already left for the day."

"You're really not gonna come back home with me?" I asked her.

"I can't," she said. "I love you, but I'm happy out here, I'm happy with Ghostshrimp. We've got Keenan and Banksy"—their dogs—"we've got the apricot trees, we've got the Draweteria." This was their daily art project where Ghostshrimp whipped up illustrations and Sarah colored them in; they sold the results on his website, often for hundreds of dollars. "Don't cry," she said, putting her arms around me. "Everything'll be okay."

"I've got to take a leak," I said, my heart twisting. "I'll be right back." I scooped up my empty half-pint R & R flask and limped up the steps to Lon's office door. Lights were on in some of the adjacent offices, but I was slightly buzzed and by that point of my West Coast visit no longer gave a fuck—I dropped trou and filled the slender liquor bottle with pee. Someone poked their head out of a door and quickly slammed it shut. A moment later, the Bangladeshi woman from the liquor store came rushing up the steps, shouting at me and waving a cordless telephone. "I'm calling the nine-one-one!" she shouted. "Police come. It's ringing right now! You must go. You must go."

"Okay, okay," I shouted back, buttoning my pants, feeling like a mutant superhero who has only good intentions but is generally viewed as a freak. Quickly, I tightened the cap on the bottle and launched it through the mail slot into Lon's office. I rushed past the old woman, my ankle flaring with pain.

"Don't come back here!" she hollered after me. "Only for office workers and their guests. Want to go to jail? No thieves allowed!"

A fuse lit within me. I turned and exploded on her: "Thieves? Lon Hackney's the thief! Your tenant, Lon Hackney. A criminal! You're harboring criminals here. You're sheltering an extortionist. You're complicit! Look, I'm a fucking police officer. Want me to call the FBI?"

She looked at me tiredly, unimpressed by my wild, nonsensical lies and impotent threats. For a police officer, I supposed, the glasses-nose-and-mustache disguise lacked a certain aura of professionalism. I tugged the rig off my face. "I'm sorry," I said. "I fell off a roof and things have been really hard for me lately. I like your liquor store. I think it's cool that you guys sell stamps. No one sells stamps anymore. And you have a really nice grandson."

"Thank you," she said, dropping her hands to her side. "I didn't really call the nine-one-one. But I guess it is time for us to say goodbye. You can find another place to be yourself."

Sarah walked me back to Eli's apartment. My flight was early the next morning. "Text me when you land in Detroit," she said, "so I know you made it home safe."

At 6:30 a.m., on the way to SFO Airport, I convinced Eli to

shoot past Lon's office on Mission Street one last time. I'd written a note to slip through his mail slot, to go with the bottle of pee from the evening before, half veiled threat, half last-ditch appeal to his conscience: "WE'RE WATCHING EVERYTHING YOU DO. DO THE RIGHT THING." But when I got to his office door and poked open the mail slot, I was stunned to see that the pile of mail on the floor was gone. I heard myself say out loud, "What the fuck?" Sometime during the night, apparently, Lon Hackney, stealthy as a ghost, had flitted through, collected two weeks' worth of contest submissions—or at least the checks from each package—and disappeared again into his bunker. After a week spent staking out his office, I couldn't believe he'd spirited past me, that I'd missed him by hours. Still, it meant he'd found the bottle I'd left for him, and that thought alone—the eel of spooky unease I was sure now circulated in his belly—kept me smiling the whole way home.

Ten months passed. Lon seemed to be lying low. Had my efforts huffed and puffed and blown his house of cards right down? It was hard to say, but all of his lit agency e-mails slipped to a trickle and then fell off completely. Maybe he'd found a new racket, I imagined, and was sticking people with balloon-payment mortgages, or peddling shady investments, or running a three-card monte game on Fisherman's Wharf—nothing to be proud of, to be certain, but all fine by me. One Saturday in the fall, a guy left his Chevy Silverado parked in front of my house, with Ohio plates and swathed in Ohio State Buckeyes bumper stickers, and I gifted him my remaining bottles of pee in the bed of his truck, with a note that said, "GO BLUE." I spent the winter in Michigan, trying to regain strength in my ankle, with mixed success, and talking to girls at the bar, trying to forget about Sarah, with no success.

In the spring, out of nowhere, I got an e-mail from Lon—not

a personal e-mail, but the standard call for submissions for his latest writing contest, the Noble Pen Awards. The bastard was back, and I saw that after his brief hibernation, he'd snaked his greedy paws to every corner of the country, expanding his empire from six bogus literary agencies to twelve, each scheduled to host an awards gala at a slew of far-flung "Future Is Now" conferences, beginning with New York City and proceeding westward. Among other contests, he'd christened his newly hatched brood the Golden Pencil Awards, the QWERTYUIOP Quest (okay, that one was clever), and, with what was starting to feel more like ill will than inattention to detail, the Cormac McCarthy Memorial Challenge. *What the hell?* Couldn't he at least pick writers who'd already died? I forwarded his e-mail to Ondrea Wales, whom I'd continued to trade messages with here and there, and she wrote back four minutes later: "Oh no! He must be stopped. Come to New York—let's vanquish him!"

Middle of June, I flew to New York, the weekend of the Noble Pen Awards and Lon's sham "Future Is Now" conference. I claimed to Ondrea that I had other business there, and I guess I sort of did, but mostly I just wanted to meet her in person and dump pee on Lon Hackney's head. The conference was now spread over two days—an awards ceremony on Thursday night at the swanky Emerald Bell Hotel, and outdoor readings in Tompkins Square Park the following afternoon. Me and Ondrea made a dinner date for Thursday evening, with plans to head over to the Emerald Bell afterwards to confront Lon.

At five o'clock Thursday, I showered and shaved at my cousin's apartment in Midtown, and transferred a pair of wide-mouth Aquafina bottles to my backpack from the gym bag I'd brought from home and checked on the plane. The blue, plastic tint of the bottles gave the pee sloshing inside them a greenish, radioactive glow. In the subway station, on the way to meet Ondrea at a sushi place she'd picked out, a police dog eyed me with grim disapproval, as though it sensed I had a bomb in my bag.

In person, Ondrea was even prettier than her picture. She had long blond hair, green eyes, rosy cheeks, and a wide, easy smile, and she wore a white lace top and a purple beret that seemed fashionable, not pretentious. The fact that she'd applied gloss to her lips and a trace of eyeliner—and were those *sparkles* dusted across her cheeks?—reassured me that I wasn't crazy for thinking of this as a date, even though in my e-mails and texts I'd held back from any romantic innuendo and had said only, "Let's grab a bite," and, "It'll be great to hang out."

What can I say? Ondrea was smart, funny, and inquisitive, entertainingly opinionated, endlessly adorable. For two hours, we tossed back tuna rolls and pounded sake. We talked about writing, our families, our childhoods, our friends, our fears, our hopes, our dreams. I told Ondrea about the old, beautiful, abandoned movie theater with a glorious marquee I'd spotted in the town of Tres Piedras, New Mexico, and how I wanted to move there, fix the place up, and share my favorite movies a couple of nights a week with the locals and whatever road-tripping folks found their way in. Ondrea said she had relatives on her mother's side who lived in a giant, dilapidated castle in the Slovakian countryside, a hundred miles outside of Bratislava, and had offered to put her up while she worked on her next book. We lapsed into silence, gazing at each other, pondering a home-and-home series: Slovakia, New Mexico.

I ordered another carafe of sake and turned the conversation to Lon Hackney and our impending collision with him at the Emerald Bell, which stirred me with a kind of open-dammed bloodlust. Ondrea wanted to know what our plan would be when we confronted him, and I patted my backpack, on the chair between us, and told her not to worry, I had the whole thing figured out.

"What do you have in there, a gun?" she asked.

I laughed cryptically. "Lon will not forget what happens tonight," I promised her. "It will haunt him. As long as he keeps it up with all the contest bullshit, this night will haunt him."

"Cheers to that," she said. She lifted her sake, and we clinked glasses and downed our drinks. I filled our cups again, and again we downed them. "Might as well finish this stuff off," she said, with the cutest of shrugs. She poured the rest into our cups and we knocked them back, like a couple of college freshmen on spring break, shooting tequila on Bourbon Street. Ondrea giggled. "I have to pee," she said. "I'll be right back."

"Okay. I'll get the check."

We headed for the Emerald Bell, walking crosstown. I took her hand, and she pulled away to adjust her purse, then reached for my hand again. My heart felt buoyant, hyperoxygenated. It was the most exquisite of gentle June nights in Manhattan. Taxis flared past; the smell of kabobs and sugary roasted almonds wafted from street vendors' carts; snatches of conversations fluttered through the air from other passersby in Greek, Mandarin, and Jamaican patois. There's no city on Earth I'd rather walk through filled with drink and holding a girl's hand. Even my bad ankle, for the first time in a year, felt brand-new.

Outside the Emerald Bell, Ondrea said, "Okay, seriously, what's our plan gonna be?"

"We're gonna ambush him," I said.

"With weapons?"

"Kind of, yes. I brought one for you, too." I pulled my backpack off, then thought twice before reaching inside, wondering if my urine bottles were too much to reveal on a first date.

Ondrea saw me hemming and hawing. "What's going on?" she said, laughing. "What's in the bag?"

I thought about how humiliated Ondrea told me she'd been in Golden Gate Park the day she'd set up her booth, about her anger at a guy who would take advantage of struggling writers, folks who had the least money to burn. It was what made a pee-bottle attack so appropriate—we'd be fighting fire with fire, lashing him back with the shame he'd splashed remorselessly on so many others.

I pulled out the Aquafina bottles and shook them up, green brew bubbling like a magic elixir. "This is gonna be the night I've been waiting for for a long-ass time," I told her. "We're gonna give Lon an extremely memorable shower in front of everybody. In the middle of the awards ceremony." I passed her one of the bottles. "Are you down or what?"

"What's in these?" she asked.

"Well. It's pee."

"Pee?"

"Like, urine."

"*Your* pee?"

"Yeah, I filled these," I said, with drunken pride.

"Tonight?"

"In Michigan."

She stared at me. "Oh my God," she said. She seemed to recognize my plan's sinister brilliance.

"We'll dump these on his head," I went on, light-headed, filled with glee. "You first, me first, at the same time, it doesn't matter. We'll let him know what we think of his scams. We'll let everyone know. Then—and this is just my suggestion—we should walk up to Central Park and climb in one of those horse-and-buggies, and kiss each other for like an hour and forty-five minutes. I really can't wait to kiss you."

Ondrea peered at me, her face frozen into the most curious expression. Over the course of the next couple of seconds, I swear I saw each tiny muscle fiber in her face—from her eyelids to her nostrils to her jaw—drop, one by one, like coins in the Plinko game on *The Price Is Right*, until she'd reached a look of confused, horrified revulsion. A dagger of instant regret gutted my insides, and I felt all the hopefulness and joy gush out of me, like a gooey knot of intestines.

"No," she said. "No! I don't think that's a good idea at all." She looked at the pee bottle she was clutching with trembling, fearful disgust, like an accident victim coming off morphine, discovering a hook where her hand used to be. "You don't even know me!" she cried. "I'm seeing someone right now. I've been seeing someone. Did you think this was—oh my God, take this from me!" She thrust the bottle back into my hand.

"I was kidding?" I said, feeling a great sadness rush in. "This is just lemonade. But Lon, he'll think it's pee!"

"It looks like pee," she said.

"That's the genius of it!"

"It's pee. Am I right? It's pee!"

"Okay, it's pee—but doesn't he deserve pee? A lot of pee? We're letting him off easy here!"

Two young West African bellhops, in their trussed-up, tasseled attire, heard our commotion and came trotting near. "Everything okay here?" one of them asked.

"It's fine, thanks," I said. "Except she's breaking up with me."

He looked at Ondrea. "Everything okay, miss?"

She nodded, but retained her look of distress.

"You two guests of the hotel?" asked the bellhop. His cohort headed away to unload luggage from the trunk of a town car.

I shook my head. "Just here for the Future Is Now conference."

"Oh, cool, man. You guys authors?"

"Yeah."

"What kind of stuff? Biographies?"

"Well, this is Ondrea Wales, she writes teen novels. They're really good—I mean, I think older readers get something out of them, too. *Girl of the Century*, check that one out, it's awesome."

Ondrea's withering gaze softened. "You read *Girl of the Century*?" she peeped.

"I read all your books."

She smiled despite herself, and looked away.

The bellhop edged between us. "Well, if you know anyone who writes biographies, if they want a crazy life story, I know someone they should write about."

"Who's that?"

"Me!" For the next several minutes, while Ondrea stood with her arms crossed, sighing and scowling, the guy outlined the strange, unexpected turns that his life and career path had taken, from a nickel mine east of Dakar to a falafel shop in Hamburg to the bellhop stand at the Emerald Bell Hotel near Times Square. His partner kept shouting for him, urging him to get back to work, to which he'd holler back in French, *"Deux minutes! Deux minutes!"* I tried to gauge Ondrea's mood—on the one hand, she seemed to think I was a fucking psycho, on the other hand, she hadn't left yet. Finally, me and the bellhop traded cell-phone numbers and shook hands, and he hurried off. I realized I was still holding the pee bottles, and quickly stuffed them deep into my backpack.

I reached for Ondrea's shoulder and she shied away. "What do you think?" I said hopefully. "Come on. Time to get Lon?"

She looked at me for a couple of seconds, her clear, green eyes widening. It still felt like anything could happen. At last, she took a sharp breath and said, "I don't think so. I'm late somewhere. I should go." She took a step back. "It was great meeting you, though. Good luck in there."

The air whooshed out of me. "I'll text you how it goes."

"Do that," she said.

"I'm here all weekend," I said. "I mean, if you want to hang out another night."

"Okay. Text me." She turned and headed off down Forty-fourth Street, without a handshake, a hug, or even a high five. Then, a half block down, she glanced back at me over her shoulder and flashed a warm, genuine smile, the kind of knowing, intimate smile that, an hour before, I'd imagined she might have had on her face after a long lovemaking session at our castle outside Bratislava.

"I'm gonna get Lon for you!" I shouted, but already she'd

flagged a cab and was hopping in. The light at Fifth Avenue slipped from red to green and the cab shot away and Ondrea was gone.

"Oh. Yeah. The Future Is Now," said a guy at the hotel's front desk. "They're in the Legacy Ballroom. Fourth floor. You can take the elevator or you can take the stairs."

I took the stairs, grand and winding, floating up them three at a time, around and around the lobby's enormous atrium, gazing at the magnificent, six-story crystal chandelier in the center, sparkling like a frozen waterfall. The steps were layered with thick, luxurious carpet and my shoes made no sound. I felt an assassin's sense of raw fury mingled with quiet, pulsing determination. It was eight thirty, and the Noble Pen awards ceremony had been slated to begin at eight. Outside the giant oak doors to the conference room, I slid my backpack around and rocked it front-pack style, tugging the zipper open; the tips of my Aquafina pee bottles quivered in the heavy, massive silence. I hauled on the doors and slipped in.

The Legacy Ballroom, for all its lofty name, turned out to be a drab and gloomy low-ceilinged hallway in the shape of three batting cages strung together end to end. About thirty-five men and women in their early fifties to mid-seventies, clothed in rumpled suits and faded dresses bearing *Hello, My Name Is* name tags, sipped wine from Dixie cups and milled aimlessly along a row of tables, where red plastic plates of carrots, celery, grape tomatoes, and cubes of cheese had been laid out, along with bowls of Chex Mix, a few boxes of Ritz crackers, and loose packets of ranch dressing. It was like a Super Bowl party for homeless academics.

"Excuse me," said a perturbed-looking woman with long strands of gray hair, grasping my arm. "Are you Lon?"

"No," I said. "I'm here to look for Lon."

She called to an older man a few feet away. "Come here, honey," she said, waggling a finger toward me, "I think I found Lon."

The man creaked near and offered his hand. "Lon? Pleased to meet ya. When's the ceremony start?"

I shook his hand. "Thanks. Not Lon, though. Thanks."

"What say?"

"I'm not Lon!" I quickly apologized, feeling bad for lashing out at the very people I was there to defend. I'd just rarely been so amped up.

"Well, who's in charge here?" said the man. He turned to his wife. "He says he's not Lon."

She looked at me. "You sure you're not Lon?"

"Fucking positive."

She gave an exasperated sigh. "Well, ain't this a fine mess."

It only took a few minutes of poking around, talking to people, to piece things together. The "awards ceremony" was hardly a ceremony at all. According to an old woman in a wheelchair who said she'd been stationed there since six o'clock, a giant, hairy, lumpy guy had shown up around six fifteen, carted in a stack of chairs, set up some tables, and spread out the food and drinks, along with the blank name tags, a couple of markers, Future Is Now pins, and certificates for each of the prize winners. He talked to almost no one and was out of there before seven. The old woman had assumed he was a hotel employee, but when I suggested it might have been Lon, the director of the festival, she said yes, that sounded right, she'd heard someone use that name with him.

Fucking Lon. He was an apparition, a wisp of smoke— Sasquatch and Keyser Söze rolled into one. I'd been to both coasts to track him down and still he kept eluding me. I roamed the hall, chatting up one kind soul after another, trying to get a line on our mystery man, but they were all as mystified as I was. For the most part, everyone's spirits were up—this was a celebration, after all, and whoever they spoke to, mutual congratulations were in order (they'd all been named prize winners)—but beneath their joviality, a creeping sense that all was not right had begun to seep into the room like a rank smell. And this was just the beginning, I knew. The next day, in Tompkins Square Park, the full extent of Lon's con would slowly become clear.

Another woman stopped me to ask if I was Lon. "I want to switch booth locations for tomorrow," she said. "I'm in the Self-Help tent, but I asked for Romance."

I couldn't bear another second of this. I'd fucked things up with Ondrea, I'd fucked things up with Sarah, and Lon Hackney, I figured, was off counting his riches somewhere, laughing at me and his legion of Noble Pen suckers.

"Well, if you're not Lon," said the woman, "you must be an author. What kind of books do you write?"

"Biographies of bellhops." I was fuming, and trying to sort out my next move.

"Neat." She reached into her shoulder bag. "Hey, would you like a copy of my novel? I'd like to give you one. I can sign it for you."

My dad, I knew, if he was in the room, would have been reduced to the same—traveling to New York with hopes of making some publishing contacts, landing an agent, and finding the right home for his book, and before long, feeling lucky just to find a stranger generous enough to accept a free copy.

The woman's book was called *Aiden's Quest*; it was spiral bound, with a sheet of cellophane over the cover, and had been printed at a Kinko's near her home in Bemidji, Minnesota, she told me. She described it as a ninth-century romantic thriller about a faerie held captive on a Scottish isle and the young monk who fights to free her. "What's your name?" she asked, peeling to the title page to write an inscription.

"You know," I said, "would you mind signing it to Sarah?"

"Who's Sarah?"

"My wife."

She gave a little squeal, and said, "I'd be happy to. Sarah with an 'h'?"

"Sarah with an 'h.'"

She signed her book carefully and handed it over, and I thanked her sincerely. Another author approached, offering me a copy of his book, and within a few minutes I'd collected a half dozen freebies before I beat it for the door. I felt my emotions crashing and burning—things with Ondrea were ruined, Lon had blue-balled my pee-bottle siege, and all that was left to do was find a bar and get smashed.

Fortunately, I didn't have to go far. A half-level below the Emerald Bell's lobby was a hotel bar called Maroon. I sat on a stool and ordered a Booker's on the rocks and watched the NBA Finals with two middle-aged Orlando Magic fans who said they were Nextel salesmen from Kissimmee. The guy next to me, chugging rum, was the smaller but rowdier of the two—he was rocking a Hedo Turkoglu jersey and waved his arms in the air when the Lakers shot free throws, going nuts if they missed, as though he'd caused them to brick it, while his bulky friend on the far side brooded and nursed a Heineken. "What's wrong, Big Fella?" I asked.

"Aw, he don't like sports," said Turkoglu. "He just wants to smoke weed."

"I've got weed," I told him.

At halftime, we went up to Big Fella's room on the twenty-second floor and I passed him a little baggie of homegrown to roll into doobies, while me and Turkoglu found the game on TV and raided the minifridge for airplane shots of Crown Royal and Jack. Soon we were all pretty fucked up. The game was a battle—Hedo and Kobe going toe-to-toe, and before long I was waving my arms along with Turkoglu when the Lakers shot free throws, and eventually we goaded Big Fella into waving his arms, too, as we all laughed and shouted.

During an ad break halfway through the fourth quarter with the score tied, I stumbled into the bathroom to take a leak, and somehow set my glass on the counter and knocked it off in the same motion, and it shattered to pieces at my feet. A second later, I slid backwards on my own puddle of ice and went crashing down—*wham*—to the floor. Something bit the side of my right hand, it felt like, and when I held my hand up, I saw dark-red blood bubbling from a long wound that ran from my wrist to my pinky—I'd sliced myself good on a broken piece of glass. I winced, but had enough drink in me, it didn't hurt too much, I just didn't want to have to get stitches. Lying on the floor of Big Fella's bathroom, I reached for a washcloth and wrapped it tightly around my cut-up hand, then began picking up all the broken bits of glass. Something caught my attention on the floor next to the little waste bucket under the sink—it was one of those long, glossy luggage tags stamped with your final destination that they slap on your bag at the airport before tossing it into the plane's belly, which you tear off and toss out once you get where you're going. But there was a name on this one, and it took me several dumbfounded seconds to process it cleanly—L. HACKNEY.

What the fucking fuck? I scrambled to my feet and charged out of the bathroom. Turkoglu turned his head from the game to look at me. "What the hell," he said. "Holy shit, you're all bloody, dude."

I looked past him, at Big Fella, and held the luggage tag high above my head, shrieking wildly, *"What the fuck is this shit?"*

"Whoa, man," said Turkoglu, rising to his feet. "I think you got overserved."

"Is this true?" I howled, waving the tag, shaking drops of blood onto my neck and chin.

"Yeah," said Big Fella. "I flew into JFK. So what."

"For what?"

"What?" His eyes were glazed and red.

"You flew in for what? *Why* are you here?"

"For the Future Is Now conference, man."

Three hours before, when I'd first walked into the Emerald Bell, the righteousness of my mission had sharpened my focus to a fine, deadly point, but now, caught off guard, drunk and stoned, I felt confused and frantic, like a man swarmed by bats. "I thought you said you sold cell phones!" I cried.

"Phil sells cell phones," said Big Fella. "I run a literary agency. What's it to you?"

"I don't 'sell cell phones,'" Turkoglu piped up. "I get retail stores to carry Nextel products. You make it sound like I'm hawking 'em out of my trunk." He turned back to the TV and cranked up the volume.

I was losing it. "But I thought—I thought you guys worked together."

"Who?" said Turkoglu. "Me and him? Naw, I just met Lon downstairs, an hour before you showed up." He leapt to his feet, cheering a blocked shot by Dwight Howard, and shouted at the TV, "Our house, baby! You're in our motherfuckin' house now!"

I stared at Big Fella—Lon Hackney—feeling sick with adrenaline, herb, sake, and bourbon. He looked like Jabba the Hutt dressed as a burned-out music producer for Halloween—long, scraggly hair, a wide, splotchy face, in a black turtleneck and black jeans. Not a salesman at all—what had I been thinking? He eyed me through hooded lids, warily, high as hell but aware that something dangerous had been set into motion. "Your name is Lon?" I asked him over the TV's roar, with a bleat of hysterical laughter.

He nodded.

"Lon Hackney?"

"Yeah. Who are you?"

I said nothing, struggling to fend off a strange rush of unexpected tears, and reached into my backpack with my unbloody hand. One at a time, I drew out the Aquafina bottles of pee.

"Here, Lon," I said. "Catch." I lobbed them across the room to him, quickly, one-two, and he caught the first and fumbled the second; it bounced into his lap, gently fizzing.

Slowly, in his weed-dwindled, morally rotted, pea-sized Jabba brain, he began to put two and two together. His face went slack, and he slumped a little, took a deep breath, and said in a flat, low voice, edged with both fear and menace, "I know who you are. What do you want from me? Why are you here?"

The quiet, eye-of-the-hurricane drama of our long-awaited face-off was lost on Turkoglu—Phil, from Nextel—who couldn't understand why we'd stopped paying attention to the game when the score was so close down the stretch. "Hey, you guys, shut up and focus! We need a bucket here!"

I felt like the German shepherd tied to a stake in the yard who for years barks ferociously at the little poodle next door, and then, when he finally breaks loose from his chain, races over, sniffs the poodle's ass for a second, and then wanders off, directionless, down the road. All of life's urgent pursuits are rendered meaningless once they're actually in your grasp—I wondered why I'd thought confronting Lon Hackney would be any different. I still had to pee. I could pee on him, I mused. I could empty the bottles of pee over his head. I could shout at him and call him names. But what, in the end, was the fucking point? Here he was before me, a washed-up fat-ass, hiding from his own conference's participants, lighting joints in a lonely hotel room, his two best friends a pair of dudes he'd just met that night, watching basketball with us though he didn't even like sports. There was nothing I could say or do to knock him any lower. Still, I'd come to New York to make him stop, to end his writing contest scam. For my dad. For Ondrea.

"Lon, you fucker, you supreme fucker," I said. "I know your fucking scam inside and out, so listen to me, you don't have to deny anything, 'cause there's no point in that. I know the scam exactly. Okay? I know. I know it all." I kept my right hand raised high toward the ceiling, clutching the washcloth, and it's possible that with all the blood dripping down my arm, I seemed crazier and more dangerous than I really was. "Here's the thing," I growled. "You got to quit. You got to quit this shit."

Phil gave me a glance, thoroughly confused by what was happening, but too intent on the game's closing minutes to worry too much about me and Lon's detente. He was on his cell phone with a buddy in Florida who was also watching the game.

"I can't quit," said Lon, very, very quietly, almost inaudible over the cries of the announcers on the TV. "I need the money. I have a wife. I have a kid." He rocked back and forth a little, inspecting the bottle of pee in his hand.

"You have real victims," I said. "Go down to the Legacy Room. Talk to them."

"It's nothing they can't afford," he said, with a hint of bitterness.

"You know what the worst thing is? You don't even read their books!" I reached into my backpack and pulled out the spiral-bound novel that the woman from Minnesota had given me, *Aiden's Quest*, along with the other books I'd collected. I felt my voice rising to a shout as I held them out and shook them in the air. "All these people, all they want is for their books to get read!"

"Guys, chill out!" snapped Phil. "Hit the peace pipe. Or take it into the hallway." He said into his phone, "Yeah, no, just the usual riffraff that can't handle their drink."

Lon sat staring at the floor. His heavy girth weighted the bed down low, and I had the thought that it must be really difficult to go through life so obese. "I'm just trying to live my life," he said. "What do people want from me."

We fell into a stalemate. In the end, even if Lon shitted on some people's heads, it wasn't genocide. It was extremely fucking lame, is what it was, and truly hurtful to some, I was sure, having witnessed just the tiniest bit of his casual destruction firsthand, but he wasn't prostituting ten-year-old girls, or abducting family pets, or selling guns to gangs—he was organizing failed literary conventions.

"Leave my room or I'm gonna call Security," he said at last.

That pissed me off. "You know," I said to him, "the only motherfucker who's more of a loser than you is me. 'Cause I'm the one who's gonna spend my life following you, hounding you, harassing you, dirtying your name, and mailing you bottles of pee, until I shut you down."

"Aaiiieeeeeeee!" screamed Phil suddenly, from between us. He slid from the near bed, by the TV, where he'd been sitting, down to the floor, hands over his face. "You can't leave that guy alone!" he wailed. "Fuck, fuck, fuck, fuck, fuck, fuck, fuck!" Derek Fisher had just drained a long three for the Lakers to send the game into overtime; they kept replaying the shot from different angles in slo-mo. "Fuck this," he said, "I'm going downstairs to watch. You guys and your lovers' spat, you're bringing me down. It's bad juju." He grabbed a beer from the minibar and padded his way out the door, letting it slam behind him.

Somehow, with Phil gone, the room felt suddenly tense and unpredictable. Lon looked at me, upset, angry, and scared, as though I might rush him. "Well," he said, wobbly voiced. "What happens now?"

"Here's what happens, I think. I'll tell you. Actually, one of two things." I was making this up as I went along. "The second thing, what I don't want, is—we fight. You're a pretty big dude, and I don't want to fight you, you'll probably get some licks in, but I'll warn you, I'm wily, I know how to inflict damage, and I fight like a cornered animal. But that's no good for either of us. If you agree to the first thing, we don't have to go to the second."

"I can't shut down the contests," he said. "I wrote freelance for twelve years. I basically lived out of my car. I'm not going back to that."

"Okay," I said. "That's not what I was asking. Here's what I'm asking." The room seemed to tilt on its side, and I wondered if my wooziness might be due to a loss of blood. "I'm asking you to drink that bottle of pee, right now," I said. "Every drop."

He lifted the bottle close to his face, as though mulling it over. "I don't know," he said at last. "Why do you want me to drink pee?"

"Everyone leaves your shitty conferences feeling burned. I want you to see what it feels like to get a bad taste in your mouth. A bad taste you'll never forget."

"Huh." He slowly unscrewed the cap off the bottle and bent his head to take a whiff. Deeply revolted, he grimaced and screwed the cap back on. "I would throw up," he said. "I can't drink this whole thing." He took a quick gander around the room, as though sizing up what objects close at hand—a lamp? an ashtray?—could be used as weapons, if things took that sort of turn.

"Drink half, then. Half is enough." I scowled and took an imposing step closer.

"Oh God," he said, burying his face in one of his meaty palms. He took a long, staggered breath, and shook his head back and forth. *"Fuuuuuuck."* It seemed to me that somehow I'd gotten through to him, and that for the first time, whatever regret he must have had for his writing contest scams was finally beginning to surface. As he sat there, head bowed, I felt a burst of quiet satisfaction. But still, I intended to follow through with my improvised punishment. "Go on," I said. "Bottoms up."

Lon raised his head and stared at the pile of books I'd pulled from my backpack. "Look," he said. "Here's another idea. You want people to read those books so bad? Fine. I'll read 'em." Quietly, he went on. "I know I can run these conferences better. It's just, I'm only one person."

It rankled me that he was still ducking responsibility by making excuses, but he had a tone of genuine self-reflection that took me by surprise. "What are you saying?" I asked.

"I'm saying I can't drink this bottle, but if you'll give me a pass, I'll make some changes. And I'll start by reading those books."

I thought about that for a moment, hesitant to let him off easy. But I wasn't sure that drinking my pee was going to lead him to any greater epiphanies. "You'll read every one of these books?"

"Yeah," he said. "Every one. Hand 'em here."

"What about all the other books people send you?" I thought of my dad's essay collection, *Brooklyn Boy*, which had surely been tossed in a Dumpster as soon as his check had been cashed.

Lon nodded. "I'll make sure they get read. That was the whole idea, from the beginning, to help people get their books out there. Mine, too." He rubbed his ear.

"Fine," I said at last. I picked up *Aiden's Quest*. "You can start with this one. I met the woman who wrote it. She's here. Downstairs. She entered it in your contest."

"What did she win?"

"Third place, I think. Historical fiction."

"Let me see."

I limped over and passed him the pages. He turned it over in his hands, reading the back cover. "This sounds more like fantasy," he said. "Historical fiction is more . . . historical." He heaved a breath. "All right, I'll read this one first."

"Cover to cover."

"Yeah. Cover to cover." He gave me a look. "No more pee?"

"No more pee."

"You're fuckin' crazy," he said, starting to laugh. "Fuckin' nutjob. Okay, I guess we've got a deal. Shit." He scooted up his bed toward the nightstand, where he'd mashed out a joint, sparked it, took a long hit, blew smoke toward the ceiling, and leaned back on a pile of pillows, fumbled a pair of glasses onto his face, and turned to page one. "Can you turn that TV down?" he said. "I can't hear myself think."

I reached for the remote and settled down on the other bed to watch the end of the basketball game.

"You better wash out that cut," said Lon. "You think you need to get it stitched up?"

"I don't think so." But I got up and went to the bathroom to wash it out and wrap it in a fresh cloth. When I came back, Lon was making little interested reading sounds—a *"Huh,"* a *"Hmmm,"* and a chuckle.

I poured myself a nightcap in a plastic disposable cup—Canadian Club over ice—and sat on the edge of the bed, sipping it down, watching the rest of the overtime, while Lon, in his bed, slowly turned through the pages of *Aiden's Quest*. With thirty seconds to play, Derek Fisher nailed another three to put the Lakers up, and they went on to win by seven, taking a three-games-to-one series lead, effectively crushing the Magic's hopes of a championship. I thought of Phil, down in the bar, or maybe back in his own room, glumly removing his Turkoglu jersey, and starting to drunkenly prepare for his presentation the next day at Nextel HQ. Sometimes in life things didn't go the way you hoped and imagined they would, I thought, resting my head back, but still, somehow, it all worked out okay.

I woke up hours later. It was maybe three or four in the morning. The room was dark and quiet, apart from flashes from the TV and the hushed voices of golf announcers. My head was pounding, my hand burned where I'd sliced it, and my ankle ebbed with a low-grade but steady ache. In his bed, turned away, webbed in sheets, hair flopped this way and that, Lon breathed heavily, a half-snore.

I stood up and inspected my hand. The wound had closed and was matted with dried blood, which looked black in the TV's dark flicker. I headed for the door. Just as I reached for the handle and turned it, a sound startled me from the far side of the room.

"Hey," Lon whispered in the darkness. "Hey, is that you? Guess what?"

"What?" For some reason, I was whispering, too.

"I finished that book."

"You did?"

"Yeah."

"That's good," I said. "That's really good."

"Yeah. Yeah, guess what?"

"What?"

"I'll tell you something," Lon said. "I got to tell you. It was pretty good."

HOW I GOT THESE BOOTS

Just past Flagstaff he appeared, a tiny, grizzled man on the shoulder of Highway 64 with his thumb out, wearing a backpack bigger than himself. I pulled over a little ways past him and climbed out of the car and watched him waddle toward me. A tin canteen and a pair of hiking boots with red laces dangled from his pack, clanking together every couple of steps. His short white hair, creased face smudged with dirt, rumpled jeans, and oil-stained sneakers gave him the look of a homeless track coach.

"Young man, thanks for stopping!" he said, thrusting out a hand. "Name's John Molloy. Where ya headed, where ya headed?"

"The Grand Canyon," I said.

His eyes sparkled. "Bingo! Me too!"

In the car, headed west again, John told me his story. For thirty-five years he'd worked in a machine shop in Lowell, Massachusetts. But his lifelong dream was to visit the Grand Canyon. He'd read dozens of books about it, studied its geology and its history; he'd even cut out pictures from *National Geographic* and pasted them to the wall above his bed.

A few weeks before, he'd been talking about the Grand Canyon with the guys he worked with, and one of them had said, "For Chrissakes, shut up already! What is it with you? It's always the Grand Canyon this, the Grand Canyon that. Look, you'll never make it there, and it's depressing to hear you go on and on about it every damn day."

John looked at me with a mischievous glint. "So I said to him, 'Okay, I quit.' Turned in my tools and walked out." He'd scraped together enough money for a Greyhound ticket as far as Amarillo, said goodbye to his mother and his teenage son, who shared his apartment, and hopped on the bus. It had taken him three days to reach Amarillo and three more days to hitchhike six hundred miles to Flagstaff. Now that he'd found a ride—me—to take him the rest of the way, he was shaking with excitement. "I can't believe we'll be there in less than two hours," he said. He clapped his hands. He drummed on the dashboard. He rubbed his eyes and whistled at the sight of each towering cactus we passed. Then he peered at me. "Say, you're pretty quiet. What you brooding about?"

I told him about my wrecked heart, the girlfriend who'd left me and moved to Scotland, how I hadn't dated or kissed another girl in two years. And now the girl I'd flown to Arizona to see—captain of the Phoenix Suns dance team—had let me down; when I'd arrived, she'd told me about her new boyfriend, an NFL punter. It was actually the punter who'd suggested I check out the Grand Canyon. "I've never been more lost," I said.

Still, I felt lucky that I was about to witness someone realize their lifelong dream. My own dreams seemed hazier and more impossible. I explained to John that I wanted to be a writer but was so caught up in an unsolvable hurt and ache, I hadn't written a word in months.

We passed the ranger station at the outer perimeter of the park, and for the next twelve miles, as we rolled closer to the edge of the Grand Canyon, John leaned halfway out his window like a happy dog gulping up the first breezes of spring. His buzzing energy buoyed me and began to tug me from the darkness. At last we reached the first overlook, and John bounded from the car, sprinted toward the edge, and gazed out across the vast chasm for a few seconds, then turned back toward me and shot two fists skyward, eyes wet, face shining. I took a picture of him and laughed out loud, exhilarated myself. We whooped it up for a minute, alone at the top of the world.

The sun hung lower, and we hiked an hour down into the canyon. John, blissed-out and bubbly, pointed out rocks and wildlife, gushing with information. This wasn't just run-of-the-mill tour-book stuff; it was endless. Not only was I blessed to be with someone in such a radiant state, I was also visiting the Grand Canyon with a guy who had, seriously, transformed himself into one of the world's top experts on the Grand Canyon. Finally, he fell into a kind of stunned, contented silence, and we made our way back up to the rim. The canyon hummed at our backs.

We found the park campground and pitched a tent in the dark. It began to snow. John passed me his canteen. "Have a sip of this," he said, grinning. "It ain't water."

In the morning, we drove down to the park office to see if we could stir up a job for John working trail maintenance or guiding hiking tours. The head ranger, astonished at his depth of knowledge, hired him on the spot. I bought John a few days of groceries and paid for his campsite through the weekend.

"Look," John said, "I can't let you just spend a hundred bucks on me. You got to take these." He pressed his hiking boots into my hands. Before I could protest, he said, "They don't fit me. I got the ugliest blisters you ever seen. I'll do better on the trail in my sneakers. Here, take 'em." He gave me a hug. "Now get on back to Chicago. I'll hold the fort down here."

A year later, when I left Chicago and drove to New Mexico to follow my dreams of being a writer, I was wearing those boots with the red laces. On my dashboard was the picture of John Molloy at the edge of the canyon, fists raised toward the sky.

SHADE

Along I-10's most dust-torn and barren stretch, in southwest New Mexico, there's an old truck-stop diner in the sad little town of Deming called the Desert Sky Café, and early one morning in November of 2003, just before dawn, I found myself parked in front of the Desert Sky in a rental Ford, my eyes wet, my hands and my shirt streaked with blood.

After a couple of minutes I pulled myself together and headed inside to get breakfast. The place was completely empty other than a no-nonsense waitress in her fifties rolling silverware at the counter and a grizzled old cook in back scraping the grill. I hopped up on a stool, and when the waitress came over, she looked me up and down and said, "Is that blood?"

I nodded. "Yeah."

"Is that your blood?"

"No."

"Should I call the police?"

"How 'bout I tell you the story and then you decide?"

She looked at me sternly, considering this. Then she plucked a pad and pen from her apron and said, "Okay. What'll you have?"

———

This was the second time I'd been inside the Desert Sky Café; the first was in 1999 on a road trip from New York City to Cali with my friend Eddie Faktorovich. But the first time I'd ever laid eyes on the place was years before, in the fall of '92, in a movie called *Gas, Food, Lodging*, which takes place in the fictional town of Laramie, New Mexico, but was filmed in Deming.

All through high school, I'd gone alone to see movies downtown at the Michigan Theater, and my visits only increased when I started college and moved into a dorm a few blocks away. One night, a month into my first semester, I went to see *Gas, Food, Lodging*, a story about a middle-aged waitress at the Desert Sky who lives in a nearby trailer park with her two teenage daughters, Trudi and Shade. In just an hour and a half, I fell so deeply and powerfully in love with Shade that when I left the theater I felt like a different person—profoundly transformed and filled with a terrible, rapturous heartache. I remember drifting through town like a ghost, lying down in a patch of damp grass, and staring at the moon for hours. I was overjoyed that I'd found my soulmate, but distressed that she was only a character in a movie—I couldn't exactly leap through the screen and introduce myself. And although it was tempting, I never confused Shade with the actress who played her, Fairuza Balk. I was sure Fairuza Balk was wondrous in her own right, but it was Shade who was my soulmate, it was Shade whom I'd scour the planet to find.

Shade was tough, tender, otherworldly, filled with a bewitching sadness. Her desolate beauty matched the New Mexico landscape, and I dreamed of visiting her town and looking for her there. I went back to the Michigan Theater the next night, my heart torqued and titillated, and then again the night after that. Crushed and giddy, I watched Shade's eyes and lips and listened to her tiny, delicate voice and the precise way she spoke. In the movie, Shade falls in love with a Mexican boy whose mother is deaf, and I figured my chances with her were increased, since my mom was deaf, too.

In the weeks and months that followed, my desire and longing for her dominated my being. My parents knew something weird had happened to me—they thought maybe I'd undergone a religious conversion since I'd mentioned visiting a mosque with a kid from my dorm. My friends thought I was 'shrooming all the time, though at that point I'd never even smoked weed. The truth was, I was seventeen years old, and I'd found the love of my life. It's been seventeen years since I came out of that theater, and I still compare every girl I meet to Shade.

Roughly three years later—December 3, 1995—at the campus computer center in Angell Hall, a few blocks from the Michigan Theater, I saw a girl sitting fifty feet from me, her boots tucked beneath her in her chair as she stared forlornly at the screen of her Mac, and I knew I'd found Shade at last. I gathered my courage and talked to her and got her name and phone number. This was Maggie Jones.

Maggie had a soft, haunted beauty. We'd lie in our own beds talking over the phone and fall into an intimate and binding silence for ten minutes at a time, watching the stars and the snow out our bedroom windows. Maggie sometimes spoke a sad, affectless sentence that sounded so much like Shade, I'd record it in my notebook. Here's one: "Trade what, bike for camera?" She'd indulge me when I asked her to repeat my favorite lines of Shade's from the movie, like, "Where'd you get those rocks?" Even Maggie had to marvel at how similar her voice was to Shade's.

Miraculously, she fell in love with me, and we had a year together that was entirely blissful, but things ended miserably. Mostly, I was too intense about my love for her, and Maggie seemed to recognize the slivers of my madness. "I'm just me," she said to me once, trying to get me to ease up. "I'm just a girl." Finally, during a year abroad in Scotland, Maggie met a French windmill repairman named Gilles and moved to France and eventually married him and had two daughters of her own.

In '99, driving with Eddie Faktorovich from the Atlantic Ocean to the Pacific, I crossed into New Mexico for the first time, and in the middle of the night, while Eddie slept in the passenger seat, I slid his green Oldsmobile off I-10 and found the ragged old truck stop from *Gas, Food, Lodging* and the adjacent Desert Sky Café. Walking inside, I felt like I was returning to a place I'd visited only in a dream—this was, unbelievably, the same place Shade had been, and to me it was as holy as a cathedral. I sat at a booth in the corner and downed french toast and OJ, studying the place, lost in a quiet, trembling contemplation. Shade's absence tore at me, and I vowed that one day I would find her and bring her back here with me. I decided to never visit the place again alone.

A year later, still searching for Shade (among other things), I packed up my car and moved to New Mexico. I didn't know a soul in the whole damn state. I'd planned on moving to Deming, but on the drive from Chicago I detoured through northern New Mexico and swooned for the high desert mountains. I found a place to live outside of Taos in a little town called Valdez, and a few weeks later, at a rave in an abandoned barn, I met Bonnie Carpenter.

Bonnie was sweet and smart and pretty, and behind her friendly laugh was a troubled sadness that reminded me of Shade. She worked the reception desk at an old motel on Highway 2 and lived with her sister in an Earthship house made of rubber tires and mud out on the mesa, across the Rio Grande. Bonnie was from Jacksonville, Arkansas, and was a graduate of Arkansas State University's satellite campus in Beebe, where her dad was a professor; after college, she'd worked at a Planned Parenthood clinic in downtown Little Rock, an hour away. She'd also been hooked on crack and heroin for four years—her move to New Mexico was a shot at starting a new life and staying clean. We spent a few thrilling weeks together but again my intensity doomed things. Bonnie needed to focus on getting through each day without getting high, and it was a constant struggle—frightening, all-consuming, and hard for me to relate to. She didn't have enough energy left over to love me back with equal force. When I came back to town after a couple of weeks away, I found out she'd taken up with a guy from her meetings at Narcotics Anonymous, a skinny electrician named Cal. She married Cal a year later, and within two years they'd had their first child. By then I'd already moved back to Chicago and, after a year there, home to Michigan.

Over the years that followed, as I rambled around the country, I briefly wrapped my arms around other Shade-like girls—Liz in Plattsburgh, New York; LeBrie in Portland, Oregon; Lindsey in Houston—all of whom shared Shade's otherworldliness, bleak beauty, and abiding sadness, but they had all faded from me like morning mist. The problem, friends said, was with my ferocious, unshakable loyalty to the mystical idea of Shade. But this devotion, no matter how unproductive, unhealthy, or stark raving mad, felt spiritual and pure, and despite my loneliness I had little incentive to ditch something that had become so meaningful to me.

By the fall of 2003, eleven years had passed since I'd first seen Shade on the giant screen of the Michigan Theater, and still she was nowhere to be found. Some nights, if I was lucky, I'd dream of her, though waking up from those dreams only tripled my despair.

Then one day, from out of nowhere, came Sarah Culkin.

Sarah lived in Tucson, three hours west of Deming. She was twenty-two, a senior at the University of Arizona, and she called to ask me a few questions about *Found* magazine for a piece she was writing for the *Daily Wildcat*. We were scheduled to talk for twenty minutes; the conversation lasted six hours. When we finally said good night, we'd already made plans to talk again the next night. I felt I'd found Shade at last.

Sarah's voice was angelic. Anytime she let out a tiny peep of laughter, I felt like I was soaring. That first week we talked every night from around midnight until the sun came up. I'd lie in my bed in the darkness, looking up at the glow-in-the-dark stars on my ceiling, Sarah's voice in my ear, and it was as though she was lying there with me. How do I describe the sweetness, nourishment, and ecstasy of those conversations? Our souls were lacing tight to each other—I was deep in it, swelled with hope and happiness.

We shared every strange, sad subchapter of our life stories and the minute details of each passing day. Sarah lived with her mom, a Wal-Mart clerk, and her mom's on-again, off-again boyfriend on the south side of Tucson. She worked at an animal hospital on the weekends, and was planning to go to grad school to study literature. One night she divulged a random fun fact: her first cousin was the actor Macauley Culkin, star of the movie *Home Alone*, but she barely knew him, since he was from New York City, where her dad lived, and she'd only been there twice.

Another night her best friend, Ivy, took the phone—"Sarah's crazy about you," she whispered fiercely while Sarah was in the other room. "And she's so *hot*! You're a lucky guy." Our future gleamed with promise—she was not battling crack or heroin addictions; she had no interest in moving to France.

Before hanging up the phone each night, we began to say "I love you." It was thrilling to be in love, while so much of her remained a mystery, still to be discovered. My curiosity about her was insatiable, and learning about even her most ordinary likes and dislikes—food, movies, books—felt revelatory. Every day, I'd go through the routine motions of my life, getting work done, picking up groceries for my Grandma Bobbie across the street, just biding my time before Sarah's late-night call and the intoxicating ring and rhythm of her voice.

My friends thought I was crazy to be getting so involved with someone I'd never met in person. "You've never even seen a picture of her? Oh, her *friend* says she's hot? Yeah, 'hot' as Lyle Alzado!" Sarah knew what I looked like from pictures she'd seen online, but there were none posted of her. She offered to mail me a photo and I told her not to bother—I felt weird asking her to submit to that kind of superficial test. Of course I was curious, but my love for her felt more righteous for being based on who she was, not what she looked like, and I figured we'd see each other soon enough. Maybe a part of me also feared that a picture would pierce the illusion, that she wouldn't be as pretty as I'd imagined, but my friends' gentle harassment only served to inoculate me against any doubts I might've had.

Before long, talk turned to how and when and where we'd meet up. A plan was hatched—in a month and a half, once I finished putting together the new issue of *Found*, I'd fly to Tucson and we'd rent a car and hit the road for a week. I suggested a visit to my old stomping grounds in Valdez, New Mexico. Along the way, I figured, we could stop by the Desert Sky Café—me and Shade, together in Deming at last, everything wrapped full circle. (Though I'd shared other intimate aspects of myself with Sarah, I saw no reason to explain Shade to her, not yet—that kind of pressure had backfired in the past.)

We made other plans, too, beyond our road trip. The tone of these discussions was somewhat playful, but we both felt so profoundly confident that we'd found our soulmate, we considered every detail seriously. We talked about where we'd move once she graduated the following spring. Part of it depended on where Sarah got into grad school, though she was also considering taking a year off first, which we thought we might spend in San Francisco or even Santiago, Chile, where her friend Ivy wanted to study. We both wanted to have kids, but not for a while. She was cool with the name Orion, my favorite if we had a boy, and I liked the name Antonya, her pick if we had a girl.

Soon the day of my flight to Arizona arrived, and Mike Kozura dropped me off at the airport in Detroit. "Good luck, brother," he said, slapping two condoms into my hands—it was an ongoing joke between us, ever since we'd seen Dr. Dre hand off a slinky-like strip of condoms to Snoop Dogg in the "Gin and Juice" video, to pass each other condoms in random moments, especially in crowded places, at school, or at work, even in front of each other's grandparents—anywhere the embarrassment factor would be high. I slipped them into my back pocket and headed for the Southwest Airlines counter.

On my flight, in a hot, emotional daze, I stared out the window at the scrolling rectangles of corn and wheat across central Nebraska, far, far below. I thought back about all the wrong turns and rut-filled detours my search for love—for Shade—had taken me, and it was hard to believe that my journey was finally over, that when I got off the plane, she'd be there waiting for me.

My mom likes to tell the story of her grandfather, who came to live with her family when she was a teenager—he was in his eighties, and his wife had died a decade before. Her grandfather revealed to her that he had a girlfriend in New York City, a two-hour train ride from Philadelphia. On Sunday mornings, he'd leave the house early, take the train to New York, and spend the afternoon with her walking in Central Park, then return home late in the evening, saying he'd been playing cards all day at a friend's house. He kept the girlfriend secret from my mom's parents—he didn't think they'd approve. Only my mom knew.

Then one morning my mom's grandfather told her that he was running off to New York to move in with his girlfriend and marry her. My mom helped him pack two bags with everything he'd need, and went with him to the train station and hugged him goodbye (but did not pass him condoms). She'd never seen her grandfather so happy. He waved to her from the window of the train, beaming, as it pulled away. Somewhere between Thirtieth Street Station in Philadelphia and New York, lost in a contented sleep, her grandfather passed away; the conductor found him when the train reached Penn Station. My mom's parents were furious when they learned that she'd been in on her grandfather's secret and had helped him pack his things that day. But she was unapologetic. "He couldn't have been any happier than he was on that train," she told them—and me, each time she repeats the story. "That's the best way you could leave this life: happy, hopeful, and headed for love."

Now I sometimes wonder: Was all my sweet anticipation on that three-hour Southwest flight the happiest I've ever been? Could I have guessed at all the fucked-up shit that was to come? I've often wished there was a way to freeze time, and that I'd known how to do it and had done it at thirty thousand feet above Nebraska—turned those three hours into thirty years, lolled for ages in that precious bath of hopefulness and light.

But nope, no luck there. A thick gray haze zipped the cornfields from sight, and ninety minutes later the plane dropped like a brick out of the clouds and screamed to a stop on the runway tar in Tucson, and I tramped up the jetway to meet my bride-to-be.

At baggage claim—our arranged meeting point—I collected my duffel bag quickly and retreated to a dark corner, scanning the crowd for Sarah. A part of me wanted to spot her before she found me so I could wade for a few seconds into that sensation of seeing her for the first time and gather myself before we engaged. I didn't know what she looked like or what she'd be wearing but felt sure I'd know who she was as soon as I laid eyes on her. But the passengers all dispersed and the luggage conveyor wound to a stop and still she hadn't appeared. Had I been stood up?

I felt a tap on the shoulder, and heard her breathe my name from behind: "Davy?"

I whipped around, and found myself facing a plain-looking stranger—long, wavy hair, a wide face and upturned nose, a slanted smile. Who else could it be but her? Still, it took me a second and a half to realize that this was Sarah.

"Well," she said, with a cute, nervous shrug, stepping to me and putting her arms around me. I hugged her back, bummed that she wasn't as beautiful as I'd imagined, and disappointed that a moment which should have been deliriously happy instead felt a bit awkward and off-kilter. But in a way I'd prepared myself for this. I knew that once we met in the flesh, I'd have to start building things with the real person Sarah was and let go of the girl I'd been imagining her to be. Even as a frightening sense of doom flitted close, I did my best to scuttle it. After all, I was happy to be here, with this girl who loved me and was up for adventure. I broke the hug off and smiled and took another long look at her.

"What?" she said shyly, laughing her wonderful, recognizable laugh, but not quite meeting my gaze. "Am I pretty enough?"

"Of course!" I said, though I felt a bit wobbly and suddenly sacked with fatigue.

"Then let's get outta here," she said, taking my hand in hers. "The rental car place closes in an hour. New Mexico's waiting!"

Our plan was to hit the road before nightfall, after an early dinner with her mom and her friend Ivy. Sarah wanted to show me a place called Old Tucson—a sprawling, Old West movie set, featured in a half dozen classic Westerns, which had been abandoned for decades but renovated recently by the city as an entertainment center, concert venue, and Old West museum of sorts. For a three-dollar admission, you could have full run of the dusty streets, drink and play cards in the saloon, and fire off pop guns in the shooting gallery. The four of us ambled down the main drag, passing a few older fellows with silver mustaches, costumed in 1880s gunslinger garb, huddled in front of a building that said BANK, twirling fake pistols, and taking turns at a real ATM. Next door, hitched to a post in front of the town's burger joint, a single emaciated pony flicked its tail at flies.

Inside, over hot wings, I chatted up Sarah's mom and Ivy, while Sarah disappeared into the bathroom and a piano with no piano player clattered a tune from the corner, its black and white keys dancing up and down as though tickled by a ghost. Sarah's mom had the gaunt, wrinkled look of a woman who'd lived a hard life in the desert and had disappointment on speed-dial. She was cordial but strangely uninquisitive—she didn't seem too concerned with who I was or the fact that her daughter was heading across state lines with a guy she'd met for the first time in person forty-five minutes before. Sarah had warned me that her mom would be preoccupied—her mom's boyfriend had moved out earlier in the week and hauled his stuff to a friend's house; this had happened plenty of times before, apparently, but each time her mom took it as hard as a permanent breakup. The fact that she leaned so hard on Sarah when she took her lumps at work and in relationships had only made Sarah seem more Shade-like to me over the phone, but in *Gas, Food, Lodging*, everything eventually works out for Shade's mom and she finds a good man—Sarah's mom, sagging and deflated, seemed to inspire less hope.

Just to make conversation, perhaps, Ivy—nose-ringed, willowy-limbed, and about forty-four percent hotter than Sarah—pointed to a quarter-sheet flyer in the plastic stand at the center of the table. "Look," she said idly, "Bubba Sparxxx is playing a show here tonight." A few times a month, I'd been told, the small rodeo arena at the back end of Old Tucson hosted local and national acts. She gave me a coquettish smile. "Hilarious. We should go!"

"Bubba who?" asked Sarah's mom.

I explained that Bubba Sparxxx was a white rapper from Georgia, kind of a southern-fried, XXXL-sized version of Eminem, but Sarah's mom had no idea what I was talking about. Then two things happened right around the same moment: Sarah emerged from the bathroom, looking a bit haggard, like maybe she'd just thrown up, and then a second later, surreally, as if cued by Ivy, Bubba Sparxxx himself—draped in a massive, shiny white sweatsuit and trailed by a crew of managers, bodyguards, and lesser-known rappers—blammed through the red swinging saloon doors and took a seat at a table in back, about thirty feet from us.

Sarah came back over and took a seat, and for the rest of the meal the four of us said little and mostly just watched Bubba and his friends, while at the same time pretending to be having our own conversation and not be watching them. Bubba had a natural boisterousness, and his voice boomed above the fray of voices at his table; we could make out the details of what food he ordered, how badly he wanted to give the Old Tucson shooting gallery a whirl, and which hot girls he half-knew in L.A. and was hoping to get on the guest list for their show there the following night.

"God, his music *sucks!*" Ivy whispered fiercely, and I jumped in to defend the guy, admitting that I had bought his first album and liked it, with the tacked-on justification that I always pulled for any small-town rapper who'd made it big. "Well, watch this," she said, swiping the laminated Bubba Sparxxx postcard from its table display and getting to her feet.

"Don't!" cried Sarah, but Ivy was already heading over to Bubba's table. She went right up to him and asked for an autograph, and the hulking bodyguard-looking dude standing behind him produced a Sharpie, which Bubba nimbly took and used to quickly scrawl his name, all without ever looking at her. Then Ivy took a tiny glance our way, and for an instant before she

looked back toward Bubba, her eyes met mine and flashed. She leaned in close and started murmuring in his ear. Bubba listened, nodded a few times, looked up at her for the first time and smiled conspiratorially, and then gestured, Godfather-like, to the bodyguard who'd passed him the Sharpie. He said something softly to the guy, and before I knew what was happening, Bubba had stood and was headed our way, flanked by the bodyguard and two others. They crowded close to our table, as though Bubba Sparxxx was our waiter and the others were trainees.

"Are you Sarah?" he said, looking at her.

She turned bright red and made a squeaking noise, surprised and embarrassed.

"Well, your friend told me the story, and I just wanted to say hi and let you know how much we appreciate you making the trip down. Kansas City, that's like, what, a few days' fuckin' drive?" He glanced at Sarah's mom. "Pardon the language, ma'am." Back to Sarah: "Our fans mean everything, you know, so this is . . . well it's the least we can do. Fellas?" With that, Bubba and two of the others launched into a half-baked and off-tune but enthusiastic version of "Happy Birthday to You" while the third answered a call on his cellie, saying, "Hold on a sec, we're singin' 'Happy Birthday' to some random chick," and then watched the others warble to the end, shaking his head and laughing, without joining in.

Then they were gone, and Ivy was grinning around the table triumphantly while Sarah buried her head in her hands. I looked back and forth between them, and had a snap series of speculative insights about their relationship: Ivy was the more attractive and more outgoing one, but also more insecure. Again and again, over the years, whenever Sarah had a big crush on a boy, Ivy would flirt, charm, and dazzle her way in, until the guy took notice of Ivy and made a play for her, which, most of the time, she would deflect. If Sarah got upset with her, Ivy would plead innocence: "I can't help it if he likes me, and besides, I know you like him, I would never hook up with him!" It didn't mean Ivy was shady, and it didn't mean Sarah was weak—it was just the nature of certain friendships and the way of the world. I'd been in Sarah's position all through high school with Mike Kozura as Ivy. Hanging around Mike meant I'd have a chance to be around plenty of girls and take a charge at his leftovers. Any gentle rank-pulling on his part was just part of the deal.

This made me feel even worse about the fact that I was now hot for Ivy and whatever physical attraction I'd tried to fire up for Sarah was tailing away. But I couldn't help myself, and I bantered with Ivy while Sarah watched us through slit eyes, unimpressed. It was so fucked up—what about all those spiritual, late-night conversations with Sarah, and the potency of our love? Wasn't she supposed to be Shade? Only a soulless asshole would fly to Arizona so full of promises, then mack on a girl's best friend. I tried to beat back, or at least conceal, my traitorous impulses by resting an arm over Sarah's shoulders, but the move felt forced and awkward, and she stiffened under its weight. A minute later, she cut Ivy off mid-sentence and said to her tersely, "Hey, let's go have a smoke."

"No thanks, I'm cool." Ivy smiled back.

Sarah wordlessly snatched up her purse and headed for the saloon doors, and I felt a bit of evil relief that she seemed to blame Ivy, not me, for the direction things had taken.

The waiter came around and I ordered a Maker's on the rocks, even though it was barely five o'clock and Sarah's mom was sitting right there across from me with a scowl on her face. But Sarah's mom said, "I'll have one, too," and Ivy smiled and said, "Hell, make it three."

The drinks came, and I took a long sip, admiring Ivy's neck like a vampire. Then I turned to look out the front windows, and in the orange light of early evening I saw Sarah with her cigarette, leaning close to the skinny pony tied to its post and nuzzling it gently. There was something so sad and beautiful and lonely and

Shade-like about her in that moment, I felt my heart swoop low. She also seemed to have purposefully placed herself in sight of us, and I knew that she was still sulking, but that all could be redeemed if I just went out there and talked to her for a couple of minutes about anything at all. Later, thinking back on it all, the fact that I didn't go to her then, that I kept sipping my drink—slouched, boiling, in my chair, half-listening to the end of a story one of Bubba's friends was telling about wrestling hogs—felt, strangely, like a greater betrayal than any of the larger betrayals to come. I watched Sarah as she teased her fingers through the pony's tangled mane, and had the thought, *Nobody can save anyone*, which was crushing, since all I wanted myself was to be saved. From Bubba's table behind me came a sudden explosion of thunderous laughter as his friend's story reached its payoff. The sound broke the spell over me and I jumped up, ready to rush out to Sarah and rescue her from the sadness of the world, but before I could take a step, she mashed her cigarette out against a *Frontiertown Gazette* newspaper box, flicked it away, rubbed her face for a second, and turned and headed back in.

Two hours later the sun had gone down and the last traces of daylight filled the sky to the west as me and Sarah rolled in our rental Ford Focus through the dead edges of town toward the I-10 entrance ramp. Our elaborate plan had already been set into motion, and there was no reason to call everything to a halt just because her friend had flirted with me and I was having a few doubts. Really, I was excited to hit the road. We'd dropped her mom off at home, and I'd had a chance to briefly meet her mom's boyfriend, Ray, who was sitting on their front porch when we got back from Old Tucson. He was wearing a nice suit but his face was sunburnt and dirty, giving him the vibe of a homeless guy at a job interview. I sat and talked with him about minor-league baseball while Sarah grabbed a few things from inside the house, and when we pulled away, I told her how he seemed like a good guy and she said, "I think he punched my mom last week and that's why she threw him out."

Sarah suggested we pick up some snacks before we got on the highway, so we bailed into a strip mall off Speedway Avenue with a liquor store and a Subway.

Inside Subway, the glaring overhead fluorescents gave Sarah's face a drab shine, and I watched her order her sandwich: "Lettuce. Tomato. Spinach. Pickles. A little bit of mustard. That's good." I had a biographer's knowledge of the details of her life, but still couldn't get used to her physical self and the idea that this girl in front of me in line was now my new girlfriend. I wished that the Mexican girl behind the counter—green eyes and high, thin brows, maybe three years out of high school—was my girlfriend instead. She had a kind of sweet and gentle gloom, and as I absorbed her, a queasying stab of nervousness daggered my insides. I kept a distance from Sarah, trying to convey that although we'd come in together, we weren't, like, *together*.

I pulled out a twenty to pay for our subs and the condoms Mike Kozura had given me a few hours before flapped from my pocket and tumbled to the floor. "Oh, it's like that?" Sarah said, laughing, as I hurried to retrieve them. "Hot to trot? I thought you wanted to drive straight through the night, but I guess we should get a motel."

"That might be necessary," I said brightly, playing along, glad that the girl behind the counter had been distracted by the ding of the bread oven and hadn't noticed, while fully aware of how appallingly thin my loyalty to Sarah had become.

Me and Sarah went next door and grabbed a pint of Dewar's and two thirty-two-ounce bottles of Sol. Whatever treachery she'd sensed in me at dinner in Old Tucson had been forgiven, and now, with her clothes and toiletries stuffed in a pink backpack in the trunk of the Ford, the gas tank topped off, and some decent liquor clanking inside the black plastic bag in her arms, she seemed a bit giddy and loosened, ready for a romantic vacation. Back in the car, I started the engine up, flipped on the radio, and found Sarah's hand squeezing my leg like a strange little crab. I looked up at her and saw her face coming closer to mine, and then we were kissing for the first time. Her lips were soft, and her tongue poked wetly into my mouth. It felt like kissing a total stranger, and there was something gross about it that at the same time turned me on. I cheated my eyes open and saw how full of feeling she was, and I remembered how important a kiss this was supposed to be—our first kiss, after two months of falling in love over the phone. I closed my eyes again, reached around her and pulled her into me, continuing the kiss, willing myself to love her as I'd loved her just hours earlier, on the flight out. But all I could think about were the odd mechanics of the kiss, her tongue flopping in my mouth like a minnow, the taste of cinnamon gum. On the radio, a guy from the BBC News was talking about the recent surprising advances in China's space program and whether or not this was a valid cause for concern. "Wait, hold on," I said, drifting back from the kiss and bumping up the volume, "I want to hear this for a second." I looked down and added, as though to further explain, "My friend's dad is writing a book on quasars"—a random lie which wouldn't have made any sense even if it had been true. We sat there for thirty more seconds, both listening carefully to the end of the report, and then I leaned in and kissed her for another five or ten seconds, to sort of wrap things up after the interruption.

Sarah smiled. "To be continued?"

"Count on it," I said, coasting forward across the lot.

Inside Subway, the Mexican girl who'd dressed our subs was wiping down the counter with a blue sponge and singing to herself, draped in a kind of brave and naked mournfulness. My heart felt bent in half. I loved that girl more in that moment than I'd loved any girl ever.

We zoomed eastward on I-10 through the wasteland towns of Benson, Johnson, and Dragoon, Arizona. The road snaked up into low mountain forests, and then, once we'd pulled free of Willcox, dropped straight down to the desert floor. I cradled my beer in my lap, taking long sips and watching the mile markers tick down as we neared the New Mexico border. In the hot darkness, talking to Sarah, it was like we were on the phone again, and her tiny voice and sweet laugh summoned up an ounce of the excitement and swooning tenderness I'd felt for her over the past couple of months. But despite these dim-wattage currents—and as much as I genuinely liked her—it was as though a switch had been thrown the second she'd greeted me at baggage claim, and no matter how mightily I fought with the controls, I couldn't crank the switch back on.

I tried to fathom how my longing for her could so swiftly evaporate. It wasn't that her looks turned me off—true, she was no model or movie star, but she had a pleasant face and a likable smile. And her personality was essentially the same as it had been on the phone, if maybe a bit mopier and less confident. The frenzied, infatuated state I'd been in since the night of our first conversation was simply gone, and in its hangover wake I felt a sense of growing, anxious dread, which my beer eased a little but not enough.

Sarah had begun to explain an aspect of literary theory that she was studying, and I said "Yeah?" and "Really?" at the right times and asked follow-up questions with persuasive tones of engagement, though in truth I couldn't really give less of a fuck and was so caught up in the mystery of our troubling disconnection, I barely heard a word of what she was saying. Then she asked a question that broke through and got my full attention: "Davy, do you think we'll get married? Like, eventually?"

I paused, and then a strange, ambiguous croaking sound came out of me, like a bullfrog tuning its pipes.

She took hold of my arm with both hands and went on. "I mean, of course this probably sounds crazy, but here's the thing. You know how sick my grandma's been getting. I've always had such a special connection to her, and I know how much it would mean to her to see me get married." She shrugged apologetically. "I figure, you know, if me and you are gonna get married anyway, maybe we should do it in six months, while she's still alive, instead of in three years. Like next spring, after my graduation. It would make her *so* happy, and her being that happy, that'd make me so happy, too." When I responded with silence, she retreated a step or two. "If you think it's too soon, or too crazy, I totally understand. I don't want to put any pressure on you, I just . . . I don't know, part of me's like, what the hell, why not? Like, we might as well, you know?" I stared ahead at the ghostly silver twinkle of passing reflectors on the side of the road. "I really hope you can meet her soon," Sarah said.

"Yeah, me too," I said finally. I felt drugged, and a little buzzed from the beer, which was weird because I usually never felt any buzz from beer alone. "Maybe we can visit her at the end of the trip, when we get back to Tucson."

"That'd be awesome!" she said happily, popping her seat belt off and launching herself close to kiss me on the ear. "I was afraid you'd think I was insane or something."

I waved my hand and sagged away. By saying nothing, I knew I was only encouraging her mislaid faith in me, but how could I be honest and let her down so completely? Our trip had only just begun, and there was still a chance, perhaps, that the spark would return. It even occurred to me that maybe all of Sarah's marriage talk was her own way of pushing past any disenchantment she might've been feeling herself. The uneasiness boiling in my stomach was now a rising panic, but my body's response to panic was always to induce a sense of severe drowsiness and dis-orientation.

Sarah sat back, refastened her seat belt, clutched my hand in hers, and closed her eyes for a nap; she'd gotten up early that morning to give her mom a ride to work. "You need anything before I hit the hay?" she asked.

"No, I'm good. Actually, pass me the Dewar's, please."

"You sure you should be drinking and driving?"

"I'm not gonna get wasted, I just need to touch it to my lips for a second and wake the fuck up."

She cracked the bottle open and handed it to me for a couple of sips, then took a sip herself and slid it away under the seat. She leaned her seat back. "I love you," she said, beginning to drift off.

I squeezed her hand.

Dreamily, she said, "This is maybe—no, definitely—the hap-piest day of my life. It almost seems too good to be true." And then she was asleep.

We passed an exit for San Simon, which put us about fifteen miles from New Mexico and just over an hour from Deming and the Desert Sky Café. As Sarah dozed, and I edged the Ford from eighty to eighty-five and then up to ninety miles an hour, I puzzled over how I might possibly escape this whole sad mess of my own design. Sarah wasn't crazy for bringing up marriage and saying "I love you"—I'd been the one to instigate that kind of talk over the phone, and had painted a beautiful, appealing fan-tasy that both of us had utterly bought into. But the fact that I'd believed as fully as Sarah in the shimmering vision of what was to come didn't let me off the hook. In the end, I was as much of a charlatan as any hustler peddling swampland to naïve retirees, and when things came crashing down, as they were bound to very soon, Sarah was going to feel suckered and swindled, dam-aged and scraped clean.

The moon rose low in the sky, casting gray light over the flat, cracked rock sea that stretched from both sides of the highway as far as I could see to the horizon. Out here, in the country's emptiest corner, sometimes ten minutes went by without seeing another car heading in either direction. The overall effect was of driving on the moon itself.

I glanced over at Sarah. An eerie green glow from the dashboard dials spilled across her face. Her chin was tucked to her shoulder, turned slightly toward me, her mouth slack. She breathed slowly and easily, one hand on her knee, the other slipped down between her legs, pressed against the zipper of her jeans. A part of me wondered if maybe I could just suck it up and spend eight days with her, try to have a good time, see how things went. Who was to say how I'd feel once we had a little more time together? The strangeness of being on such an intimate journey with someone who felt so foreign might subside. But I knew I wasn't attracted to her, and our whole chemistry seemed off. The idea of having to fake it for another week filled me with a discomfort so deep it edged into terror. Then again, ending the trip early—and having to find a way to explain it to Sarah—felt too horrible to really contemplate. I banged once, hard, on the steering wheel, marveling at the trap I'd set for myself, and filled with painful exasperation. With no clear path at hand, all I could do was to simply keep driving.

Another few miles down the road, a small maroon sign flashed off the shoulder: *Now Leaving Arizona, Come Back Soon!* Two hundred yards farther down, a wide billboard loomed from the median dirt: *Welcome to NEW MEXICO, The Land of Enchantment.* We whooshed past, and I felt the border sweep over us like an invisible membrane as we entered my magic land. I thought of Shade, and longed desperately for her to be in the passenger seat of my car instead of this impostor.

I needed a cover story, it seemed to me, a way to end our trip that didn't feel personal. And the truth was, it wasn't personal, not exactly. It wasn't her fault that I'd built her up as some kind of idealized soulmate. What I craved and had been chasing, again and again, for the past eleven years, I began to realize, was the exquisite misery I'd felt when I'd first seen Shade on the screen. That wrenching longing was its own perfect drug, and as long as a girl kept me at arm's length and maintained a distance, some veil of mystery—as Maggie and Bonnie and all of the others had, even when we'd come together—then my excruciating and exhilarating ache could be preserved. But when a girl threw open the gates and let me in, as Sarah had, no matter how charming, smart, and pretty they might be, the intensity would drain from me and I wouldn't be able to gas it out of there quickly enough and start my search for the next girl to call Shade.

Past tiny Steins, New Mexico, I began to see signs for motels and truck stops in Lordsburg and Deming. I knew I couldn't go as far as Deming, not with Sarah. But I didn't want to pull off the highway and turn around until I had a plan in place. Slowly, I pieced together what I would tell her. It hurt my heart to think about how she might respond—with anger, with grief, with shock? Sarah's face, dipped in moonlight, was so placid, her sleep so peaceful, I couldn't help but think of my mom's grandfather on the train to New York and his waiting bride. I hated myself for what I was about to do.

I resolved to get off I-10 at Lordsburg, but at the first exit I faltered at the last second and stayed headed east, and a mile later, at the next exit, I was boxed out by an enormous tractor trailer hauling a single ninety-foot windmill turbine blade that looked like a dragonfly wing made of metal. I braked hard but couldn't get over in time, and the pint of Dewar's shot out from beneath Sarah's seat and wedged itself against her left foot. There was no third exit, just an amber dusting of streetlights from Lordsburg's central square disappearing in the rearview mirror, and magnificent, sad, sacred Deming puffing heat from twenty miles ahead. I thought of my last visit to the Desert Sky Café, my promise to myself to return only with Shade. How many times since then had I dreamed of what that moment would be like? It was agonizing to be so close and yet so far away.

I wasn't even sure if there'd be another exit before Deming. I dropped my speed to sixty-five and started looking for a gravel turnaround with access to the westbound lanes. The Dewar's bottle at Sarah's feet made a sloshing sound as we coasted over breaks in the road, and I slipped off my seat belt and stretched my right hand toward it. If I was going to turn the car around and wake Sarah up and lay some bad news on her, I needed some scotch in me first.

I got my fingers around the bottle and plopped back into my seat, but just as I began to unscrew the cap, a dead horselike beast, big as a Clydesdale, flashed suddenly into sight thirty feet in front of us, stretched on its side across both lanes. "Holy shit!" I cried, pounding the brakes and yanking the wheel hard to the left. We rocketed onto the left shoulder and into the hard dirt beyond, then fishtailed wildly and shot back onto the road. The bottle of Dewar's had jumped from my hands and landed down by the pedals.

As I reached again for the bottle, Sarah bolted upright and shouted, "Watch out!" Ahead of us, in the same lane, was a car's entire steel fender and grille, massive as a canoe. I swerved hard to the right, almost lost control again, and finally came to a stop in the middle of the road. "Oh my God, what just happened?" Sarah said, frightened and full of alarm. "Are you okay? Wait, are you drunk?"

Adrenaline firing through me, I eased the Ford up a long, curving incline, past an old Chevy Cavalier parked on the shoulder with its hazards blinking and its windshield and front end completely demolished. I pulled in behind the rig with the gigantic turbine blade, which had stopped on the same shoulder a hundred yards in front of the Chevy. "I think someone hit a fucking unicorn!" I shouted. "Come on, let's make sure they're okay."

I leapt out of the car and saw a trucker in jeans and a T-shirt heading our way from the rig, swinging a flashlight. He called out, "You hit it?"

"Just missed it," I said.

He reached me and Sarah, who'd climbed outside and was rubbing her eyes. "Well, you guys're lucky," the trucker said. He was perhaps in his late forties, rail thin with an enormous shaggy beard. He waved his flashlight down the road. "I hope they ain't hurt too bad. Let's go see."

I trotted after him, pulse throbbing in my neck, Sarah just behind us. "What was it?" she peeped. "The animal."

"Elk," said the trucker.

The Chevy had apparently smashed into the thing dead on—its windshield was splintered into a thousand shards, and behind the wheel an old Native American man sat picking bits of glass from his face, blood spotted here and there, while in the passenger seat, a boy no older than twelve stared out at us in a daze. "I didn't even see it happen," he told us as we unclipped his seat belt and helped him out his side door. "I was sleeping. It was just, you know, *boom*." His eyes were wide with amazement. He ducked his head around and said something I couldn't understand to the old man in the driver's seat and the old man glanced at him and nodded and said a few words back. "My grandpa's okay," the boy said. "He's just upset about the car. He doesn't have insurance."

The trucker said to Sarah, "You got a phone? Stay here with these guys and call nine-one-one. They need a wrecker for sure, and maybe an ambulance." Then he pointed his flashlight down the slope toward the dead elk and said to me, "Come on, we need to get that thing out of the road."

We started down the shoulder, and in the moonlight I could make out the elk's giant black carcass as we closed to thirty yards. A pair of headlights rose into sight a half mile back, and the trucker pulled back. "This is a bad place to be," he said. "Wait a second." He started frantically waving his flashlight at the oncoming car, but they kept hurtling toward us, only gaining speed, it seemed. At the last second, before crashing into the elk, they banked right, just clipping the thing, and roared directly toward us along the shoulder. I dashed down into the ditch while the trucker held his ground, swinging his light. The car whipped back into the right lane of the highway and went screaming past, nearly sideswiping the Chevy where Sarah stood talking into her phone, before shifting back to the left lane and disappearing out of sight up around a bend.

"Hey, get your ass back up here!" the trucker hollered to me.

"I don't want to get hit, dude," I called up.

"There's rattlers down there," he said. "For fuck's sake!" His voice was ragged with urgency; easily convinced, I galloped back up beside him.

Another pair of headlights was drawing near. Again, the trucker waved his light wildly, but this time it was a big white van, not easily maneuverable, and they broadsided the elk without even slowing down. There was a deafening crunch and a boom as the van lifted half a foot into the air and came slamming back to the pavement. For a moment, the van skidded toward me and the trucker sideways. Then it struck the Chevy's mangled, detached bumper, sending up a geyser of sparks, and spun off the far shoulder, coming to rest in the median.

People die all the time because they are in the wrong place at the wrong time, and standing on the side of the road while full-sized Dodge vans and Pontiac Chargers whirled this way and that was about as fucked up a place to be as I could imagine. I was scared shitless, my heart jangling in my chest like a dinner bell, but the trucker said with absolute calm, "Come on, no cars, let's roll," and in that moment I would've followed him through a firefight in Mogadishu rather than reveal myself to him as the coward I actually was.

We hurried down the middle of the highway and reached the huge, twisted hunk of metal that had been torn from the old man's Chevy. The trucker grabbed one side and I grabbed the other and we lugged it to the shoulder and heaved it far into the rocky ditch, where it crashed like a cymbal and clattered on down the hillside, presumably waking hundreds of rattle-snakes. We continued down the road, and as we got close to the animal itself, the air was filled with an overpowering barnyard stench.

The van's direct hit had sheared off the elk's back half and spewed pulverized pieces across fifty feet of pavement like lava from a volcano. Slippery innards were splashed everywhere and the road was black with blood—the smell stung my eyes and I was careful not to breathe in through my nose. The trucker booted what looked like a hoof out of his way and raced over to the elk's front half, and I came up fast behind him. Without hesitation, he took hold of one of the front legs; with sickened chills, but also a degree of morbid fascination, I took hold of the other. The animal was remarkably undamaged, at least its head and front legs and shoulders, and its leg felt like what I imagined an elk's leg might feel like if the thing were alive—muscly, with a layer of coarse, fuzzy fur over an oily hide. Its eyes were open, its face stupid and blank. Me and the trucker both tugged as hard as we could, but the beast was heavy as a coffin filled with ice and only budged an inch. Then, from the darkness, two big guys materialized at our side, a father and son perhaps, who'd climbed from the destroyed white van. All four of us hauled to-gether and the elk slowly moved with us across the asphalt, leak-ing guts and ribs from the seam in its belly. We kept straining backwards until we'd dragged the thing clear of the road and most of the way off the shoulder. "That's good," said the trucker. When we all let go of the legs, they kept their upward angle, which gave the elk the posed, oddly comical look of a man bow-ing to the floor and praising God.

The trucker laughed. "What a waste," he said. "If I had my pickup, I'd take that meat home." He looked at the father and son. "I feel bad, fellas. Another minute or two, we coulda had that thing outta your way. How's your vehicle?"

"Done for," said the burly dad, with matter-of-fact remorse.

"Damn." The trucker rubbed his head with his forearm. "Well, let's get the rest of it, too."

For the next couple of minutes, the four of us roamed the empty lanes, hurling chunks of elk off the road. I picked up a bloody, knotted leg, roped with veins and tendons, and foul, squishy organs, including one so nasty-smelling that I gagged and almost threw up. It was easily the grisliest task I'd ever been a part of, but in a weird way I was grateful to be picking up elk parts, instead of the grislier task of talking things out with Sarah. Finally, a couple of semis lit into existence at the bottom of the hill, and the trucker said, "That's probably good," and the four of us stood off to the side as they howled through. It was strange that all the sharp danger had drained from the scene so quickly, and left only a few unremarkable patches of roadkill blood.

The trucker and the father ambled along the median and got on the ground with flashlights to look at the underside of the totaled van, while the beefy son pulled out a gallon jug of water, splashed it over my hands, and passed me an old raggedy towel to dry them. I asked if they needed a ride or any more help, but they said they were cool, they'd call a friend with a tow truck in Deming, so I headed up the road toward Sarah and the wrecked Chevy. As I got closer, I could see the moonlit silhouettes of her and the little boy and dimly make out their voices, talking and laughing, and I felt a sudden gaping sadness open up inside of me.

"What's your boyfriend's name?" the boy was saying to her.

From the darkness, Sarah replied with reverential softness, "His name is Davy."

Ten minutes later, we were back in our car, ready to drive on. I'd pulled off my shirt covered in elk blood, tossed it to the rattlers, and thrown on a fresh one, but my hands and elbows were still smeared with blood and instantly the new shirt had streaks of its own. My shoes, bloody on the soles, smelled like pig slop; luckily, as I took a few sips of Dewar's, its sweet pungency helped cancel out the odor.

I started the Ford, peered east toward Deming, and then, with a wave of guilty upset, pulled onto the road and swung a wide left, bumping across the sandy median and back onto the highway, pointed west. Sarah was too abuzz with all that had just happened to recognize that we were heading the wrong way. Her unsuspecting ease reminded me of a ladybug I'd lured into a pot as a kid before frying it with a magnifying glass. She filled me in on the Native American boy's story—he'd been living with his mom on an Air Force base in Twentynine Palms, California, but his mom had just been cycled into service in the Middle East, so his grandfather had picked him up the day before and was bringing him out to live in New Mexico. "I bet he'll always remember this night," she said. "God, that poor kid. I mean, his grandpa seemed nice enough, but a change like that's always hard."

We passed Lordsburg again. Sarah started laughing. "You really stink, you know. It's the elk. That is the weirdest smell. But, I don't know, there's something kind of manly about such, you know, hands-on work. I like that you're not afraid to get dirty. You're like one of the whalers in *Moby-Dick*." The dashboard clock read midnight.

Our headlights danced across a small roadside sign: SAN SIMON, AZ 22; TUCSON 168. I saw Sarah take notice of it and sit up a little, and my stomach swished in slow, cramped circles, like an eel in a goldfish bowl. "Wait a second," she said, "I think that sign said Tucson. Are we going the right way?"

I gripped the wheel, suddenly choked up. My plan was all set to go, but its irreversibility was chilling. Once I launched into it, I'd have to see it all the way through. It wasn't too late to change my mind—I could still act like I'd made a mistake and turn back around. But I pictured myself in an hour at the Desert Sky Café with Sarah and knew that would be far worse for both of us. The only thing less kind than what I was about to do would be to drag it out over the course of several days. Better to tear a bandage right off than to rip it off slow. I hardened myself, trying to work up the necessary coldness to do the deed.

"Yeah, and there's an I-10 West sign," Sarah said. "I think we turned around twice or something?" She looked over at me, and our eyes caught, and in that tiny moment I think she understood what was happening. A quiet shock registered in her face, and somehow, once that first dart had pierced her, I felt free to follow with a hundred more.

"I've got something really terrible to tell you," I said, my voice starting to break. "I am so, so sorry. I can't believe I'm doing this to you." And suddenly the long, complicated lie I'd dreamed up began to pour out of me. I told her I'd had a longtime girlfriend named Liz who I'd loved more than anything, but who'd struggled with drugs and mental problems until our relationship had dissolved. Just recently, I explained, in the past couple of weeks, Liz had come back into my life, and we'd decided to try to get back together. I should have said something before coming to Arizona, I told Sarah, but the reunion with Liz had happened so suddenly, I hadn't known what to do. Now, though, I saw that I had to get home to her. I assured Sarah that my fondness for her was very real, but also that I knew this wasn't our time and that I couldn't in good conscience continue the trip. I could just as easily have tried a more honest approach, but I didn't fully understand what I was feeling myself, and I was afraid Sarah would think that any missing spark was a sign of shortcomings on her end, instead of my own, and that the rejection would bear a more bitter sting. Besides, the heart of the story was true—there'd been a girl named Liz, the one from Plattsburgh, New York, and I'd been devastated when things with her fell apart. Had she wanted to get back together, I would've jumped at the chance. But I hadn't heard from her in over two years. As I yammered on, I pretended to cry and then found myself really crying. Up ahead, a pair of signs coiled from the sand, thanking us for visiting New Mexico and welcoming us to Arizona.

If Sarah had grown angry and started calling me names or had burst into dramatic sobs, it might have been easier. But she just cried very softly for a minute or two, covering her face with her hands, and then with her thumbs she rubbed the tears from her eyes and stared quietly ahead into the desert night. I kept apologizing and sniffling and sputtering until at last she said, "Stop saying you're sorry. It's my fault, too. I should've never believed that this kind of thing could happen."

"No," I protested. "You have to believe. These things do happen. Magic can happen." But I knew I didn't really have any right to be making that particular case to her. "Just not this time, or not right now."

"Whatever." Her face crumpled into a crying face but she wouldn't seem to let herself cry.

Something about the way she was blaming herself and trying to bury her sadness broke me. I burned in hot self-hatred, wondering how I could ever forgive myself for so casually inflicting such pain, while at the same time selfishly worrying that I would always be this alone, unless I could track down the Mexican girl I'd seen at the Subway in Tucson. For the next hour, we didn't say a word to each other. A couple of times, Sarah broke down in tears for a bit and then steadied herself. She leaned her face to her window for minutes at a time, looking into the endless dark, and then sat back, watching the hood gobble up each white, stubby dash painted along the center of the road. Time moved very slowly, and each mile seemed to last an hour or a week or a year. Only the towns whirling back past us—San Simon, Dragoon, Johnson—revealed that the car was actually moving.

In Benson, I stopped to fill up on gas, and when I went inside to pay, I ducked into the bathroom and tried again to scrub the elk blood from my hands, mostly in vain. I grabbed a Milky Way bar for Sarah, which she'd mentioned in one of our early conversations was her favorite. We got on the highway, headed west still, and strangely we began to chat about not much at all, amicably, as though nothing had happened. The breakup and tears had brought us somehow closer together or at least removed the weight of expectations I couldn't fulfill, and the next forty-five minutes passed quickly as we reveled in each other's easygoing company. Soon Tucson's orange-y glow filled the night sky, and Sarah got quiet again and said, "Not this exit, but the one after this."

She guided me through her ghost-town neighborhood back to her mom's house, and when we reached her street she said, "Just pull over here." I cut the engine and killed the lights. "Look at that," Sarah said. She pointed all the way down to the end of the block, where her mom's boyfriend, Ray, sat on their front porch, twitching a bit under the white chute of a single streetlamp, like a man on the stage of an empty auditorium.

"That's weird," I said.

She sighed. "That's just Ray." Then, a second later, she'd squeezed onto my lap and we were kissing fiercely. Her lips moved to my chin, down my neck, and after a minute she pulled up my shirt and starting kissing my chest. With one hand, she traced along the insides of my thighs, slowly up, and I felt myself getting hard. The possibility seemed to teeter before us to have sex right there in the car. I was in such a daze, and so lost and warped from the past twelve hours and our queer round-trip, I might have simply gone for it. But from nowhere, a fat gray cat dropped onto the hood of the car with a loud, clanging thud and crouched at the base of the windshield, tossing its tail back and forth and sizzling us with a freaky death stare. Sarah laughed a sad, shy laugh. I reached for the keys from the ignition. "Let me get your stuff out of the trunk," I said.

"Do you want to sleep here tonight?" Sarah said. "We've got a sofa I can give you."

"I think I'm just going to cruise around, find a café."

"God," she said, "I don't know how I'm going to tell my mom about this. I've been talking about you nonstop for the past six weeks. I feel totally lame."

"Me, too. The same."

We bailed outside and I opened the trunk and handed over her pink backpack. We held each other for a bit and kissed again. I felt connected to her in a way I'd never quite felt connected to any of the Shade girls I'd been involved with over the years, like she'd seen me at my ugliest and basest and most plain but still thought I was an okay guy. Her forgiveness and compassion struck me as incredibly generous and nothing but genuine. "I am so happy that I know you and that you came into my life," I told her, trying to keep grateful tears from sprouting up. "I'm sorry I fucked this all up so bad, but I hope you know how much you mean to me, and that I really do love you."

"I love you, too," she said, taking a sharp breath. "Call me when you need me." She spun and walked toward her house without looking back.

I climbed into the car and watched her go. When she reached her front porch, she said hi to Ray, and slipped through the front door. I sat there for another few minutes, looking at Ray, looking at the gray cat on the hood, and flipping for no reason through the sports pages of a *USA Today* I'd picked up on the plane, like I was on a stakeout. Finally, Ray stretched and stood and went inside, and I started up the car, swung it through a clumsy four-point turn in the street, and headed once more for Deming.

Before I got back on I-10, I had one stop to make—the Subway off Speedway Avenue. By now it was almost three in the morning and the lot was dark. In front of the liquor store next door, a man was passed out next to a slew of empty bottles, draped in a chopped square of old carpet.

I ripped a sheet of paper from a notebook and began a note to the Mexican girl who'd been working behind the counter earlier in the night. I knew I was crazy—at the peak of my dementedness, really, my hands spotted with dried elk blood—but I also longed for the girl desperately, and it seemed to me that if this whole sad affair with Sarah had led me, ultimately, to my sweet Subway angel, and things worked out for us, then the universe might still have a logic to it and not simply be a place of chaos and meaninglessness, as I was beginning to fear.

When I was done with the note, I read it through, amazed that I could author something so bizarre and creepy that was at the same time so hopeful and honest:

> To the girl with green eyes who was working tonight (you also had silver-hoop earrings)—my name is Davy, I came into Subway around 8:00 tonight with my friend Sarah. (I had a brown hat and a black T-shirt that said WCBN. Sarah was the one who asked you which bread was the freshest and gave you a hard time because she didn't think the bread you gave her was fresh enough.) Anyway, I thought you were beautiful and I wish there was a chance we could get to know each other. I don't even live in Tucson, I live in Michigan, but if you ever feel like talking on the phone sometime or even want to write me an e-mail or send letters back and forth, I would really love it. I'm not a weirdo or anything, just someone who trusts deeply in intuition. I hope to hear from you sometime! All my info is below. Love and Respect—Davy

I climbed from the Ford and walked over to the door of the Subway, looking for the best place to tuck the note and trying to decide if I should actually leave it. I could imagine the endless ribbing the girl might get for it from her coworkers. And the chances of her actually responding seemed remote. Then again, the chances of her calling or writing to me if I didn't leave the note were even less, so really I had nothing to lose. Still, as badly as I ached for her, I wasn't so crazy as to miss the irony of the situation and my own manic tilt—I'd ditched one Shade candidate and inside ten minutes was trying to break through to the next. A lonely feeling wobbled me, and I stood there rereading the note again, sacked by a sudden hopelessness.

The man wrapped in carpet coughed and groaned in his sleep, and in my moment of self-pity it seemed that very little separated the two of us. It was easy to envision that one day soon I'd be rolled up in a carpet of my own. At last, I went ahead and slid my note through the Subway door, jumped back into the Ford, and hit the highway, pointed east.

Quickly, the lights of Tucson faded and the mountains swallowed me up. A piece of downtrodden jazz came through the radio, a fluttering signal from a station in Bisbee. Two hundred miles in front of me, the Desert Sky Café sang its siren song. All of my senses felt heightened, and I welled up with crisscrossing currents of emotion, relieved to be on my own again, inside the familiar soreness of my longing for Shade and away from the messy scramble of actual interaction with a girl. My aloneness felt holy and pure, proper for a pilgrimage. The moon settled behind a bank of low clouds and a million or so stars tumbled into sight.

Through the darkest part of the night, the same small desert towns I'd passed twice already scrolled past a third time. It felt like I'd spent lifetimes driving this same stretch of road. There were no other cars for miles at a time. Odd, mournful memories scudded in like fist-sized meteorites—standing at the end of the North Avenue Pier at midnight, overlooking downtown Chicago and Lake Michigan, a hot wind in my face; a man with a hook for a hand I'd picked up hitchhiking in Lafayette, Louisiana, and delivered to his estranged daughter's house in Lake

Charles; the old Scottish woman who'd tried to comfort me as I cried on the bus from Edinburgh back to London the night Maggie Jones broke up with me. Soon a great weariness began to blanket me. All I wanted was to pull into Deming, coast over to Shade's house, climb into bed beside her, and kiss her hair and the back of her neck as she slept, then hold her through the night.

Past Exit 1, I pulled over to the left-hand shoulder to take a leak, and found myself looking up at the giant *Welcome to NEW MEXICO* sign and a packed zoo of constellations beyond, stepping from the sky. I entered a kind of waking dream, high off the majesty of the stars, and floated there in the desert cool for what might have been five minutes or an hour, soaking up the glorious night. Gentle cyclones stirred through, carrying the taste of sage and piñon pine. Animals in the far, far distance cawed, hooted, and mewled.

Finally, I lashed back into the Ford and pressed on into New Mexico. I cycled through a hot triptych of feelings—joyous, sad, and lonesome. I felt Shade's presence so near, it was strange to consider that I'd flown down from Michigan to travel with Sarah, not with Shade. Past Lordsburg, I dully registered the wash of my brights on the dead elk's carcass at the side of the road, and the Jackson Pollock–like tangle of brown blood and entrails across both lanes, already faded.

One at a time, the stars snuffed themselves out, and the sky ahead pooled from black to deep blue with the first hint of dawn. Tiny houses and ramshackle trailers dotted each desert crest, marking the outskirts of Deming. Five minutes later, I bent right off I-10 onto the service drive, and after coasting through a few sets of lights the truck stop rose into view, a couple of rigs arranged side by side in the lot, the Desert Sky Café glowing in the middle under a pair of streetlamps, one pink and one orange.

Before I went in, I sat in the car for a bit, misty-eyed, heart ablaze. A low, sustained foghorn hum buzzed through my whole body, like I was still in motion. I'd sworn not to return to this spot without Shade, but here I was, without Shade. Without Shade, I was completely hollowed out and done for. Without Shade, I felt I might crumble to dust. But fuck it, first I'd get breakfast.

Forty minutes later, I finished telling my story to the waitress and she was disappointingly—almost comically—unmoved. She'd never seen or heard of *Gas, Food, Lodging*, didn't have a daughter named Shade, and was nearing the end of a double shift. She peeled some Wet-Naps from a shelf under the register and passed them over. "There's a john through the kitchen," she said. "Go on and wash up. But if you don't mind, let me cash you out first."

In a dirty sink in back, I rubbed the last dried traces of blood from my hands and forearms. I decided not to stay in Deming to try and find my soulmate, who was a character from a movie, but instead to head on to Albuquerque—if I made good time, I'd be there by noon, and could crash out on my friend's sofa while he was at work.

Outside, in the bright morning sun, I popped the Ford's trunk, tried to douse the dead elk's persistent stench with a fresh swath of deodorant, and started to change my shirt once more, when a state trooper's black SUV crawled into the lot and came to a stop right behind me, pinning me in. An older man, Hispanic, tall and broad-shouldered, in a brown uniform and black boots, stepped out and walked cautiously over, surveying me closely. "Good morning," he said, hand at his hip.

"Good morning," I said.

"Getting cleaned up?"

"Yeah."

He moved closer. "What you got on that shirt?"

"Blood. I was clearing some roadkill off the interstate."

"That's what you told Carol, huh?" He nodded toward the diner. Apparently, the waitress had put in a call. My drawn-out story must have sounded insane to her—how was she to know the difference between elk blood and human blood? Also, I supposed asking her to break a hundred-dollar bill might not have been the best idea. Spattered in blood, flashing C-notes, it must have seemed like I'd robbed a stagecoach. "Can I see some ID?" the trooper asked. I handed over my driver's license, and he said, "You mind sitting in my vehicle while I run this?"

"I guess not." He gave me a quick check for any weapons, led me to the back of his SUV, and I climbed inside. Somehow the pain I'd inflicted on Sarah earlier in the night felt linked to this police action, which muffled any resistance I might otherwise have had. The cop shut the door, walked around to the driver's seat, protected by a thick pane of wire and Plexiglas, and called my info in over his radio. Now that I was safely in his custody, he seemed to relax a bit, and introduced himself as Officer Maez. He asked me to repeat the story I'd told the waitress, and I found myself recounting the whole weird journey my long night had become, explaining the reasons I'd come through town in the first place—Sarah, Shade, the whole enchilada. He listened with thoughtful care, raising his eyebrows, shaking his head, and occasionally chuckling at appropriate moments. He told me he knew *Gas, Food, Lodging* inside and out; he'd even been an extra in a scene filmed inside the diner. After the complete disinterest of the waitress at the Desert Sky, it was nice to open myself to someone as curious and attentive as Officer Maez.

His radio came to life and he exchanged a few words with someone at HQ. Then he told me, "Sorry, this could take a few more minutes. We run everything twice—Border Patrol has its own database. Got to run the plates, too."

We kept talking. Maez turned out to be kind of a sweetheart—he owned a bean farm with his wife, he told me, and wrote poetry sometimes in a little notebook when work was slow. At last, he eyed me in the rearview mirror. "I understand about Shade," he said. "I get it. I used to be like you. Chasing phantoms." He laughed and rubbed at his graying temples.

"So what'd you do?"

"I married my best friend. Rhonda." He pulled out his wallet and dug through for a photo, then pushed it against the glass, upside down. "That's Rhonda."

"She's pretty."

"Yeah, she can be mean when she wants to be, but she's a good one. I got lucky." His radio crackled to life, and after a minute he said, "Okay, looks like we're all set here. Thanks for your patience." He stepped out and opened my door. Then, once he'd passed my license back, he looked me over and rubbed at his chin. "You know, come to think of it," he said, "there was a girl named Shade who used to live right here in town."

This sideswiped me. "*What? Where is she?*"

Maez explained the story. When Rhonda's youngest daughter was in high school, she'd had a friend named Evangeline, and after *Gas, Food, Lodging* was filmed in Deming and the movie landed in theaters, Rhonda's daughter and the rest of their friends had started calling Evangeline "Shade" because she looked so much like her and had so many similar interests and just seemed to share her very essence. She'd even washed dishes at the café for a couple of years in high school.

Naturally, my heart was on fire. "What's her last name?" I asked Maez. "Where can I find her?"

"Well," he said cryptically, "I'll show you something." He marched me back into the Desert Sky Café, and deep in the rear corner, between a pay phone and a dusty pinball machine, he pointed out a small plaque on the wall, with a picture of a beautiful, dark-haired girl at the top and an inscribed gold plate below:

EVANGELINE 'SHADE' CHRISTIE

§

June 19, 1977 – December 30, 1999

§

*'I think of you as watching from a time and space beyond the
sky, a place where we might someday come'*

§

'Earth has no sorrow that heaven cannot heal'

"Sorry," Maez said softly. "I just thought you might want to
see that."

I felt a gulf of sadness open up in my chest. "How'd she die?"
I asked him.

"Had a wreck on Highway 26, out toward Rincon. They
added a traffic light there. A little late, though." He seemed to
gauge how affected I was, and rested a hand on my shoulder.

Was Shade Christie the Shade I'd always been searching
for? Maybe. Probably. Who knows? I've learned more about her,
and everything I learn about her makes me think that yes, I
would have been crazy about her—I would have married her—
I would have loved her for a thousand years. But who knows how
she would've felt about me? She'd had a boyfriend anyway, a
fairly serious one. If she hadn't died, she probably would have
ended up marrying him.

What kills me sometimes is the knowledge that she was
there in Deming, still alive, the first time I visited, on my road
trip with Eddie in the spring of '99. Some nights I think about
Shade Christie, haunted by the thought that I could've found her
and we could've been together, if only I'd stayed in Deming and
told Eddie to continue out to California without me.

These days, it still happens from time to time—I'll get bowled
over by a dizzying love for a girl I've only glimpsed: the bartender with tattoos on her neck who fills in some nights at the

8-Ball Saloon, just down the street from my house; a Denny's waitress in Wheeling, West Virginia, working a mop and bucket in back when her shift is through; a girl with pink hair on the Greyhound bus from Chicago to Detroit, wearing two hoodies and listening to headphones, writing in a journal, taking long sad looks out the window at the passing scenery. Once, I would have tried to talk to each of these girls, made contact in some way, hoping to break through and build something, the way I'd left a note for the girl who worked at that Subway in Tucson. But after the night of the elk, the long drive with Sarah Culkin, and the next morning at the Desert Sky with Officer Maez, that was it for me and Shade. I'll always love her more than anything, and I can't help but size up any girl I hang out with and compare her to Shade, but there's nothing much to be gained by continuing the quest. I won't find Shade in this lifetime. Shade is dead.

That morning, after spending some time with Shade Christie's memorial plaque, I headed back out to the parking lot with Officer Maez when he tapped my arm and pointed at something. I followed his gaze and saw, perched on a rusty post twenty feet away, a strange and beautiful owl staring back at me with whirling eyes, tender and probing. In my billowing sadness, just beginning to understand that I would never hold Shade in my arms, I had the odd but persuasive thought that Shade had died and come back to Earth in the form of this owl. I'll always remember the way that owl looked at me.

NIBBLE, LICK, SUCK, AND FEAST

In May of 2004, a New York publisher put out a book I'd put together called *Found*, based on the annual magazine I produce, which collects love letters, to-do lists, journal entries, photos, and other personal notes and ephemera that folks around the country have plucked off the ground or the street. To help spread the word I bought a van on eBay and hit the road with my little brother for an 8-month, 50-state, 136-city tour. The publisher's publicity team managed to get me booked on local morning TV shows in most of these cities. How it worked, I'd show up at the station around 6:30 a.m., a producer would clip a little microphone on me, and somewhere between weather and sports, one of the morning-show anchors and I would talk about the book for two to three minutes.

Early on in the tour, I took these gigs pretty seriously. After all, the publicists and TV stations were clearly doing me a huge favor by pimping the book. In Philadelphia, Boston, and New York, I made sure to arrive plenty early, act energized, and be prepared with cool *Found* notes to share. But by the third week of the trip, I was starting to wonder who exactly, if anyone, was watching the local news at 7:00 a.m.? Also, while a couple of the hosts of these shows were real cool and genuinely enthusiastic about the book, most of them didn't get me, or the whole idea behind *Found*—yet this only increased their chipperness and jaunty dawn enthusiasm. "Those pants are so fun!" they'd say, looking me up and down. "Plaid pants! You're fun, huh?"

What kept me excited about these TV gigs was getting to meet and hang out with the other folks who were my fellow guests on the morning shows. These were local chefs with recipes-of-the-week, mayoral candidates, a team of Irish dancers, a kid with an eighty-pound pumpkin. In Baltimore, on FOX 5's *Good Morning Baltimore*, I did my little *Found* song and dance, and then the anchor asked me to stay on her couch while she brought on the next guest—Baltimore's Best Mom. This was right before Mother's Day. Baltimore's Best Mom turned out to be an eighty-seven-year-old woman named Darnelda Cole. She sat next to me on the couch, and on the far side of her sat her fifty-year-old son, Dice. Darnelda had no idea why she'd been asked to come on TV; they'd plotted this as a surprise. The anchor asked Dice Cole to read the letter he'd written nominating his mother for the prize. Darnelda grew weepy. At last, the anchor declared Darnelda Baltimore's Best Mom and produced an oversized plaque from somewhere and presented it to her, at which point Darnelda fell sobbing into my arms; I gave her a wild bear hug, caught up in the moment. The anchorwoman quickly joined our embrace. Dice, meanwhile, had lit up a cigarette, which an alarmed producer raced over and doused with a splash of sparkling water. Darnelda took this in and began hollering at her son and whacking him with her new plaque—"Dice, you can't smoke in here. This is TV we're making, what you thinking, boy! Put that damn thing out!"

There were other high points, and by high points I mean low points for the stations and their guests. In Cleveland, two city parks employees showed off an injured hawk and falcon they'd rescued and rehabilitated. Then the falcon got loose and started flapping about, crapping on everything. The anchors had to forge on through the local news and sports and weather while the falcon continued to dive-bomb them, rationing its poop so it had enough to drip a few drops on them with every sortie. It was fucking amazing. In Chicago, a young soccer champ whom they'd invited on to demonstrate his fancy moves booted a ball off the wall of the set, knocking it over backwards, revealing the fact that we were not actually in the hosts' living room, as it might appear, but in the middle of a big, dank, concrete hangar. In Phoenix, I was sandwiched on-air between Cedric the Entertainer and the governor of Arizona. Cedric came on right before me, dropped a couple F-bombs, and then sheepishly left, telling his chaperone, "I didn't mean to say that shit, it just came out, I swear to God!"

Often, my brother and I would do a *Found* event in one city, hit the road for seven hours, taking turns driving all night, and get to the TV station parking lot in Louisville or Milwaukee at around 4:00 a.m. for a couple hours of sleep before it was time for me to unfold myself, clomp inside all rumpled and bleary eyed, and do my thing for ninety seconds on-air. In the wee hours, security guards in the station lots would poke flashlights in our van windows and roust us, and I'd explain that I was going to be a guest on the morning show, and they'd disappear for twenty minutes to check into it, then come back and wake us again to tell us that things had checked out and everything was cool.

In Seattle, after a young security guard played this game with us, I asked him if I could come inside to use the john. We ended up talking for a while. His name was Pico. It turned out that the station was moving soon to brand-new, larger digs, and that Pico was going to be replaced by an automatic gate with a swipe card reader. Pico asked why I was going to be on the morning show and I explained to him the whole idea behind the *Found* book—all notes and letters and photos that people had found and sent in to me, little scraps that gave a glimpse into the lives of strangers.

Pico got excited. He told me that earlier that very same night he'd been sifting through boxes that were being tossed out before the station's big move, just looking for mugs, T-shirts, old calculators—anything of value—and he'd found a bunch of racy notes from the morning show's old, dour anchorman to a young camerawoman. We galloped out back to the Dumpsters and mucked about until we found the stack of steamy pages. "You should read some of these on the show!" Pico cried. I resisted for a bit, but Pico was vehement. "This guy's a class-A asshole," he said. "I'm telling you. He got a janitor fired for throwing out his lucky tie that he left on the bathroom floor. She worked here eight years."

Three hours later we were on the air, and the anchorman was turning to me with a grumpy look. "So tell me about this book. You collect trash, is that it? You like trash? Trashy trash? One person's treasure is another's treasure?" He might very well have been drunk at seven fifteen in the morning.

"Yes, sir," I said. "People are finding this stuff all over the country, all over the world, really, and sending it in to me. Some of it's hilarious, some of it's heartbreaking. It's amazing how powerfully you can get a sense of someone just from a little ripped piece of paper you pick up off the grass. Like *this one*, for example." I held his note up high and read it aloud. "'Stacey, you've got a rack on you, now that's a pair. I will nibble, lick, suck, and feast on them. Quit playing hard-to-get.'"

What an expression that fellow had on his face! Back in the lobby, Pico stood with two janitors by a big TV set, and as I walked past them, out into the bright, blurry morning sun, Pico smiled, gave me a little nod, and said with quiet pleasure, "Good job, man, good job."

CANADA OR BUST

My friend Tim Nordwind is the bass player for the band OK Go, and he'd been invited one Sunday night to DJ at a bar on Sunset Boulevard called Hyde Lounge; since he knew I was visiting L.A., he asked me to come down and hang. I'm usually a dive-bar sort of guy, but I'd heard that Hyde Lounge was L.A.'s fanciest, most exclusive club and I was pretty sure that getting my name on the list at Hyde Lounge would impress Missy Freeze, the beautiful blond-haired girl I'd met earlier in the week. Missy had grown up in rough-and-tumble Youngstown, Ohio, but now lived in Beverly Hills and worked in special promotions for St. Pauli Girl, the beer, which meant that she dressed up as the St. Pauli Girl at conventions, movie premieres, outdoor rock concerts, and other events and served beer to people. I'm always drawn to girls in the service industry—waitresses, baristas, bartenders, concierges, strippers—basically anyone who's working for tips. I dream of burrowing through their lacquered shell of professional friendliness to investigate the soulful edges I glimpse underneath.

OMG, Missy texted back instantly. How'd you get on the list at Hyde???!!!

Her excitement was promising, and at dinner she amazed me

with stories of her childhood in Youngstown among hardened pool-hall types with names like Wrench, Smoke, and Burn, but once we were through the doors at Hyde, she saw a guy she recognized, handsome and nattily dressed, and whisked off with him upstairs without a look back. I kicked it briefly with Tim in the DJ booth, but he was busy spinning records, so I left him alone and skulked around the bar for a half hour, sipping a twenty-dollar drink, half-looking for Missy, and soaking up the atmosphere—young Hollywood agents in silver suits mixing it up with waifish models in slinky dresses. At thirty-three, I was probably the oldest person in the room, and I felt myself attracting odd looks, like an old, craggy barfly who's sure to cause a fight.

In a dark corner, looking equally lonesome, was Pau Gasol, the Spanish basketball star who'd just been traded to the Lakers. I asked if I could join him, and for twenty minutes we chatted amiably about Barcelona (he confessed to bouts of homesickness) and absently watched as his new teammate, Sasha Vujacic, swayed on the dance floor with a girl in high heels he'd apparently just met, relentlessly sucking face. I explained to Pau the term "sucking face" and told him that I'd always hated it because it seemed vulgar, when kissing can be so tender and exquisite. But he argued that in this instance it was fiercely apt. He repeated it a few times, tickled by the expression: "'Sucking face.' Wait, is it 'Sucking *the* face?'"

"No, just 'sucking face.'"

Finally, Vujacic broke off and headed for the john, and I caught sight of Missy on the dance floor with the guy she'd bumped into, laughing and smiling, tugging at his tie.

"That's her!" I cried to Pau, pointing.

"Who? The girl you were telling me about? Oh shit, that's not good." The guy had pulled her close, and as we looked on, they began to furiously make out. Pau shook his head solemnly. "Sorry, man," he said, downing the rest of his drink. "Damn. 'Sucking the face.'"

Missy, I figured, could find her own way home. After a couple of shots with Pau, I barged out of Hyde and on the sidewalk out front ran into two black teenagers selling bootlegged hip-hop CDs. We talked for a couple of minutes and they introduced themselves as Tito and Score. Tito was the wilder of the pair, light skinned, with long dreadlocks. He asked if I played an instrument and revealed that he was starting a metal band, though he still needed a drummer, bassist, and guitarist (he would supply all the vocals). Score, dark and gangly, stood shyly behind him, nodding along. They said they'd been drifting around the country and now were headed north, toward Canada. Their next stop, they hoped, was the Bay Area. As it happened, I'd decided in the previous few minutes—as I'd watched Missy swirling tongues with a guy who hadn't just bought her dinner or gotten her into Hyde Lounge—that L.A. had grown old and it was time to head for San Francisco to check in with some friends up there. I gave Tito and Score my phone number. "Call me tomorrow," I told them. "You guys can ride with me."

My phone started ringing at eight in the morning. But it was neither Tito nor Score; it was Missy. I let it go to voice mail, then instantly listened to the voice mail she'd left: "I am *so* sorry about last night," she said, sounding legitimately distressed. "I can't believe what I did to you. I used to date that guy Martin, and I was drinking, and I just got all—anyway, that was really fucked up of me, and I'm sorry. I hope I can make it up to you later this week."

With that, my planned trip to San Francisco was canceled. I went back to sleep for several hours and had forgotten all about Tito and Score and my ride offer when my phone rang again in the mid-afternoon from an unfamiliar L.A. number. It was Score, calling from a pay phone. His real name, he said, was Hakim. He still wanted to get up to the Bay Area, but there was a problem—he couldn't find Tito. They'd arranged to meet at Hollywood and Vine, he told me, but it was three hours later and Tito still hadn't shown. I explained that my trip was on hold, and he said, "Oh," with such disappointment and skepticism that I sat up straight. I could sense his train of thought: *Yeah, like some random white dude was really gonna give a seven-hour ride to a coupla hoodrats he'd met on the street.* His lost faith in me felt like a challenge worth rising to. Besides, what the hell was I doing hanging around L.A. waiting on the St. Pauli Girl when I'd likely have a better chance with any girl in any bar in San Francisco?

"Tell you what," I said. "Fuck it. I'll give you a ride to the Bay. Find Tito."

But Score—Hakim—stunned me. He explained that he'd just met Tito the night before. How weird! The night before I'd thought of them as an inseparable team—Tito and Score, Score and Tito—the dynamic duo. Somehow in my drunken state, I'd believed that they'd been friends for years. I'd imagined them playing themselves as the swashbuckling protagonists of a road film called *Tito & Score*, which I hoped to one day write and direct. Now Tito was nowhere to be found. No matter. I told Hakim I'd pick him up at ten o'clock that night. "Where do you want to meet?" I asked.

"How 'bout the parking lot of the Verizon store? I think it's, like, Sunset and . . . I don't know." He had a 'shroomer's spacey affect. "Hold on," he said. I heard him calling out to a passerby, "Hey, what street is this? Western? Okay, thanks." He giggled into the phone. "Okay, Sunset and Western."

"Cool. See you there." I hung up and began crafting a text to Missy, working hard to seem chipper, and careful to allude to vague creative projects in the works with collaborators in the Bay, so that it would appear that I was bolting north not as a spurned suitor but as an impulsive globe-trotter whose artist lifestyle sometimes demanded last-minute travel.

She texted me right back: Ill come with you! St pauli event in palo alto tues!!

A few hours later, I caught sight of Hakim in the parking lot before he saw me and Missy, while we were still at the light at Western, a quarter block away. He wore a camo backpack and had a small blue duffel bag hanging off one shoulder; in his arms, he cradled what appeared to be a lone, raggedy turntable, its cord dangling behind him like an untied shoelace. We were half an hour late, and he was searching the passing traffic with the hopeful but anxious and half-defeated look of someone who fears he's been stood up. The light changed, and when I roared up beside him in my borrowed Jeep Liberty, he lit up with a gigantic, relieved smile. I jumped out and gave him a little handshake and half-hug, and we placed his duffel bag and turntable in the backseat. He hopped in on the other side, and the three of us got on the 101 headed north.

Hakim—smiley, somehow both shy and talkative, perhaps a bit blazed—told us his story. He was nineteen, and had grown up in a rough part of Las Vegas. He'd finished high school the previous June and soon realized there wasn't much for him to do in Vegas besides get into trouble. He'd always loved DJ culture and underground hip-hop, and a dream had formed inside him like a hot, molten rock—he wanted to get a pair of Technics turntables and go to Canada and become a DJ. Why Canada? He'd once had a conversation with someone who'd been to Vancouver, and it sounded like a paradise—lush, racially tolerant, and highly cultured. He also appreciated its lax marijuana laws, and what he perceived to be its general laid-back vibe. Also, he imagined that there were fewer DJs in Canada than, say, L.A., and that it would be easier to break in as a young DJ.

Along the way, though, he had some stops to make. He wanted to visit a library in Oakland that he'd been told his grandfather had helped to open. He wanted to try to find some other relatives in the Bay Area who he hadn't seen in a decade. And he wanted, eventually, maybe after a spell in Canada, to find his dad, who he'd never met his whole life, but who he knew lived in Newark, New Jersey, at an address he kept on a deeply worn and creased pink Post-it note which he pulled from his back pocket to show to me and Missy. "They call him Score, too," he told us. "That's kind of how I got the name."

Hakim had left home nine months before and started his journey in L.A., where he'd been ever since, living on the streets for weeks, even months at a time, and then getting a room in a house for a month or two, when he could afford it. He'd been hustling CDs on the street and working as a canvasser for environmental groups. He was Internet-savvy enough to negotiate Craigslist for jobs and temporary sublets, but still had spent most nights sleeping in parks and on the beach, or in abandoned buildings occupied by squatters and crackheads. He seemed to simultaneously be a homeless street kid and an undercover reporter observing the lives of homeless street kids—he was full of keen observations and funny, affecting stories about other kids he'd met, like Tito.

After about ninety minutes of rapid-fire talk, we'd wound our way up the mountains on I-5 just north of the city and were headed down the long decline on the other side into the central California plains. Hakim produced an old Gang Starr CD from his backpack and asked me to put it on, and thirty seconds later he was in a deep sleep.

I kept driving. Missy smiled over at me, the blue, iridescent lights of the dashboard dials casting her in a soft glow. With her large eyes, button nose, and shining teeth, and her childlike kindness and innocence, she reminded me of Ariel from *The Little Mermaid*. There's no feeling like gliding down the interstate through the desolate flatlands with a beautiful girl in the passenger seat, especially one you hardly know. The world was ripe and swirling with mystery and possibility.

Missy outlined her schedule for the week: she was working a tech convention at Stanford on Tuesday evening and a UFC match on Thursday at an arena in San Jose—her St. Pauli Girl costume was packed in a small green vintage suitcase way in the back. The folks she worked for had reserved hotel rooms for her from Tuesday night on, she told me, but it wasn't clear from the way she said it if she was inviting me to spend the whole week with her or not. I was pretty sure that the work on my project in San Fran could be shuffled to the following week, since it had been made up in the first place. When we got to the Bay, I suggested, Missy could crash with me at my friend's apartment, and I'd roll her down to Palo Alto the next day.

Soon her lids grew heavy and before long she was sleeping, too. I cranked the music up and opened my window to let in some night air, dank with cow dung and fertilizer but blissful nonetheless. We pushed north past Bakersfield. I kept peeking over to watch my passengers sleep. It felt like Missy was my wife and Hakim was our kid, though I'd only known them for five days combined. Still, on a drive like that you get a sense for how joyous it might be to have a family of your own.

Around three a.m., at a gas station outside Fresno, I stopped to refill the tank and grab some snacks. Hakim roused awake long enough to request a bottle of water and a granola bar, but by the time I came back out he was already asleep again. It was as if he hadn't really closed his eyes in six months. After another hour, the highway widened and orange streetlights sprouted along the shoulder and the median, signaling that we were close to Oakland. At the tollbooth for the Bay Bridge, a woman in her fifties blasted soul music on a tiny radio and wailed along, almost oblivious to us as she took a ten-spot from me and passed back the change.

Hakim sat up and rubbed his eyes. We rose up onto the bridge, the whole Bay spread out before us, the buildings of downtown San Francisco clustered slumbering in the dark. Day or night, this vista has always been one of my favorite views of any city anywhere. I turned and said, "Welcome to San Francisco, Hakim." He nodded, with a look in his eyes that I couldn't quite identify but took for quiet joy at being one step closer to his destination: Canada.

But what would happen once he reached Canada? Missy and I had talked about it for a bit after he'd first fallen asleep. It's appealing to imagine that if we can just get that one thing in our life to work out—if we can get the job we want, finish writing that book or making that movie, get the right girl or get to Canada—that everything will be solved, absolved, good to go for good. I slipped into that way of thinking way too often, I admitted to Missy, even though I knew that sometimes in life all of a sudden there you were—standing with your Technics turntables just across the Canadian border, and you're not a new you, you're just you, but in Canada.

It seemed, from the way Hakim dreamily talked of it, that Canada, to him, was not so much a place but a sensation he was seeking, a sense of being home. He'd alluded to his mom's drug problems, told us that he'd come home from school some days to find that she'd hocked his CDs and Sega games at the pawnshop. Before leaving home, he told us, he'd essentially been responsible for taking care of his fourteen-year-old sister—the turntable he'd found on the street and set gingerly in the back of the Jeep was to be a birthday gift to her; she aspired to be a DJ like her older brother. Living on the L.A. streets, while full of adventure and interesting characters, was exhausting. The Canada of his imagination was a place where he could find community, maybe an established DJ to take him under his wing, and, above all, a tranquil home.

Maybe in Canada he'd find what he was looking for, I thought. Surely he would. He was friendly, if a little shy, bright, creative, not caught up in drinking or hard drugs. But it was a bit of a crapshoot—starting fresh in a new place where you know nobody is never easy. I'd helped Hakim get a few hundred miles closer to his destination but couldn't even provide him with a home for the night. I'd scored a couch for me and Missy from some girls I barely knew, and I didn't think I could show up at their place at five a.m. with a drifter I'd met the night before. More pertinently, I didn't want to jeopardize the possibility of sucking face with Missy once we landed.

In the Castro there's a dingy but always-hoppin' twenty-four-hour diner called Sparky's—ten years before, I'd spent some lost, lonely nights there, sipping OJ and reading novels in a corner booth till dawn. I remembered flirting mildly with the guys in neighboring booths, not because I wanted to hook up, but because I just wanted to feel wanted by anybody. It was a lame place to abandon a new friend, but I couldn't think of anywhere else to drop Hakim off.

He grabbed his backpack and his little blue duffel from the back of the truck, and I offered to hold on to the turntable for a while so he wouldn't have to lug it around with him. I gave him a *Found* magazine T-shirt and a couple of magazines and the bottle of water and granola bar I'd bought for him at the Roadside 76 station. I felt a sad wave crash over me, like a parent dropping their kid off at college. Hakim assured me he'd be fine. "Get outta here," he said. "Go on. It's late. Tell Missy it was fun talkin' to her." She was dozing in the passenger seat.

"Call me tomorrow afternoon!" I said.

He smiled. "I will."

We hugged, and I waited till he went inside and found a

seat—at my old corner booth, as it happened—then I hopped back in the truck and drove off through the silence and the stillness of the city, where only a rat scampered across the street and an old man stocked newspaper boxes with the morning edition. At my friends' apartment in the Mission, me and Missy lurched quietly upstairs and headed for the couch they'd made up for us with fresh sheets and sofa cushions tucked into pillowcases. We sat a couple of feet apart. After a long drive through the night, when you finally sit down the world always feels like it's still in motion.

I took Missy's hand in mine, my heart pounding once, heavily, like the drunken wallop of a bass drum. She pulled her hand back a bit and whispered, "I think we should sleep head-to-toe."

"What's 'head-to-toe'?" I whispered back, a sudden sense of dread squeezing my insides.

"You know," she said sweetly. "Your head's on one side, your toes down there." She gestured with her other hand. "My head's over there, and my toes over here."

"Okay. Why?" I said. "My feet probably smell bad. Yours are probably worse." This was me trying to keep things light.

"Then come on," she said, "let's go wash them off."

She pulled me into the bathroom and we sat on the edge of the tub and ran some hot water. While our feet soaked, Missy explained that she was planning on trying to get back together with her ex-boyfriend Martin, and that she wouldn't feel right sleeping head-to-head, toe-to-toe with me. "I'm afraid of what might happen," she said, with a mischievous smile.

"What, I might gouge you with my toenails?"

The hot water rose to our ankles. Missy's feet looked like they could've belonged to a porcelain doll; mine looked like they belonged to Bilbo fuckin' Baggins. There was no real need to ask her why she'd decided to get back with Martin or at what point over the course of our drive she'd made the decision, but I did anyway, trying my best to stifle my disappointment.

"It wasn't even like I decided," she said. "I just fell asleep while we were driving, and when I woke up, it was like Hakim going to Canada, I just knew."

In a way, this was hardly unexpected, and I didn't so much hurt as feel profoundly tired. Still, I wished I'd ditched Missy at Sparky's so Hakim could've slept on the couch instead, while I curled up on the thick rug across the room. It sucked that he was fending for himself in an unknown city while the St. Pauli Girl soaked her feet in a tub. Weirdly, though, even as I felt burnt and rejected by Missy, my tenderness for her grew. I had the sense that Martin had been the one to break things off with her before, and that by trying to rekindle their romance, she was putting herself in a painful and vulnerable position.

I followed her back to the living room and we arranged ourselves on the sofa, head-to-toe. I clasped her feet in my hands and caressed them and kissed them. They were like warm, polished ivory. She held my feet, too, and caressed them and even kissed them. It was oddly intimate and ecstatic.

I thought about Hakim and his journey north. I wondered if he was still in that booth at Sparky's, or if he'd left and was roaming the city. I could picture him walking up Market Street as night faded and morning edged in, all the way downtown, while bits of trash and clutter kicked against the curbs and skidded across the sidewalk as though pulled by strings, players in a grand choreography. His wanderings reminded me of my own wanderings, and I hoped and prayed that he would make it to Canada.

He never did.

Three years later, I was in Honolulu, loping down a dark beach around midnight with a few drinks in me, feeling sorry for myself for being all alone in such a tropical paradise, when I stumbled upon a sprawling party in the sand: a circle of tiki torches; a hundred kids dancing to old-school hip-hop. Not a tourist vibe, these were locals: artists, college kids, surf rats. Someone handed me a beer, and I stood on the edge of the circle, brooding on things. In the middle of the party, a few lanky guys with dreadlocks stoked a fire. Deeply tanned, bare-legged girls with hoodies over their swimsuits clustered around them, laughing as they passed a couple of joints back and forth. I watched the DJ on the far side, behind his turntables, juke his shoulders and pump his arms, and felt jealous of the guy—it seemed like he'd found his place in the world, while I was as unmoored as ever. The allure of being the DJ finally registered for me—you can be with others and be alone at the same time, and feel good about it. As I continued to watch him, he turned my way with a smile, and his features melted from those of a stranger into those of a friend, and I realized that—unfathomably—it was Hakim. "Hakim!" I rushed over and gave him an insane hug. "What are you doing here?" I shouted in his ear, incredulous.

"Oh, what's up, Davy," he said. "Just spinning for another half hour or so. Then I'll probably get something to eat." He seemed unfazed by the serendipity of running into each other years after we'd met, a couple thousand miles across the globe.

Later, near the University of Hawaii campus, on the quietest corner of a rowdy intersection, we sat on a curb with falafel sandwiches, while stray dogs and drunk students weaved past, and Hakim caught me up on his journeys. He'd spent his first two months in the Bay living at a homeless shelter for older teens, and then had hit it off with a graphic designer with whom he sometimes played chess in the park. The guy had found him work in his office as a receptionist, which after a few months Hakim managed to parlay into an entry-level design job. It turned out he was a natural. When the company relocated to New York, he'd made the move, too.

Hakim told me about going to visit his dad for the first time in Newark. "I don't know what I was expecting," he said. "But this wasn't it." His dad had opened the door, stepped outside, spoken with him warily for a minute on the front stoop, and sent him on his way. "He knew who I was, I think. He said he knew who I was. But what kind of guy does that, his own flesh and blood?" Hakim's voice cracked, even as he claimed not to care. "Well, it's his life, I could give a fuck."

Hakim liked being part of a team, and the people at work told him he showed great promise, but life in an office wasn't for him. About a year ago, he said, he'd come to Hawaii on vacation with a musician friend, and they'd both decided to stay. Hakim found some freelance design work with local businesses, launched a DIY music label, and over the past few months had finally carved out a niche for himself as a DJ, spinning at bars and small clubs all over the island, even flying to Maui for a monthly gig. Not bad at age twenty-two. He had a tight crew of friends and shared a house with twelve of them deep in the mountain jungle, a few miles outside of town. His sister was planning to join him in a few months, once she finished with high school back home in Vegas. Though he'd never reached Canada, his dream of finding community and creative fulfillment seemed—against tall odds—to have been rapturously realized, which gave me a prolonged, satisfying rush. We giggled, thinking back on the night we'd met, and our overnight drive from L.A to the Bay with Missy Freeze.

"You still with that girl?" he asked.

"Never was." I took a breath. "Well, kissed her feet once." I languished in the memory's bittersweetness.

Hakim cocked his head to the side. "You know," he said, "I still don't really know what I'm doing, or what life is all about, but, man, I was pretty lost back then, and I'm not as lost now. I keep telling my sister: There's no key to the universe, you just have to point your way in one direction, keep going, keep going, keep going, and see what happens."

"Canada or bust," I said.

Hakim smiled. "That's right. Canada or bust."

NAKED IN NEW YORK

"Yo, look at that white dude."

"Dang, he all *naked*!"

I opened my eyes and saw two young teenagers peering at me from a distance of about fifteen feet, their necklace chains dazzling in the blinding morning sun. An instant later, I realized with a jolt that the nude white dude they spoke of was me.

"Watch out, he waking up!" one of them cried, and they tore off out of sight in genuine terror. I sat up hazily and looked around. I was in a tiny park somewhere in New York City—a few wooden benches, some trees, a drinking fountain. Beyond, the world bustled, honked, and shrieked. Whatever extremely drunken notion had inspired me to abandon my clothes the night before, the logic was lost on me as the glamourlessness of my situation slowly dawned. I was completely naked except for a pair of dirty socks—no money, no MetroCard, no cell phone, just a wailing headache.

I cobbled together a plan of action—first, find some clothes; second, figure out where I was; third, find a way back to my friend Seth's apartment in the East Village, which was home for my six-week stay in the city. But how to find clothes? I sifted glumly through a pair of trash cans at the center of the park—no pants, no sheets, no newspapers, only a giant pizza box. I wrapped the thing around me and ventured out of the park to the crowded sidewalk. Shoppers, students, and businessmen streamed past without even a curious glance. Naked people, I soon discovered, are simply not given much credibility when they appeal for help from strangers on the street.

I stopped an enormous man walking a tiny dog. "Listen," I said, "I know this sounds crazy, but last night was my birthday— well, today is my birthday, but we celebrated last night—and, well, I'm naked now. Can you help me? I need some pants. Do you live around here?" The guy wheeled spryly past me, dragging his little dog, which began to bark at me furiously as though outraged by my nakedness.

Mutts aside, it was like being given the silent treatment by the whole damn world. Everyone burrowed into their headphones as they passed me and looked dead ahead. I couldn't even get anyone to stop long enough to explain my predicament; instead, folks clamped cell phones to their ears and said things like, "Wait, I can't hear you, there's a weird naked guy trying to talk to me."

In the peripheral attentions of people rushing from one place to another, I registered no differently than any other skinny, bald hobo dressed in dirty socks and a pizza box, who, if engaged, would probably ask for eight bucks or want to discuss aliens, secret gamma rays, and CIA plots. Speaking calmly and sanely only seems to amplify your deranged vibe when your outfit comes from Sbarro's.

Shopkeepers shooed me away from their shops. One actually waved a broom. "Go home!" he said, as though I was a stray cat. I tried my luck at the entrance to an office building. "Look," I said to the security guard, "I'm in a ridiculous situation. If you could fish something out of the Lost and Found for me, I'd be hugely grateful."

"We're not in that business," he said.

"Well, what business are you in?" I shouted. "The business of ruining my life?!" I felt like I was going mad. Soon I'd forget about pants; I'd only be concerned with CIA plots. "Come on," I pleaded, suddenly desperate, "I'm just a regular person. Okay, a regular person who *happens* to be naked. Man, help me out! It's my birthday!"

A squad car pulled to the curb and I raced over. The officer on the passenger side rolled his window down about three-quarters of an inch, wary, perhaps, of pee. "We can arrest you or you can get out of here," he said.

"Please, sir, don't you have a blanket in your car, an extra towel in the trunk, anything at all? Please help me out."

I saw then that he was eating a slice of pizza; in the same moment, he took a closer look at what I was wearing—this seemed, somehow, to cause great alarm. His face darkened. "I can arrest you, buddy, that's all I can do."

I retreated back to my bench in the park, ashamed, frustrated, and depressed. My self-identity was shifting. I felt like the kind of person who gets drunk and ends up naked in a park with just their socks on, which I now was. I didn't know what to do. My friends were all at school or at work; I couldn't barge in to their offices like this. Their cell phone numbers were all stored on my cell phone, I didn't know any of them by heart. The only numbers I knew were ones like the request line for the crappy alternative rock station I always listened to at home in Michigan, or my grandma. I imagined how that collect call might play out. "Hi, Grandma, no, everything's fine, I just lost my cell phone. Listen, quick favor. Go to Kinko's, okay? Kinko's. It's a copy shop. Ask them to help you create an e-mail account, I need you to e-mail some of my friends in New York and tell them to come meet me somewhere. Yeah, e-mail. You know? Okay, look, at Kinko's they'll know. E-mail. No—'*E*'! As in 'Emperor's New Clothes.'"

Grim reality sank in. The only solution was to somehow

make it to Seth's apartment building and find a way to get in. I was at the lowest tip of Manhattan, a few miles from Thirteenth Street and First Avenue. No cabbie was going to stop for me. The subway felt out of the question. I'd have to hoof it.

It was a long walk. After a dozen blocks, I got sick of holding the pizza box awkwardly around myself and pitched it. The breeze felt good. I started singing out loud a little. No one seemed to notice me or my nakedness. In Ann Arbor, where I grew up, it was a tradition each year after the last day of classes for the college kids to run a nude midnight romp through town called the Naked Mile. For a youngster, the night was always full of marvel—who knew that private parts came in so many different shapes and colors and sizes? But what I loved most was after the race was done, the way naked folks kept milling around town for hours, naked at the ATM, naked going into Taco Bell, naked tossing a frisbee, like it wasn't no thang. All those naked people made me—the clothed one—feel like an oddball. Clothes, and taboos against nudity, seemed, for a moment each year, absurd. Striding up Broadway, flopping about, nakedness made sense to me. It was my birthday; I'd wear my birthday suit if I goddamn pleased!

At last I made it to Seth's apartment. After an hour on the front stoop, his upstairs neighbor came home, recognized me, and let me inside the building. Soon I had on a pair of fresh boxers, sweatpants, a T-shirt, and clean socks. It was both a tremendous relief and a strange, fleeting disappointment to be back in the land of the clothed. I ordered a pizza.

TARANTULA

Nobody wakes up and thinks, *Today is the day I'm gonna cheat on my girlfriend* (or boyfriend or husband or wife). The shit just kinda happens—a series of small, bad decisions that leads to one larger, pivotal collapse. There are some guys who do it once, and then break down to their girlfriend or spouse in a fit of anguished remorse. Life really sucks for them for a long time after that—nothing is more difficult than trying to recover a broken trust, though I'm told that if you put in enough work the eventual rewards can be worthwhile. Then there are the rest of us, who carry our treacheries in silence for weeks, months, and years at a time, like a low-grade fever, always aware of our own rotten cores, but not too caught up in it all to blunt the joys of everyday life. Still, when you're cheating on someone, whether it's now and then or some ongoing affair, it's hard not to feel shitty about yourself, self-poisoned, and want to do something self-destructive from time to time, like close your eyes on the highway and count to ten, or drink gallons of whiskey at the bar on a Sunday night until you hit the floor.

It was 2002. I'd moved back to Michigan and was living in my folks' basement, though I was close to thirty years old. Six blocks away was a bar called Brewskie's, in a drab, frayed strip mall on Packard, crammed between Aladdin's Market, which sold Middle Eastern food products, and a defunct pet store called Age of Aquarium, where I'd spent hundreds of hours as a kid, watching the old man who owned the place feed spiders and baby mice to the snakes, and peering in at kittens, rabbits, and ferrets stuck in their cages while they peered right back out at me. As kids, me and my friends had no malls to go to within easy reach, no Coney Island (where my dad and his friends had strutted their stuff)—all we had were the dilapidated shops on that sad two-block stretch, each with its own unique, unidentifiably sour odor—DJ's Pizza, East Ann Arbor Hardware, Orange Panda Chinese Restaurant, G & H Barbers, Video Watch, Mary's Chicken & Fish. To this day, I'll meet people who grew up on the southeast part of town, and we'll go back and forth, gleefully reciting the names of those decrepit stores as if they were old friends (or at least old, friendly neighborhood hobos). What's weird, though—surprising, unlikely—is that most of those places are still there, including Brewskie's, the old, windowless bar, which was the one place as kids that we were never allowed inside, and therefore the subject of endless fascination.

Living with my parents again, me and Brewskie's began making up for lost time. At first it was just the nights that the Pistons were on, but pretty soon it was the off nights, too. Inside, it was cozy and dark, the oak-paneled walls lined with framed jerseys of obscure 1980s Red Wings, decades-old softball trophies perched below. I ran into all the kids from the neighborhood I'd grown up with—playing basketball, baseball, and hockey, riding the same buses to school—but they were no longer kids, they were thirty years old, too, and most looked far older. They had scars on their faces and walked with limps. We sat on stools up at the bar and spilled our stories over beers and shots of Jim Beam. One guy had done serious jail time, another had lost four fingers and half a foot in some vague accident, and the next had four kids and had already gone gray. Most worked for their dads or had taken over their dads' businesses—Trenkle's Towing, DiBella's Flooring—and many nights their dads sat further along the bar with their own crew of buddies, razzing us, and sending over shots secretly doused with Tabasco sauce. "That bitch is on the take," one of my new/old friends would mutter, spitting out the drink and nodding at the girl behind the bar. "She oughtta warn us, not sell us down the river."

"That bitch" was Kori Boss, and she'd grown up a couple of streets down from me, just a few hundred feet behind the bar. From grade school to high school, I'd nurtured a secret crush on her older sister, Amanda, and a few times over the years had left flowers for Amanda on their doorstep, along with anonymous mash notes. On an overnight school camping trip in tenth grade, I'd finally come clean to Amanda that it had been me all along, and inside the cab of an abandoned crane we'd found deep in the woods, she'd kissed me for hours, but just that once and never again. Now Amanda was a military wife on an Air Force base in Oklahoma, and Kori was serving me drinks every night at Brewskie's.

Kori was less pretty than her sister Amanda, but—in an appealing way—far wilder. Anytime someone ordered a round of shots, she poured herself two. She was tall—as tall as me—skinny as a signpost, and had long black hair, gray eyes, and a sideways smile. She dreamed of apprenticing at her friend's boyfriend's tattoo shop in Redford, then moving to California and opening a shop of her own. I knew I had a chance with her by the way she drank up my tales of all the places I'd lived since high school. Some guys that came through Brewskie's had fat rides, others had handsome grins and a Marine's physique, but I had stories about go-go clubs in D.C., raves in Albuquerque, and epic reggae beach parties in Del Mar, outside San Diego. I understood the currency these stories had with her and slid them across the bar, a couple every night, gently wearing her down. Kori was engaged to a carpenter who'd moved up from Knoxville, but that didn't stop her from catching me on the way out of Brewskie's some nights, wrapping her arms around me, kissing me on the corner of the mouth, and breathing the words hot in my ear: "When you leave town, take me with you."

"How do you know I'm going anywhere?" I'd ask. "I live here."

I'd feel her lips on my cheek and on my neck. "Fuck you!" she'd cry. "Just take me with you."

The night me and Kori first fucked, and all that other crazy, strange, really sad shit followed, happened to be the night before Thanksgiving, but it began like any other night: I called my girl-friend, Tasha, a sweet, dazzlingly beautiful and sparklingly bright arts reporter for the *Toronto Star* who I'd met on my first big *Found* magazine tour and had been dating medium-distance for a year, and talked to her for an hour. Then I went to Brew-skie's, watched the Pistons blow out a team on the West Coast, and celebrated with the usual cast of characters—Franz DiBella, Bam Walbridge, Randy Wix—and our usual lineup of drinks—beer, tequila, and whiskey—while Kori drank along and passed out a couple of free rounds to top off the night. But on this night, when Kori hugged me goodbye, she said, "In the back of my truck there's a tarp. Hide under it." So I did. And twenty, maybe thirty minutes later, I heard her footsteps get close, and her door open, and the truck start up, and we rattled away, down Platt Road, it seemed to me, though I couldn't see a thing. Eventually, I peeled off the tarp and lay on my back looking at the dull com-ets of orange streetlights overhead, until we hit a dirt road and they trailed off, replaced by a few cooling stars. Thinking back, this was probably the only worthwhile, positive part of the night—that thrumming anticipation, the cold air ripping over my face, the truck's surefire *vroom-vroom*s as we tore like a shot arrow toward somewhere mysterious.

At last we ground to a stop and Kori hopped out and slammed her door shut. I climbed down and looked around—we were surrounded by trees, in the driveway of a giant, ramshackle mansion, bats swooping this way and that past a yellow front-porch floodlight. Kori fell against me and shoved her tongue in my mouth. What can I say—it felt pretty hot, and this had been a long time coming, especially if I imagined her to be her sister Amanda, which at times over the next couple of hours I did. She led me inside, and straight to a tiny bedroom in the back of the house, decorated with posters of pro skaters and teen pop punk stars, and lit by only a purplish black light at the foot of the bed. "Whose house is this?" I asked. I knew she lived closer to town, with her fiancé, the carpenter.

Kori was already stripping down to her white bra and panties. "You can't tell anyone this happened," she said. "Nobody. Promise."

"I'm not gonna say a word," I said. "I've got a girlfriend. I'm not trying to put this on the airwaves."

"Good," she said. "We've both got something to lose."

"And you got to promise me, too," I told her. "I don't need any psychos coming after me, showing up at my house."

"I promise," she said, her whole body blue in the eerie light. "This never happened."

We pounced on each other. I'd always been the tender sort of lover, and tended to lean toward slow, emotion-filled kisses and a fair bit of soulful staring into a girl's eyes. With Kori that night, it was the exact opposite—we fucked each other like beasts. All that was missing was the Nine Inch Nails soundtrack. She grunted and growled and moaned. "Fuck the hell out of me!" she screamed. "Fuck me, you fuckin' fucker!" I bent her over and fucked her from behind. I threw her on her back, pinned her shoulders down with my knees, and, upon her instructions, choked her with my dick. I did all kinds of shit I really didn't know I was capable of doing, but it didn't seem ridiculous, it fucking made sense and felt right, like I was accessing a part of myself I'd never known before. In the black light, Kori's teeth gleamed like rows of fangs, and the gray of her eyes turned completely opaque so that her eyes were all white, with no pupils. It was like fucking a witch or a vampire or something undead. Finally, as our cries crescendoed, she shouted, "Come on me, come on my fucking neck!" and I pulled out of her and came on her neck and her chin, and she laughed like she was possessed, then took me in her mouth until I was hard and ready to go again.

After that second time, Kori fell abruptly asleep, and I lay next to her, staring down past my limp, chafed, and stinging dick at my glowing toenails. I slowly became aware of movement at the foot of the bed, and to my horror I saw that the black light was actually housed inside a large glass tank that held a massive black tarantula, nimbly straining for freedom, its back arched, legs outstretched. I cried out and yanked my feet away, supremely spooked. The thing scurried back and forth along the glass, its body curled unnaturally throughout, as though it didn't want to take its eyes off of me. Then, after twenty seconds, it held still, continuing to stare, its hairy legs bristling and making tiny, slow-mo jabs. "Kori, what the fuck!" I hissed, but she was totally passed out, facedown in the pillow.

I hurdled over her, peeled my pants from a pile of clothes on the floor, tugged them on without boxers, and fled into the kitchen and found a light switch. I opened the fridge, plucked out a beer, popped it open, and stood gazing at pictures taped to the side, still three-quarters drunk. I recognized young, teenage versions of Kori and Amanda in many of the pictures, and also a wedding picture of Amanda with her Air Force husband, in uniform—at Brewskie's, the same shot was on display, framed, behind the bar (for years, she'd worked there, too). I looked around the kitchen and it came to me that I'd been inside this house before—it belonged to Kori and Amanda's aunt and uncle, who owned a costume shop called Fantasy Attic, a few blocks from Brewskie's. A couple of times the summer after high-school graduation I'd ended up at parties here, though I'd barely known Kori at the time, and Amanda had kissed me just that one time and had long since moved on. On the fridge were others I recognized, sort of—the aunt and uncle who owned Fantasy Attic, on a pontoon boat in a lake, and also Kori and Amanda's teenage cousins, a boy and a girl, on a Florida-looking beach, balancing on a felled tree in the woods, at a table in a restaurant blowing out candles on a cake. Presumably it was one of their bedrooms in which I'd just fucked Kori—or a demon claiming to be Kori—and so it must also have been their giant spider that had freaked the fucking shit out of me. My money was on the girl. In their pictures, the boy looked like a straight-up jock, but the sister had a black guitar and purple hair, evidence of a goth streak that might attract her to creepy-ass critters.

I plucked a recent picture of lovely Amanda off the fridge and studied it—from the past couple of years sometime, in a crowded parking lot, waving a pair of sparklers at dusk, with a gentle smile—and thrust it into my back pocket as a kind of heart-bending souvenir. But then I spotted, peeking halfway out from the empty square where the first picture had been, another picture, with a face in it that stunned me—my own. Carefully, I teased it loose, scraping at the yellowed Scotch tape which bound it to the fridge, and held it up close for inspection. In the picture, I was a teenager myself, maybe thirteen or fourteen. I stood among a dozen others next to a swimming pool in someone's backyard, a beaming, untroubled look on my face. This was a birthday party, perhaps. Kori and Amanda were in the picture, too, just twelve and fourteen, it seemed, along with a bunch of other kids I recognized but couldn't name. A strange feeling overcame me, and I found myself crossing to the back door and opening it to the cool autumn night. In the dark, I saw steps that led down to a cement deck, lined with abandoned flower beds, and beyond, a waist-high chain-link fence. Barefoot, my beer in one hand, the picture in the other, I padded my way down the steps. The wind gusted, sweeping cold air across the curls of hair on my chest, crusted with dried sweat, and slamming the back door shut behind me. I was chilled, but the fresh air was rejuvenating, and I felt alive and alert and at the edge of a mystery.

I let myself through the fence, and as my eyes adjusted to the darkness, I could just make out, in the thin light from the kitchen windows, the dim shimmer of a large in-ground swimming pool, layered in dark-brown dead leaves, a black plastic pool cover scrunched in a heap at the far corner, half in the water and half out. This, I understood immediately, was the same pool from the birthday party in the picture, and all at once time seemed to fold in on itself. I couldn't rope in the details, but I knew that, yes, there'd been a birthday party, and that I'd gotten myself invited through a friend because I'd heard Amanda Boss would be there. Even when I'd been back to this same house years later, after high school, I probably hadn't realized I'd been there before. I held the picture up to study it again, but it was too dark out there to see a thing.

I brushed the leaves, acorns, and twigs off a decayed vinyl deck chair and stretched out to sip my beer and try to make sense of things. My toes discovered a dry, raggedy towel on the deck beneath a leg of the chair and I tugged it loose and wrapped it around myself like a shawl or a cape. I thought of how badly I'd truly longed for Amanda Boss—and for how many years—and then I thought of Tasha, my beautiful, talented, kindhearted girlfriend, who actually loved me back, and was a better fit for me than Amanda Boss could ever be, and who was surely, at this moment, sleeping soundly in her cozy apartment off Queen Street in Toronto, or maybe even at this point, an hour before dawn, had woken early to straighten up her apartment before work, since I was due in for a visit that weekend. I felt suddenly sober, desperately regretful, and sick to my stomach. And yet, some part of me also rejoiced at the strangeness of life, at its darkly comic twists and turns, which had stranded me as a kid at a birthday party chasing unrequited love for a girl I'd never get, and then fifteen years later deposited me beside the same pool to sip a beer, having just railed that same girl's sister under the watchful eight eyes of a lurking tarantula. As shitty, lowdown, and ugly as I felt about what had just gone down, I couldn't say for sure that, given the chance, I would rewind the night back to closing time and skip the ride in the bed of Kori's truck and just head home instead. I wanted badly to be a good boyfriend, not just good but faithful; at the same time, I wanted to live, and this, I felt— buzzed, downing a beer in the woods somewhere, pelted by falling acorns and pine cones, my loose dick tingling, thinking on the past, and hating myself a little but not too, too much, while owls hooted in the night—this, I felt, was living.

I stood and crept to the edge of the pool and dipped in my right big toe. The water was colder than I'd expected, and my whole body seemed to suddenly take notice of how cold it was outside. I turned around to head back in and figure out my next move, when something at the edge of my awareness prompted me to turn back and face the pool. When I squinted, I could see, in the middle of the deep end, tangled up in the pool cover's submerged folds, just teasing the surface, a large, dark, and re-flectionless shape. A sense of dread billowed deep within me. I made my way down to the end of the pool for a closer look, but it was too dark to see much. My toes bumped against a skinny pole on the ground—one of those long-handled pool-scoopers with a flat mesh screen at one end, used to trawl the water for leaves and other lightweight debris. I held it by the base of its handle and stretched my arm out until I felt the screen end bump against the thing in the pool, which felt hard, made of metal, and I exhaled, deeply relieved. It was, perhaps, an old granny's walker, or an empty croquet rack, tumbled in by the wind. What had I been afraid of, anyway?

Balanced on my heels, toes out over the water, I reached again and caught the edge of the scooper on the half-floating thing, and drew it slowly, slowly toward me. As it got within a couple of feet, it took on the shape and form of a small bicycle, and at last I was able to grab hold of it by the handlebars and haul it onto the deck. Water peed from its joints onto my pant legs—just one of those mini BMX bikes kids rocked at the park to do tricks on and impress their friends, until at fifteen they got a fast-food job and could upgrade to a motor scooter.

Still uneasy for reasons I couldn't quite place, I decided to finish a quick circuit around the edge of the pool. From the far side, the kitchen lights, through crooked-armed trees, reflected quietly off the pool surface, pocked here and there with black clumps of leaves. Toward the shallow end, I saw another dark shape, bobbing a few feet from the edge of the pool, like a black towel draped over a kickboard. I returned for the scooper and hustled back across the marbled deck, twirling the pole like a quarterstaff and making ninja sounds for no one, trying to scatter the weird vibe worming around in my belly.

At the shallow end, I poked the black floating thing with the screen end of the scooper. The feel of it—heavy, firm but giving—made me shudder. I poked again, and saw that the thing was bigger than I'd realized, that the bulk of it was submerged, with just a small black fabric-y part above the surface. A part of me wanted to drop the pole and run right then, grab my shoes, and head for the road, but another part of me—a disturbed, morbidly curious part of me—already knew that this thing in the pool was a person, a dead human being, and wanted to stick around to investigate and find out what would happen next.

I used the scooper, oarlike, to pull the floating thing in toward the edge, and it spun gently. One submerged part of it hit the bottom of the pool or the near wall, and the whole thing rolled softly on its side, revealing a man's pale face, eyes closed, mouth halfway open. The pole clattered to my feet as I recoiled, full of terror. "What the fuck!" I shouted to the night. "What the fucking *fuck*?" I backed slowly away, feverish, unblinking, not really believing what I was seeing, feeling like I was in a dream, and at the same time all too aware of every sensation— the smell of wet birch bark, the zooming trill of trucks on some highway beyond the woods, the slimy, wriggling feel of a slug squashed under the arch of my left foot. Finally, I turned and ran for the house, slipping and sliding on the slick, leaf-covered deck. I dashed through the kitchen into the bedroom where Kori was asleep, the tarantula glued up high to the glass of its tank like a black, severed hand.

I shook Kori awake, frantic. "There's a fuckin' dead guy in the pool!" I shouted. "I swear to fucking God, he's dead out there."

She was half-dead herself and hardly seemed to know who I even was. "What?" she said raspily, covering her eyes.

Then, before I knew it, I was racing back through the kitchen, out the back door, and down to the pool. Without shedding my pants, I took a flying leap and splashed right in beside the floating man, grabbed him around the shoulders, and heaved him with all my might up onto the deck, but he was so heavy, I barely got him out of the water. He slid back toward me, smashing his face on the edge of the deck with an awful, forceful slap, and sank backwards, into the pool again, all the way underwater. I gripped him from under his armpits and heaved once more. This time I got the top half of him out of the water. I seized his legs and pushed them up on the deck, so that he was lying facedown along the edge of the pool, his right arm draped in. I climbed out and knelt beside him and rolled him toward me, onto his back. His head lolled to the side and dark, foul-smelling water gurgled from his mouth. I shook him. I cried, "Wake up, dude! Are you all right? Are you all right?" This, I recognized, was the lame first-responder script I'd had drilled into my head in seventh-grade health class. My brother Mike had once come across a

giant of a man on the Metro in D.C. who'd suffered a heart attack and had slumped over, unconscious, no longer breathing.
Miraculously, Mike and another passenger had breathed the life
back into him, and an EMT team appeared, took over, and fully
revived him. Months later I met the guy at one of Mike's photography shows. Obviously still grateful, he'd bought up half the
pictures in the gallery.

But this guy was not asleep, not unconscious, not in a
coma—he was clearly long gone. His face was slack and ghostly
white, his sopping, dark hair mashed and swirled against his
scalp. I heard myself gasping and sputtering. Not wanting to
acknowledge how helpless I was, I put my hand close to his mouth
to feel for breath, pressed my fingers to his neck, and finally
gripped his wrist, searching for a pulse. Nothing. His hands were
cold, clammy, a little bit slick with an oily film. For all I knew,
he'd been in the pool for a week. I backed off a few feet, still on
my knees, disgusted by the layer of unfathomable ickiness that
was now on my hands, and lashed suddenly by a bout of stinging
sadness.

A new set of shadows swam over the dead man's face, and I
looked over my shoulder and saw Kori's silhouette close by,
maybe ten feet from me. She was barefoot, in just the Bell's
Pizza T-shirt I'd pulled on before heading for Brewskie's earlier
in the night, which felt like years before, from another time. In
one hand, she held the world's weakest flashlight, which she
aimed at my face before speaking. "Who . . . who is it?" she said,
haunted and afraid, voice cracking.

"I don't know," I said, whispering for some reason. "Give me
that thing."

But she held her ground, frozen in place.

"Please?" I said. "Don't shine it in my face. Here, let me see."

"I can't," she said, whispering now, same as me. "I can't come
closer."

"Slide it over." I could've just gone to her and gotten it myself, but I was frozen, too, keeping still and barely making a sound, abstractly scared of something sinister that remained hiding in the night.

"It's not my uncle, is it?" she asked, lowering the beam from my face.

"No," I whispered, trying to readjust to the darkness. "It's not your uncle."

"Is he really dead?"

"He's really dead."

Kori knelt down and set the flashlight on the ground and gave it a quick shove and it squirted across the deck, past me, right into the pool, disappearing with a tiny *ploop*, immediately extinguished. I heard it come to rest on the bottom with a tiny tap.

"Fuck," I said. I got to my feet and moved away from the dead man, and Kori scampered quickly back, withdrawing toward the house, as though I was the one who'd killed the guy and she feared she would be next. Honestly, I feared her equally. Was this what she did with dudes she was fucking on the side? Bring 'em back to her aunt and uncle's house, fuck 'em senseless, let the tarantula dig its fangs in, and then ditch 'em in the pool? I wondered how often drowning victims were surveyed for spider venom. But of course, I knew, neither of us intended to harm the other. "We've gotta call the police," I said, hurrying after her, away from the dead man. I caught up to her, put my arm over her narrow shoulders, and ushered her up the steps, through the back door, and into the kitchen.

My phone had been in my pants when I jumped into the pool and it was as cold and lifeless as the dead dude on the deck. I asked Kori for hers and she told me she didn't know where it was. It was maybe in the truck, she told me, though sometimes she just left it overnight in its charger at work. I scrubbed my hands off under scalding water in the kitchen sink, then hunted around the room until I found a cordless phone in its cradle by the door to the den. "What are you gonna tell them?" Kori asked.

"That there's a fucking dead guy in the fucking pool."

"But here's the thing," she said very slowly, eerily deliberate. "No one can know you were here."

"What?"

"If you call the police, and they come, and you're here . . . Tony's gonna find out." Tony was her fiancé, the brawny but gentle-seeming fellow I'd caught glimpses of but had never officially met.

"This is fucked up," I told her, my voice rising. "This isn't something to fuck around with. It's a crime scene. Or something. I can't just take off. I mean, I touched him. My fingerprints are all over that guy. I mean, seriously, are you crazy? We have to call the police! An ambulance, too. Maybe the guy's still alive even!"

"Stop shouting at me!" she cried. "God, what the fuck's happening?" She retreated to whichever cousin's room we'd fucked in and slammed the door shut. I could hear her begin to sob.

Fuck it—I was sure the guy was dead, but I knew that any chance he could be saved, no matter how microscopic, was being squandered with our half-drunk, predawn madness. I dialed 911 on the cordless, and wandered into the kitchen, back to the fridge, with its collage of old snapshots. A dozen Amandas of all ages flashed me broad smiles.

At that moment, just as a dispatcher picked up, Kori came flying out of the bedroom toward me and snatched the phone from my hand. "I think someone died in my aunt's pool," she said into the receiver, suddenly calm. "No, I don't know who it is. I just saw the body." She gave her full name, her aunt and uncle's names, and their address, thanked the woman on the other end of the line, and hung up the phone. "Please," she begged me. "*Please* get out of here."

"It's a bad idea," I said.

"Cheating on your girlfriend's a bad idea—that didn't stop you."

"Fuck you. You're being fucking crazy."

"No. I'm not," she said. "You know what's gonna happen if Tony finds out you were here, if he finds out what happened?"

"He'll kill me?"

"No. Worse. He'll kill *himself.* I'm not gonna hurt him that bad. I'm not gonna let him find out what happened tonight. Your . . . visit. Let's just try it. If something really goes wrong and I need to tell the cops you were here, I'll tell the cops you were here. They'll understand why we tried to hide it."

I felt sick, as torn up as I'd ever been in my life, and also aware that the clock was ticking, the police were on their way. "I don't know," I said.

"Would you want your girlfriend to know you were here?" Kori pleaded.

"No."

"Well, think if you were in my shoes." She paused and then added, desperately, "Look, free drinks for life at the bar."

It was what she'd said the moment before—imagining if I were in her shoes, if I had to risk Tasha discovering my treasons— that swayed me. In that moment, I couldn't imagine ever going back to Brewskie's, free drinks or not. "Okay," I told her. "Grab my shoes, will you?"

"Thank you!" she cried. She hurried off to the bedroom while I stalked barefoot out the back door and down to the pool.

The tiniest tease of dark-blue morning light played through the trees in the eastern sky. I stood beside the dead guy and went down on one knee and grasped him by the shoulders and shook him with real violence. "Wake up!" I shouted. "Wake your fucking ass up!" But he was dead, he was definitely dead dead dead, his body heavy as a sack of stones. There was no way, I knew, that skin-and-bones Kori could've ever wrangled him from the pool—a

Kmart store detective could've figured that out. There was only one thing to do. My heart brayed. "Oh God," I said under my breath, and then I lifted with both hands, straining as hard as I could, and rolled the guy back into the pool. He slipped in smoothly, without a splash, like an alligator easing back into the bog after spending an afternoon working on its tan.

Oddly and powerfully adrenalized, I loped a quick lap around the pool before heading back into the house, scanning the ground—the same kind of "idiot check" sweep I always did before leaving a motel room. It was a good thing I did—the picture I'd swiped from the fridge of junior high me *avec* crew, poolside, at the birthday party a decade and a half before, sat shinily on the deck by the deep end, among leaves, next to the minibike. I plucked it up, folded it in half, thrust it into the back pocket of my drenched corduroys, and tossed the bike back into the pool. Then I raced into the house. Kori was there with my shoes. "What did you do?" she asked me fearfully.

"I put him back in the water," I told her darkly, slipping my shoes on and grabbing my winter coat. "The bike, too."

"What bike?"

But I was already out the front door, trotting past her truck and on down the long driveway toward the road, shirtless, my coat hanging open. I took a left when I reached the road and, a minute later, heard the wail of sirens. I scrambled through a ditch and into the woods, and watched an ambulance and a police car roar past, and, two minutes later, two more police cars and a fire truck. It was then that I realized I'd left not only my shirt but my underwear and socks and favorite hat behind, all evidence of my presence at the house. But there was no going back. I ran along the dirt road until I hit a paved one, took a right, and jogged another mile, past rusty mailboxes and roadkill raccoons, until I washed up on a gigantic empty parking lot and realized where I was—the Meijer's on Ann Arbor–Saline Road.

From a pay phone, I called my folks' house, and my brother

Mike answered, having just arrived home for Thanksgiving weekend an hour before, after thirty-two hours of travel from Kazakhstan, where he'd been reporting for a Russian newspaper on Central Asian ethnic conflicts. With a groggy laugh, he agreed to bail me out of trouble and twenty minutes later picked me up in our mom's battered-but-still-eager-for-a-fight '89 Aerostar. "What happened to you?" he asked. "You're completely soaked. Here, put this towel over the seat." We coasted back across the lot the way he'd come. The sky was turning orange and pink. "You all right?" he said. "You look pretty insane."

"I'm fine," I told him. "Just had too much to drink last night. Way too much to drink. You know. Biggest bar night of the year."

Thanksgiving, at my family's house, is generally fairly easygoing, but not without its traditions. As always, me and my dad put the Lions game on and at halftime muddled down to the basement and into the tiny, spooky, cobweb-filled room under the stairs to retrieve a dozen aluminum folding chairs, plus the four wooden slats which extend our dining table to banquet-table size. I was brutally hungover, and felt rattled in minor, intermittent doses, expecting the cops at any moment to show up in our yard. I kept picturing that man spread out on the deck beside the pool, in his waterlogged black hoodie and jeans, one shoe off and one shoe on, and felt seared with the notion that he was somebody's son, somebody's father, somebody's husband or boyfriend, perhaps, certainly somebody's friend, and that now he was dead. At times, it was all I could do not to start crying.

As dusk fell, thirteen of my mom's longtime meditation students showed up at our door, one by one—the kind, centered, understatedly spiritual folks who, since my childhood, had played the part of my extended family, since we had no blood relatives within a ten-hour drive. Every year, after the potluck feast is over and everyone's stuffed, we all sit around the living room, playing our family's 1983 edition of a game called Scruples, where you read ethical questions off of a card and try to guess how each person will respond. "Okay, this one's for Davy," said my mom's good friend Karen Shill in her musical Cape Town accent. "'You suspect a neighbor's son of vandalizing cars. When confronted, he admits his guilt, but begs you not to tell, for fear of corporal punishment. Do you inform the neighbor?'"

I chewed on that for a second. "Yes," I said evenly. "Let the son of a bitch fry."

The house phone was ringing. Since it was already past eleven I figured it was probably for me, and scrambled out of the room to answer it in the garage, which had been converted years before into the meditation hall where my mom taught her classes. Kori was on the line. She sounded shaken. "What's wrong?" I said. "Is everything all right? What happened when the police came?"

"I'll tell you about it in person," she said. "What are you up to tomorrow?"

"I'm going to Toronto to see my girlfriend."

"Oh. Okay." She paused. "What time are you leaving?"

"Like three. I gotta drive to Windsor, and I'm taking the train from there."

"Shit. Okay. Well," she said, "I'm working lunch, but how 'bout when I get off I give you a ride to Windsor?"

"Yeah, if you want to. That's cool."

"Okay," she said. "I'll see you then."

"Wait, hold on," I said. "Is everything cool? Are we in trouble or anything?"

"Jesus." She took a deep breath. "A guy is dead."

"Shit. I know. Look, I know, okay? I'm sorry." I could see how, from her point of view, my fear of the cops seemed petty, but the dead guy had been dead long before I found him, I was pretty sure, whereas I still had plenty of years ahead of me and didn't want to spend any of them in prison just for being shady and stupid at her behest. At the same time, a part of me felt shrouded in darkness, like I'd killed the guy myself. Cheating on Tasha was one thing—one fucked-up thing, yes, but just one medium-sized fucked-up thing, and, no surprise, this wasn't the first time it had happened. But the other thing—pushing the guy back into the pool, no matter how dead he was—I was having a hard time spinning that one to myself.

Kori sighed. "I'll see you tomorrow."

"Wait, can you bring my hat?" I asked her. "It's my favorite hat."

"I'll bring your fucking hat," she said.

The next day, a cold front moved in, and the featureless gray sky promised snow. Around quarter after three I watched through the front window of my parents' house as Kori's truck pulled into the driveway. I walked outside with my gym bag full of clothes, slid into the cab beside her, and gave her a hug. "Want me to ride in the back, under the tarp?" I asked.

"Very funny," she said.

We headed west on 94, past Rawsonville's abandoned auto plants and salvage yards. Peering over at Kori as she fiddled with the radio and hit the blinker, shifting back and forth between lanes, it was hard to make sense of the fact that all of the crazy shit we'd done in her cousin's bedroom was real, and not some demented dream. Kori told me the police had been at her aunt and uncle's house all Thanksgiving morning and half of the afternoon. The dead man's name was Clint Wilkerson III. He was a veteran, forty-three years old, had had some problems with drugs and alcohol, and had twice served time for burglarizing homes. He lived with his mom and sister in a trailer park through the woods behind Kori's aunt and uncle's house—this, I knew, was on land that had once been a drive-in movie theater called That's Entertainment, where as a kid I'd seen *Jaws* and *Gremlins*.

The mom and sister had been called, Kori said, and they'd come by the house, spoken to the detectives in the front yard for a while, then came inside, sat in the living room, and wept. They'd asked Kori about what had happened, and she'd repeated the story she told the police—that she'd come outside for a late-night beer and had spotted him in the water. The police assumed he'd been watching the house, knew that Kori's aunt and uncle and their kids were out of town, and had planned to break in but had fallen into the pool instead, too drunk or high or panicked to pull himself free. But Clint's mom and sister told Kori, privately, that they felt it was suicide. Clint's ex had just moved to Mobile, Alabama, with their two sons. "He was acting so strange," the mom told Kori. "He kept telling me and his sister how much he loved us. He kept saying, 'If anything happens to me, take care of my boys.' Like he was back in the service, headed overseas." They hadn't seen him in a few days, and thought he was staying at a friend's place over in Jackson.

"Did the cops say how long he'd been in the water?" I asked Kori.

"No," she told me. "They said the medical examiner would be the one to know."

We passed the Detroit airport, planes lifting off and disappearing into the gloom. "I'm going to the funeral," Kori said. "It's Sunday." She was starting to cry a little.

"I'm sorry I can't be there with you," I said, touching her arm.

She pulled her arm away. "No, it's okay. How would I explain that? Tony will be there."

"Right."

Detroit's elegant, sage downtown skyline came into view, beaten up but still standing strong. Kori asked if she should cross the Detroit River to Windsor over the bridge or through the tunnel.

"Tunnel's faster," I told her. In the dark of the tunnel, fluorescent lights strobing over Kori's face, she began to really cry. I took her hand in mine on the center console. "It's okay," I said. "I promise, it'll be okay."

On the far side, from the comfort of his immigration booth, a Canadian officer in dark glasses asked for our IDs. It occurred to me that if by some chance the cops *were* on my trail, fleeing to another country would look really, really bad. But of course, more likely, Clint Wilkerson's death had already been filed away as an accidental drowning and the detectives assigned to the case were at home with their families, eating leftover stuffing and downing scotch.

"How long will you be in Canada?" the customs official asked, elongating his vowels like any good Ontario native.

"Just the weekend," I said.

"I'm just dropping him off at the train station," Kori added. "I'm not going with him."

"Reason for your visit?" he asked me.

"Visiting my girlfriend in Toronto. She writes for the *Toronto Star.*" Even when I'm guilty of nothing, I reflexively invoke specific details when talking to authorities out of some faith that it will deepen my story's aura of integrity.

"Your girlfriend, eh?" The officer stared through Kori's window, between the two of us, where our hands were joined, down by the gearshift.

I pulled my hand away. "Yeah."

The officer smirked and waved us through.

At the VIA Rail station, Kori pulled to the curb and said, "Well, have a good trip." Her eyes were still wet, and in that moment, as we said our goodbyes, she was more beautiful than she'd ever been. I leaned in and put my hand on the back of her neck and we shared a long, intense kiss.

"You know we can never do it again," she said. "You know, the other night."

"Of course not," I said. And we didn't, not for two years, and when it did happen again, it was just once—I was dating another girl, and Kori had moved on from Tony and was living with another guy.

We traded another little hug and I bailed out of the truck and slung my gym bag over my shoulder. "You know how to get back to the U.S. side?" I asked.

"I'll figure it out," she said. "Say hi to Toronto for me." She flapped her hand at me.

"Will do. Peace out." I walloped the door shut and headed for the train.

There's a certain kind of hangover that lasts two days. The second day is actually worse than the first, because on the first day you're still slightly drunk, and you can kind of coast through, but on the second day you feel the way I felt now—dizzy, sad, and profoundly exhausted, dead to the world. I found a window seat and the train chugged out of the station, eastbound through empty factory yards and dried marshes, as night fell.

Slumped to the glass, my own bald, red-eyed reflection stared back at me from inches away. I closed my eyes, feeling small but persistent waves of guilt, remorse, and nausea lapping at me. How could I have done what I'd done? Tasha was an angel and deserved none of my careless, reckless damage. There was nothing cool or playa-listic about my ability to deceive her, it was purely sociopathic. I wondered how something that had seemed so thrilling, adventurous, and deeply enticing at the time—on the ride to Kori's aunt and uncle's house in the back of her truck—could later feel so absolutely sickening, once the liquor had finally worn off. I liked that my life was at times unpredictable and mad, and that I'd learned how to craftily feed my addiction to new experience, but I hated that I was a liar and a cheat and a fucking fraud. I hated Kori, too, for being as awful and deceitful as me, and dragging me into the mire. I thought of Clint Wilkerson III, drifting facedown in the pool, while inside, ten yards away, I fucked Kori from behind with my finger in her ass. Acid, rueful tears welled from deep within me and burned the corners of my eyes and I pawed them quickly away.

I made a series of promises and compacts with myself—I would never do this shit again; I would respect the woman I was with; I would drink less, because drinking, I knew, was too often what threw open the gates and welcomed the storm. All in all, I knew how lucky I really was: I'd fucked up—many, many times over the years—but still I had a beautiful, smart girlfriend waiting for me once my train reached Toronto, and as long as I could get my mind right, I could dig in fresh when I arrived, slate clean. I'd turn over a new leaf, like my friends that had kicked eating disorders, gambling, and heroin, but without all the pesky meetings and rah-rah Jesus bullshit.

Past London, Ontario, I dozed off for about forty minutes, and when I woke up, my hangover had magically lifted. I still felt faded, but no more than after a night closing down any bar, though I also had a spiky kink in my neck tossed in from sleeping with my head at an odd angle. The darkest parts of the last thirty-six hours—Kori's howls as I fucked her, her vagina's vinegar smell, the dead man's waterlogged body and vacant face, gummy to the touch—had all been expunged from me, or if not expunged, just heated to a thousand degrees and melted down into one strange, vivid, and unshakable image—that fat-bodied, wiry-legged, blacker-than-black tarantula in its black-lit purple tank, staring out at me. The train screeched and squealed along the tracks and blasted its deafening whistle as we hurtled through Toronto's western suburbs, while I sat rubbing my neck, looking out the window, lost in the vision of that gigantic, terrifying goddamn spider.

Tasha was there waiting when I stepped off the train, and we kissed and whisked off in a cab to an art opening on Queen Street, where a friend of hers from work was showing off canvas-sized drawings of robots fighting samurai warriors. The gallery was mobbed with friendly hipsters and young professionals who cried each other's names out and traded funny hugs, careful not to spill each other's wine or plates of crackers and cheese. A guy in horn-rimmed glasses and an argyle sweater chased his friend down and shoved a handful of pretzels and Pepperidge Farm goldfish down the back of his collared shirt.

"I'll kill you," shouted the victim merrily, whirling into a ka-rate pose and continuing to silently move his mouth, as though he were an actor in a Japanese movie that had been dubbed into English.

"Not if I kill you first!" shouted the guy in the sweater, facing off against him, while the crowd circled around them to watch their mock combat.

I made my way to the far end of the gallery and stood inches from a painting, my back to the room, my eyes even with the gleaming tip of a samurai's sword, savoring the prickly sensation on my tongue and in my throat as I took down a full glass of white wine. Alcohol is the nectar of the gods—every cut, rip, puncture, and abrasion of the soul is mended once the first drop hits.

"There you are!" said Tasha, coming up beside me, grabbing my arm above the elbow. "I thought I lost you for a minute." She gave me a look. "I am so sorry. We don't see each other for weeks, and the first thing I do is drag you to a place with, like, nine hundred of my friends. We should really just find a place to be alone, huh?"

"Yeah. That would be nice."

Her brow furrowed. "What's wrong? Did you get hurt? Why are you rubbing your neck like that?"

I dropped my hand; I hadn't realized I'd still been rubbing it. "It's nothing," I told her. "It just hurts. I think—I think I got bit. I think I got bit by a giant spider."

"Aww," she said, her eyes going soft. "You poor thing. Give it a few days. It'll go away."

I smiled down at her, brimming with feeling. "You know, Tasha, I really love you."

"What do you mean 'really'?" She pretended to be mad. "Like 'actually'—like you didn't really mean it all the times you've told me that before?"

"No, that's not what I mean," I told her. "I just mean that I love you a lot. I *really* love you."

"Oh." She smiled, looking deep into my eyes. "Well, guess what? I really love you, too."

SOUTHWEST

Some folks fall in love gradually; for me it always happens in an instant. I was at the airport in Albuquerque, headed for California, when I saw a beautiful and sweet girl dressed in white, maybe twenty-three years old. I watched her at the check-in counter—she was sad but radiant, and she moved and spoke delicately, like an arctic bird on a fragile bit of ice. With her was a gumpy guy in a hot-pink NO FEAR T-shirt. He was pestering the lady behind the counter with questions about the plane: Was it a 747 or a 767? The lady had no idea, but he was determined to pry an answer from her. I prayed that this guy was not the boyfriend of my sweet girl. It seemed inconceivable, and yet I knew the world was filled with strangenesses, so it was hard to say. The pair finished their business at the counter and, to my delight, said goodbyes and headed off separately. I noticed for the first time that the girl was wearing a cumbersome plastic boot on her right foot, as though she'd broken a bone or torn a ligament, causing her to lurch and sway with each step. This effortful gait, combined with her sad glow, twisted something in me, and my heart hurt, and I was in love.

It's been my peculiar blessing that every time I see a beautiful girl in an airport, she ends up sitting next to me on the plane.

This has led to a number of thrilling flights filled with excited conversation, followed by an exchange of e-mail addresses at baggage claim. But what do you e-mail to a girl who lives in Pensacola, Florida, or Vancouver or Dublin? Ships crossing. It never adds up to much. So it was no surprise but a kind of painful wonder when I got on the plane in Albuquerque and found myself sharing a row with the sweet and limping girl in white. She had the window, I had the aisle. Between us, her purse and my backpack shared a seat and gently caressed.

Our plane rocketed into the sky and the girl stared sadly out the window. I waited for her to glance my way so I could begin the conversation that I guessed would end painfully when we parted ways in San Diego, but she was so lost in her aching and faraway thoughts that she never turned from the window, even when the beverage cart rolled past with pretzels and Coke. To busy myself, and because it was the only other thing on my mind, I pulled out a long story I'd been working on for three weeks and had just finished that morning and printed out, and went through it, making little changes, turning the pages loudly in hopes that the girl would peek over. But my efforts seemed to go unnoticed. Her lips were pursed, her eyes cut at the clouds. In a way, she was too nicely dressed for my taste, but that bland elegance was exotic to me and made me hunger for her more. I looked back at the typed pages in my hands—I was still in that fleeting honeymoon phase you'll sometimes have with a just-finished story, where for a moment everything about it feels perfect and snugly in place. Finally I said to the girl, "Hey, what's your name?"

She smiled at me, which was a surprise. Her name was Kara. She was a student in Seattle. I asked about her boyfriend's interest in planes. Boyfriend? At the check-in. Oh, no, she explained, that was only her cousin; she'd been visiting family in New Mexico. I'd thought her sadness would make conversation lurch and buckle, but everything sailed smooth as could be—she acted oddly grateful to me for the small talk, and she seemed to occasionally hold my gaze for an extra sixteenth note. But how could I parlay this chance meeting and warm chemistry into a lasting love? I told Kara I'd be right back and took the riddle with me to the back of the plane. Among portholes and strange cabinets I stretched my legs and listened to two male flight attendants tease each other about some misadventure involving a motorcycle and a birthday gift. I needed to give Kara something that would keep us in contact, but what? Then I knew at once—I'd give her the story. It would communicate something of me and, more importantly, it would give her something to respond to, a reason to stay in touch.

I glided back down the aisle and took my seat again. Kara laughed. "Wondered if you were coming back."

"Got held up in traffic," I said. "Listen, do you like to read?"

"What?"

"Reading, do you like to read?"

She paused and thought about it. Granted, it was a stupid question, but not a complicated one. At last she said, "No."

"No? You don't like to read?"

"No," she said, apologetically. "I hate reading."

"You hate reading."

"I just don't like it."

"You just don't like it." I laughed. She clearly wasn't kidding. All I could do was repeat after her, like an idiot.

"Sometimes I read magazines," she offered hopefully. "I like to see what the models are wearing."

Sadly, shamefully, pathetically, I forced my story on her anyway. I tried to explain what it was about, but the crashing down of my fantasies made me tongue-tied and weary. I wrote my e-mail address and my cell-phone number at the top. "In case you want to let me know what you thought of it," I said.

Kara smiled brightly and folded the story carefully into her purse, like a drawing given to her by a retarded child. Later,

I imagined, she'd rid herself of the thing in the ladies' room trash can. Still, her eyes seemed to express to me that she wasn't ruling out the possibility of staying in touch.

In San Diego, I was headed for baggage claim and she was off to catch her connecting flight. We hugged. She had no scent at all. I knew—for that reason, somehow—that I would never hear from her. "Keep in touch," I said.

"I will," she said. Then her face took on the dark look she'd had when I'd first seen her. She turned and I stood watching as she shuffled away down the long corridor until at last she disappeared out of sight.

NEW YORK, NEW YORK

The morning the World Trade Center towers came down, my friend Maggie Smith was modeling for a drawing class at the University of Michigan School of Art and Design. She was naked, perched on a stool high atop a table in the middle of the room, and trying her best not to move. Without warning, a school administrator burst into the room and called the professor out into the hallway. A couple of minutes later, the professor slipped back in, ghost-faced and shaken. "Okay, listen everyone," he said. "I've got an announcement to make." He choked up a little. "The United States," he said with great authority, "has been attacked by China."

He went on: "New York City's been completely destroyed. Washington, D.C., too." A handful of students, apparently those from New York and D.C., began to sob and some fled out the door in hysterics. "Now, listen," said the professor, his voice rising, "we can all stop what we're doing and rush out of here and join the madness of the world . . . or we can stay right here for the next hour and a half and *create art*." Half the class grabbed their packs and hurried out, but the other half stayed, and Maggie felt compelled to stay, too. Naked and terrified, tears streaming down her face, she held her pose for an hour before the professor finally relented and sent everyone on their way.

Meanwhile, one time zone west, I was at my apartment in Chicago, watching the news all day, teary, heartsick, and angry, though not at China. After dialing and redialing his 917 cell number for an hour, I finally reached my friend Seth in the East Village. Dazed, he described standing on the roof of his apartment building and watching the second tower fall. "It absolutely did not feel real," he said. "I'm on my roof right now, I'm looking at this massive cloud of smoke and dust, and still, I can't believe any of this is happening."

I took in about eight hours of live coverage on TV, and at last shut it off and wandered outside with my tape recorder and microphone. I'd just started doing stories for the radio show *This American Life*, hosted by Ira Glass, and talking to people on the street, I imagined, was not only my job in this kind of situation but would also give me a break from the queasy sadness and horror of CNN, watching the planes hit again and again and again. Some of the folks I talked to said, "Let's bomb 'em back to the Stone Age," even if they weren't sure yet who "'em" was; others were already worried about American retaliation and all of the civilians in foreign countries who were sure to suffer the consequences.

Strangely, though, many of the folks in my neighborhood had no idea that an attack had even occurred. I lived in a neighborhood occupied largely by Mexican, Polish, and Ukrainian immigrants who spoke little or no English, and dozens of times I found myself struggling to explain the events of that morning to a pair of old women wrapped in scarves, or to a group of young day laborers, sweaty and worn out from a twelve-hour shift, who all just wanted to go home and didn't seem to believe my story. It was like trying to convince them that the Loch Ness Monster had just poked its head from the drain in my bathtub. "See, look!" I'd cry, pointing at the sky, which was ominously quiet. "All the planes have been grounded; all the airports are shut down." But a scruffy white dude with gigantic headphones, waving around a sixteen-inch stick mic and spinning *"The sky is falling"* yarns, held as much interest to them as a discarded cigarette butt; they seemed to suspect I was either mentally ill or trying to get money out of them, or, most likely, both.

Among those who had heard, misinformation was rampant. One woman thought white supremacists were the culprits. A Turkish guy said he'd heard it was the Greeks. A pack of Cuban teenagers told me that Chicago itself had been targeted, and that the Sears Tower had been vaporized. I dragged them a half block down to the intersection of Augusta and Wood, where you could see the whole downtown skyline, and pointed out that everything was still standing. This provoked an ugly argument between them in Spanish and led to some pushing and shoving until a police car rolled by and they all split in separate directions.

When night fell, I got a call from a girl named Susannah Cotton, a sweet, pretty writer from Nashville I'd been hanging out with for the past few weeks and was deeply into but hadn't yet kissed, and I picked up three cheap bottles of wine and hiked out to Western Avenue to see her. She poured us each a giant glass and lit a bunch of candles and we sat close on her floor as I played her some of the on-the-street interviews I'd recorded earlier in the day, which she found as moving and oddly funny as me. The mood was both somber and sort of lovey-dovey—a few times she started to tear up and I'd put an arm around her. Still, Susannah's body language seemed to indicate a certain resistance to getting too close. She was recently out of a relationship, and she'd made it clear that she was reluctant to get involved in another anytime soon. But to me there was something meaningful about the fact that she wanted my company on a night like this. At the time, if you remember, no one knew if this was the beginning of a sustained wave of attacks on American soil or the terrorist version of a one-night stand. A frightening, mysterious end-of-days chill hung in the air like a dark mist, and there was the unspoken possibility, however fuzzy and indistinct, that all of us would be dead or colonized by Halloween.

The phone rang and Susannah jumped up to check the caller ID, then answered the cordless, "Hey, you," and dashed into her bedroom and shut the door. This was her ex-boyfriend, I was sure. It wasn't the first night he'd called her while I was hanging out at her place. I lay on the couch, swigging wine and listening to her speak in soft tones from her room, though I couldn't make out the words. My brother Mike called my cell and for a half hour we compared notes on which family members we'd heard from in New York; it seemed that all of our aunts and uncles and cousins, thankfully, were safe. I hung up with Mike just as Susannah emerged from her bedroom.

"Sorry," she said, "I was just talking to my mom. She's pretty upset. Who were you talking to?"

I saw her lie and doubled down. "It was Ira Glass," I said, invoking the name with careful emphasis, since I knew she was a fan. "They want me to go to New York and report on what's happening." This slipped out completely spontaneously, and the idea itself was somewhat ridiculous—if *This American Life* wanted folks on the ground to cover one of the biggest news stories in history, they had plenty of veteran reporters already in the area whom they could turn to. I guess at some level the hours I'd spent earlier in the day recording people on the street had lit in me the urge to head east and report from the thick of it all, and it must also have felt like one of the few things I could say in that moment to impress Susannah and get her full attention.

And it worked, kind of. For the rest of the night, she treated me like a soldier headed off to a war zone, doting on me, letting her hand rest on my arm and my shoulder and my knee. By four a.m. she invited me for the first time to stay over at her apartment, and as I lay in her bed, holding her in my arms, she even let me kiss her neck and her left ear and her cheek, but not her lips. That, I imagined, would have to wait until I came back from my phantom reporting assignment. Every fire needs room to breathe, and a week or two away, involved with what Susannah believed to be dangerous and meaningful work, seemed a surefire, unmistakable route to her heart. But with every airport shut down and a car that could barely be relied on to make it down the block, I had to wonder: How would I even get to New York?

They say that America was at its best in the days after September 11, but that's not what I experienced in the late afternoon of September 12 at the Greyhound station at Harrison and Wells in downtown Chicago. People had been stranded everywhere around the country and were far from their families and understandably desperate to get home, but I wasn't sure what was to be gained by, say, hammering a fist against the Plexiglas window at the ticket counter and shouting, "Just get me to fuckin' Philly, you dumb motherfucker!"

Outside, arriving buses were subject to even greater abuse as they disgorged a handful of passengers and fresh mobs fought to board like it was the last chopper out of Saigon. After an hour or two caught up in this clusterfuck, I had the idea to catch a bus a few blocks west as it slowed to a stop coming off the I-94 exit ramp. I pounded on the door and when the driver opened it, I scrambled up the stairs and past him, down the aisle to the back of the bus. Once we reached the station, I took a seat vacated by a middle-aged couple, and watched out the window as the driver fended off the hordes hoping to board. A few passengers squeezed on, and a young black woman in a pink track suit took the seat next to me on the aisle and introduced herself as Laquisha.

MY HEART IS AN IDIOT

"How'd you beat them out?" I asked, nodding toward the parking lot throngs.

"I've got sharp elbows," she said. "And I gave the driver forty bucks cash."

The guy must have been racking it up—he filled every seat and let another half dozen folks on, strewn along the aisle. In the massive rearview mirror, his shaggy beard, scarred, misshapen face, and tattered yet strangely ornate uniform gave him the look of a traveling carnival worker dressed as a pirate captain for Halloween. He eyed us all as he jerked the bus into reverse, then laid a few blasts on the horn, fixed on his side mirror as he backed slowly through the crowd, and at last crunched into low gear and headed for the highway, bound for Cleveland and points east.

Laquisha was twenty-two. She was from East Harlem, and had come to Chicago to spend a week with a guy she'd met a month before at a club in Lower Manhattan, blocks from the World Trade Center. He'd even paid for her plane ticket. Only after she'd arrived had the truth of his situation become clear—the guy was obviously married. He parked her at a low-rent South Loop hotel and stopped by now and then to have sex with her, on his lunch break and briefly each day after work. Afterwards, he'd invent an excuse to rush off and tell her he'd see her the next day. A massive, diamond-encrusted wedding ring appeared occasionally on his left hand, and when challenged he'd said, "What, this? This is my class ring!" She'd spent the week feeling duped and forlorn, browsing stores for clothes she couldn't afford, wandering through museums, and watching *Jurassic Park III* each night at the theater on Navy Pier. After the hijacked planes hit their targets, she never heard from the guy again, and now she just wanted to get back home. "But my life's boring," she said with a sigh. "I really don't get why you're taping all of this."

I was taking my radio assignment seriously, invented or not.

A bus full of people headed home to New York in the city's darkest hour? That seemed like potent stuff to me. Any colossal event is always expressed most poignantly through the experience of a few individuals, and carrying a tape recorder and microphone gives you license to engage with strangers and ask any questions that come to mind, no matter how silly, bleak, or personal they might be. As the sun dipped out of sight and nightfall doused the golden Indiana wheat fields, I roamed up and down the aisle, kneeling here and there to collect stories from other passengers: Where had they been the morning before, when the planes struck? Where were they headed now? What did they think the future held for all of us? There's something dizzying and intense about interviewing people with a crystal-clear mic and weighty headphones clamped on your ears. All other sound is negated, and the person's mouth appears to be moving silently, with their voice streamed right into your ears, directly inside your head, as though they're magically transmitting their thoughts. Your face is within a foot or two of theirs, and as you look into their eyes, you can see individual emotions swirling to life; you're point-blank on their laughter and their hurt; you can watch a tear begin to form. I swear, I could interview strangers about watery farts and come away feeling moved.

For the most part, everyone was still in a strange kind of shock, as though they expected to wake from this shared nightmare at any moment and be thrust back into their relieving, pedestrian concerns. They all offered earnest, thoughtful responses to my questions, but for many there was a sense of detachment, like they were talking about a football game that hadn't gone the way they'd hoped, while for others it was a struggle to lay out their feelings without simply repeating things they'd heard Peter Jennings say, or the plain truth that this was one of the most horrible tragedies they'd ever seen. More interesting to me were the individual details of how they'd each ended up on this bus—the business trip to Denver, the family reunion in Des Moines. As it turned out, few of the passengers were headed to New York City itself. Some lived in Boston, some lived in Connecticut. One hippie couple, an environmental activist in a Mexican poncho and his young, dreadlocked bride, were just hoping to get as close as possible to their home in Halifax, Nova Scotia. About half of the folks on the bus were a group of retirees from Wilkes-Barre, Pennsylvania, who'd flown into Vegas on Monday, the tenth, for a six-day casino junket. Tuesday morning, an hour after the World Trade Center buildings had collapsed—while my friend Maggie had continued to pose nude in that university art class, I imagined—they'd boarded this bus, and apart from a few stops for gas and food and to drop off passengers and pick new ones up, it had been a thirty-six-hour straight shot, with at least another twelve to go.

"What's your stop?" I asked the white-haired old woman I was kneeling next to.

"Harrisburg," she said.

Her husband, leaning over, cut in, "We're still trying to work that out."

Most of the old folks just wanted to be left alone to sleep and play cards. Laquisha, on the other hand, was down to talk for as long as I wanted, and about anything that I cared to bring up. We compared favorite movies, favorite comedians, and favorite singers. Laquisha told me that for the past six months she'd been working at the Sbarro's in Times Square, and to learn about new music, she'd made a policy of asking customers what they were listening to on their headphones—if it sounded cool she'd write it down. Often, tourists from Minneapolis, San Francisco, Tokyo, and Berlin had simply popped the CD out of their Discman and passed it to her to keep. Her friends thought she was weird because she listened to indie rock, techno, and opera, and not just hip-hop and R&B.

Laquisha told me she was taking one class a semester at a community college in the Bronx, and hoped to eventually transfer to a four-year school to study psychology. I learned that back home in New York she was raising a ten-month-old girl, though it wasn't her baby; the baby actually belonged to her mom. Laquisha's mom had been in and out of drug rehab for years, and the previous winter had given birth to Laquisha's baby sister, before disappearing back onto the streets. "She wasn't even around long enough to give her a name," Laquisha said with a frown. Laquisha had named the girl Destiny. This sorry, failed trip to Chicago was the longest she'd ever been away from her. I loaned Laquisha my cell phone so she could call the cousin she'd left in charge of her baby sis, and casually eavesdropped as she gave an update on her slow progress toward home.

Outside of Jamestown, Indiana, the bus driver pulled off the turnpike into a sad-looking truck stop and said in a raspy southern brogue, "Bathroom break. Have a smoke. You're not back on the bus in fifteen minutes, you get left behind."

Hungry, Laquisha and I went inside to poke about, and she revealed that she'd emptied her wallet bribing the bus driver to get aboard. I bought her a microwaveable bacon-and-cheese sandwich and a Diet Mr. Pibb, nabbed a pile of granola bars and dusty fruit for myself, and we sat in the scraggly grass outside, with the Greyhound bus in view, and had ourselves a strange, postapocalyptic picnic, as other drivers pulled into the truck stop and filled their gas tanks, all looking slightly dazed. The midnight air was oddly warm, and a hot, flip-flopping breeze swept Taco Bell wrappers and empty soda cans this way and that across the lot.

"Did you see that white woman in the front of the bus?" Laquisha asked me. "The one with the black coat and the pink scarf who keeps crying?"

I knew exactly who she was talking about. She sat directly behind the driver with her face buried in her hands, at times weeping softly, and at times completely still, maybe even asleep. The bus was so full that some people had squeezed three to a row, with a handful seated in the aisle toward the bathroom all the way in back, and yet no one dared to share a seat with the crying woman. I'd thought I might approach her with my tape recorder and my microphone—not solely because the job of a journalist is to intrude on people in their moment of grief, though it is, but because I'd also learned that it sometimes brought comfort to people in pain to have someone to talk to, instead of being shunned. As a rule, if I see someone crying, anywhere, I try to enagage them, or at least see if they want to be engaged, since I know how much I've appreciated it when a stranger has done the same for me. But when I got near, and summoned the courage to put a hand on her shoulder, ready to explain myself and ask if I could sit with her and talk, she lifted her head from her hands and stared at me with a look of such utter heartbreak, misery, and revulsion, that I quickly said, "I'm sorry," and hurried away in retreat, spooked and ashamed.

"I don't know if it's true," Laquisha said, "but I was talking to this girl at the bus station in Chicago, and she told me she was on the bus with that woman coming in from St. Louis and heard her talking to someone. And I guess what she said was, her son was in the towers. Or that's what she thinks. He was a waiter or a cook or something in that restaurant at the top of the thing. And I guess he's missing. She still hasn't heard from him."

"Wow. Oh my God." Naturally I'd suspected that the woman had been affected by the attack in a way that was more personal than, say, the band of retirees from Wilkes-Barre, but still, the specificity was shocking. "That is so fucked up."

"Right?" said Laquisha. "I can't imagine if Destiny was missing and I didn't know if she was alive or dead or what." She teared up a bit herself, and when I draped an arm over her shoulders, my tiny gesture of compassion seemed to trigger a greater release. "It's just all so fucked up and crazy," she said, her voice breaking as she started to really cry. "I can't believe this is happening."

"Me neither." I squeezed her shoulder and watched our fellow Greyhound passengers begin to stream out of the truck stop, back onto the bus.

We sat there for another minute, rocking gently, and then Laquisha sniffled, wiped the tears from her eyes with two fists, and laughed. "This has been the most fucked-up week of my life," she said.

"Come on," I said, standing. "Let's make sure no one steals our seats." I pulled her to her feet and followed her back to the bus and up its steep interior staircase, past our buccaneer-looking driver, who closed the doors behind us, flipped the ignition, and brought the engine roaring to life. Spontaneously, as I moved past the woman in the black coat, her head sunken low, I touched her shoulder again. She lifted her head to peer up at me, eerily blank, and I wordlessly offered her a banana and a granola bar in my outstretched hand. For a moment she paused, and then she took both, and managed, in a whisper, "Thank you."

I found my window seat, Laquisha took the aisle, and after a few minutes back on the highway, Laquisha, and just about everyone on the bus, it seemed, had fallen into a heavy sleep. I popped a can of Tecate and watched out the window as dark trees, deserted billboards, and the dull lights of sad-sack, forgotten towns trickled past. We crossed into Ohio. I closed my eyes. Over the hum of the engine, the tinny treble of Laquisha's headphones, and the barely discernible twanging notes of country songs on the driver's radio, I could hear the woman at the front of the bus wailing softly to herself. It was the world's saddest sound.

In Cleveland, around three a.m., our bus coasted down a highway exit ramp, wound its way through desolate downtown streets, and turned a corner into a wide Greyhound station parking lot, bright with pinkish fluorescent light. It was the middle of the night, but the lot was a hive of activity, where ghostly throngs waited and roamed, smoking, eating, playing dominoes, and kicking a soccer ball back and forth, while others flopped on the sidewalks, jackets pulled over their heads, using each other as pillows. The overall effect was of a refugee camp.

As soon as we pulled in, a cry went up and people grabbed their backpacks, duffel bags, and suitcases and began to crowd toward us, lurching like zombies. Reflected in the rearview mirror up front I could see our driver swiveling his head, taking the scene in with visible fright. Before allowing the bus to come to a complete stop, he thought better of it, and instead laid on the horn, gunned the engine, and cranked the wheel hard to the right. The crowd parted as we rumbled through, into a wide alley, and with a jolt we dropped off a high curb, emerging onto a tiny side street behind the bus station. A few fleet-footed hopefuls had given chase, hammering on the flanks of the bus as they ran alongside us, dodging hydrants, newspaper boxes, and telephone poles. The driver cut left onto a wider street, and floored it for several blocks until those in pursuit had fallen away. He swung a right, rolled through a maze of side streets, and finally pulled into an empty warehouse parking lot and killed the engine. "This is Cleveland," he said over the loudspeaker, a bit rattled. "Anyone getting off?"

A scattered few came awake and shuffled up the aisle, and the driver climbed outside and helped them wrestle their bags free from the luggage compartments beneath the bus. Then he scampered up the steps again and said, "I'll be back in fifteen," and I watched as he guided the disgorged passengers away in the direction of the bus station. I dozed for a few, and when my eyes fluttered open again, the driver was back, tramping through the warehouse lot, followed by a ragtag band of five or six new riders, surging after him with pained, desperate faces, lugging duffel bags and steamer trunks behind them. They loaded their stuff under the bus, came aboard, and settled down into the few remaining empty seats or any vacant real estate they could find in the aisle.

Laquisha shifted around and squinted at me with one eye. "Are we there yet?" she asked.

"Cleveland," I said.

She gave a cute little *harrumph*, settled back, tugged her headphones back over her ears, and pressed play on her Discman. Soon we were off again, back on the turnpike. I watched the moon rise over an open field and couldn't help but think of my favorite Simon & Garfunkel song, "America." I'd always dreamed of finding the right girl and running away with her on a Greyhound bus to somewhere new and thrilling, like the young Michigan couple in the song. But everything had been turned upside down—as much as I had Laquisha's back and felt that she had mine, there was no romantic energy between us, and we were headed to New York not because a new part of our life was beginning, but because the world, for all we knew, was ending, and we were determined to be there to see it fall.

The next morning was cool and bright, and at the Highspire Rest Area in central Pennsylvania, I found myself strolling out of the men's room, zipping up my jeans, and blinking in disbelief as the Greyhound bus—with my backpack, recording equipment, and everything else still aboard—rolled away through the parking lot, down the entrance ramp, and back onto the turnpike, before disappearing around a distant bend. Laquisha came galloping toward me, breathless. "That crazy fucker ditched us!" she cried.

It took about half an hour and a round of excitable discussion with the other two dozen passengers who'd been left behind for some kind of explanation to emerge. The dude from Halifax had noticed around dawn that one of the old-timers from Wilkes-Barre kept roaming up the aisle to talk to the driver. Someone pointed out that the entire retiree contingent, all trying to get home from Vegas, had remained on the bus when we'd arrived at the rest stop, while almost everyone else had gotten off to hit the john or see what kind of breakfast they could scrounge together out of the vending machines. It wasn't hard to guess that the gang of seniors had bribed our driver for a direct trip home to Wilkes-Barre, two or three hours north through the Pocono Mountains.

As we all stood around, still trying to make sense of things, a shy ten-year-old Amish boy, who was traveling with an older teenage brother, piped up: "The bus driver, he came and told me to get off the bus, right before they left. He said, 'Tell everyone I'm sorry and I'll be back for them.' He said, 'Make sure you tell everyone I'll be back.'"

So there it was—we'd been ditched all right, but perhaps only temporarily. A gruff older man who'd refused to let me interview him the night before folded his arms across his chest and said, "Well, I'm sure as shit not gonna spend the day hanging around, hoping he comes back for us. I'll find another ride." He stalked away, toward a line of semis waiting to refuel. A handful of others, muttering curses, headed back inside the rest area to call rental-car companies or try to hitch with strangers. As for me, I wasn't going anywhere without my brand-new, top-of-the-line audio gear and all of the tapes I'd recorded the day before, and everyone else seemed equally reluctant to leave without their stuff, so we all decided to just dig in for the day and make the best of it.

The woman with the black coat and the pink scarf, who'd been standing at the fringes of our huddle as we tried to understand why we'd been left behind, cupped a hand over her mouth, hustled off on her own, and settled onto a picnic table at the edge of the woods fifty yards away, while the rest of us sat close together in the shadow of a towering, moss-covered elm. We read tourist brochures. We slept. We chatted in the grass. To other travelers we must've looked like the oddest group ever, our affiliation impossible to decipher—young, old, black, white, Hispanic, and Asian, with a pair of Amish boys tossed in for good measure.

The young Amish kid uncovered a chewed-up green-and-orange tennis ball in the grass and started a game of catch with his older brother. A few others joined in, someone grabbed a sturdy stick, and soon enough the game of catch had morphed into a full-on game of stickball, with two teams of six or seven, sweatshirts and jackets as the bases, and an old Somali lady from Queens as the home-plate ump. Others who'd pulled into the rest area to take a leak or walk their dogs rotated in for an inning or two and then subbed out and headed on their way. The short baselines and shallow outfield favored the offenses—if you poked the ball into the gap, it bounded into the parking lot, underneath cars, for an almost certain inside-the-park home run. Shouting, laughing, and moving our bodies seemed to be exactly the release everyone had sorely needed, though every ten minutes or so I'd eye the woman in the black coat, posted at her picnic table, eyeing us, and feel a simmering splash of guilt for having too much fun.

At one point, a Sikh man with a heavy beard in white robes and a magenta turban stopped to watch us, along with his two teenage sons, who wore jeans and T-shirts, and after Laquisha extended an invite, the boys asked their dad if they could play. He nodded, and the boys joined the team at bat and waited for a turn at the plate. With the bases loaded, the younger of the two, who was maybe fourteen, picked up the stick, took a couple of mighty practice cuts, and crowded the FUBU-hoodie plate, making playful boasts in Punjabi to his dad and his older brother. The guy pitching for my team was a retired cop from Long Island who'd made no secret of his freshly hatched hatred for Arabs when I'd interviewed him during the long haul through Indiana the night before. "Yeah, those Japanese internment camps during World War Two?" he'd said. "Maybe that seems wrong now, but I'll tell you one thing, who knows what would've happened if we hadn't locked them all away? We should be doing the same thing right now with the Arabs." He might've been more intense and outspoken in his anger than anyone on the bus, but his general sentiments weren't unique, especially among the older, white, Wilkes-Barre crew, who'd since abandoned us. Now, his eyes flashed as he checked the runner at third, squeezed the tennis ball in his right hand, and peered in toward home.

"Hey, man," said the hippie from Halifax, making a quick move toward him from first base. "Mind if I toss a few pitches?"

The retired cop waved him away, growling, "I got this."

Laquisha, at second base, glanced over at me, and seemed to glean my growing concern—I'd already given her a rundown on which passengers I was entranced by and which ones saddened and spooked me. "Let's go to the bullpen," she called. "Let's give someone else a turn on the mound."

But the cop was already going into his motion. The whole game, he'd served up nothing but juicy batting-practice lobs, but now he reared back and fired a fastball right at the Sikh kid's head. The kid ducked and the ball sailed harmlessly past. "What the hell, man?" cried the kid's older brother, jumping to his feet from the picnic table where he waited on deck.

I took a few steps toward the mound, but the guy from Halifax had already raced over to confront the cop. "What was that about?" he demanded.

"Take it easy, bud," the cop said, waiting for someone to retrieve the ball and toss it back to him. "It just got away from me. The thing's slippery. It's a dog's old chew toy." He smirked and rubbed his palms together. "Come on, let's play ball."

Warily, I repositioned myself at third. The Sikh kid stepped back to the plate and hunched into his stance with a sad, fierce look in his eyes. The old cop glared at him and kicked the dirt at his feet. He wound back, and unleashed another whistling burner. The kid ducked hard, dropped the stick from his hands, and tried to turn inward, away from the pitch, but it caught him right in the side of the face. He let out a little cry and crashed to the ground with a thud. His dad rushed to his side and knelt over him, and his older brother dashed over, picked up the fallen stick, and took one menacing step toward the mound. This was exactly what the cop seemed to be hoping for. Puffing out his chest, he strode forward, shouting, "You want some of this? Come get some of this!"

"Fuck you," the older brother said, hurling the stick in the opposite direction, where it disappeared onto the roof of the little brick building that housed the women's restrooms. He turned and helped his brother—who was more stung than actually hurt—get to his feet.

I hurried over to them to urgently apologize, but the dad hissed at me to leave them alone. He put his arms around his boys' shoulders and guided them swiftly into the parking lot, where the three of them clambered into a yellow Ford Focus hatchback and wheeled away.

The game instantly disbanded. The cop commiserated with the few passengers who believed he'd made a heroic stand, while the rest of us put our hands in our pockets and wandered away, crushed and dispirited, aware of the ugliness and divisions of our new reality, but seeing no point in talking about it. Laquisha and I found another spot in the grass to kill the rest of the afternoon. "It smells like dog doo-doo," she said. "I don't even have my Discman." She leaned back, wrapped an arm of my sweatshirt over her eyes and ears, and heaved a troubled sigh. "This sucks," she said. "I'm missing my shows. I'll tell you what. Terrorism can suck my dick."

Around six in the evening, our Greyhound bus groaned into the lot beside the shady grove where we'd spent the last few hours dozing and mashing mosquitoes, and the bus driver opened the door and sat fiddling with a pair of nail clippers as everyone filed silently aboard—what was there really to say to him? Once we hit the highway, though, the guy from Halifax went up to give him a piece of his mind. It was wrong, he said in a loud, pitched Canadian accent, for the driver to have gone off-route and stranded us for most of the day. "I appreciate you coming back for us," he said, "but for some of us, it's very urgent to get home as quickly as possible." He nodded toward the woman in the black coat in the front seat.

"Where you from?" the driver asked.

"Halifax."

"Where's that?"

"Nova Scotia."

"Canada?"

"Yeah."

"Well, look," said the driver, "this is America. Money talks. I'll get everyone home in good time. Anyone that makes it worth my while, they get home first. Wilkes-Barre's not off-route— this whole bus is off-route. You know what my route is? Vegas to Phoenix and back. Look, I'm on injured leave. I've got metal rods in my spine. Tuesday morning, they call me in, pull this bus out of retirement, and tell me to get people where they need to go. So here's my advice: sit down, shut up, and just be happy that *our* country's a target, not yours."

Defeated, and still steaming, the guy turned and made his way slowly back down the aisle. His shy, dreadlocked wife said, "Lee, I told you it wouldn't help to—"

"I know," he said, cutting her off with a raised palm, and swinging into the row behind her. Now that all the old fogeys had been chauffeured home, and a few other folks had foraged off on their own, the bus was two-thirds empty. There was enough space for me and Laquisha to each have our own row, but I was grateful for her quiet fellowship, and the fact that she still made a point of holding down the seat next to me.

Night fell, and I found myself, predictably, gushing to Laquisha about Susannah Cotton for an hour, dissecting every phone call and sort-of date we'd had the past couple of months, explaining why some moments had given me hope while others had drained me of it.

"Guys play too many games," Laquisha said. "If you like her, you don't have to keep it a secret from her. It's like you're trying too hard not to show your hand."

"You know, I'm probably the furthest thing from her mind right now," I said. "When things are this fucked up, you just want to feel safe. I bet you anything she's gonna get back with her ex-boyfriend. In fact," I said, dropping to a hush, "I bet he's behind this whole World Trade Center thing. All part of his plan to win her back."

Laquisha slapped me on the arm. "That's not funny," she said, laughing. Then she tugged on my elbow. "Why don't you call her?" she asked. "Just call her and say hi and tell her you're thinking about her."

That was a bad idea, I said, and defied the whole point of going on this trip—to give Susannah space and make her realize how much she missed me when I was gone. But the idea of calling her had now been planted in my mind, and it raged liked an infection until at last I gave in, dug out my cell phone, and punched in Susannah's number. My heart hammered with each ring. Laquisha leaned close so she could hear, grasping my sleeve with a terrified look on her face, like she was at a midnight horror flick at the drive-in.

Finally, Susannah picked up, but there was no "Hello," just the rowdy, unmistakable din of a Thursday night at the Gold Star, the hipster bar on Division where she and I had first met. I could hear her voice, talking merrily to someone over the ruckus, but I couldn't make out any of her words, only the crash of glasses, the squeaks and squawks of the people around her, and the heavy chords of the Fugazi song "Waiting Room" and its grinding chorus blasting from the jukebox: *"I don't want the news, / I cannot use it. / I don't want the news, / I won't live by it."* What had happened was clear to me—she'd seen who was calling and had tried to duck the call, but had pressed the wrong button before dropping her phone back into her purse.

"It's okay," said Laquisha. "She's partying. Who's gonna answer their phone when they're out at the club?" She sat back. "What're you doing? Aren't you gonna hang up? Hang up!"

"I'm just gonna listen in for a while," I said. "See if I can figure out who she's with, or if she says anything about me."

"You're weird," Laquisha said. "But I guess I'd do the same thing."

I leaned against the window, the phone clamped to my left ear, the right side of my face pressed to the cool glass. It was strangely wrenching to be transported inside the Gold Star, through sound alone, and be at Susannah's side, while out my window green mile markers ticked down toward Philadelphia, and red lights on distant radio towers flared and faded in mute code. I appreciated that everyone back in Chicago was having a fun night, but a part of me also felt repelled—didn't they know what was happening in the world? Didn't they know that festivity, for now, was tasteless? And why hadn't Susannah at least answered her phone and said hi, that she was at the bar, and that she'd call me back later? There were male voices around her and there were female voices, but it was impossible to tell who she was with or if a hand was resting casually on her hip or her thigh, though I guessed that one was. I listened for twelve full minutes, with creeping heartbreak; then my phone made a low *bee-bee-beep*, which meant we'd passed out of cell-tower range and into roaming mode—often responsible for a monthly kick in the nuts on my Sprint bill. I hung around on the line for another forty-five seconds, and finally, heavyhearted and full of an unnamed sorrow, dropped my phone into my lap, and our bus pressed on through the night.

"Wake up," Laquisha said. "We're getting close." It was almost dawn on the morning of September 14, and the eastern sky had filled with shades of purple and red. "We just passed Newark," she told me. "We'll be in the city in like half an hour."

I rubbed my eyes, still caught in a web of unsettling dreams, and as we floated in stop-and-go traffic, I began idly counting the cars on the New Jersey Turnpike, watching people handle their morning routines—eating bagels with cream cheese and sprouts, brushing their teeth, putting on makeup, and singing along to the radio. The normalcy of it all was movingly reassuring—the terrorists had wreaked horrific havoc, no doubt, but they sure as hell hadn't won.

"I'm writing my phone number down," Laquisha said, tearing the corner off a page of her softcover psychology textbook and scribbling with a pen. "Here," she said, passing me the torn scrap. "You'll be in town for two weeks, right? Use it. You got to meet my little girl, Destiny. She's the cutest."

"I'd love that," I said. "I feel really lucky we ended up sitting next to each other."

"Me too," she said with a smile. "And don't worry about that crazy little ho you were tellin' me about. You got bigger fish to fry. If I was ever gonna date a white boy, it'd be you." Pleased with her own brashness, she swiped her phone number back from me, added a little black heart, filled it in, and passed it back.

"How soon is too soon to call you?" I said, glowing a little and flirting right back, still a little dazed from lack of sleep and our whole ragged journey.

Before Laquisha could answer, though, the Greyhound's brakes let out a high, whining squeal, and everyone at the front of the bus began to gasp. We both sat up straight and craned forward to see what was going on. Through the windshield, as the bus came around a high, three-sixty curve leading to the entrance of the Lincoln Tunnel, the full Manhattan skyline had come into view, and the sight of it, just across the Hudson River, was one of the most awful and shocking things I'd ever seen. All of Lower Manhattan was engulfed in a yellowish haze, and at the far end, where the World Trade Center had been my whole life, there was simply nothing, only billowing plumes of black smoke rising all the way to the clouds.

Up front, the woman in the black coat and the pink scarf broke into sobs, and soon everyone on the bus was crying, too, me included. Nobody said a word, and as we wound our way around the ramp and the tunnel swallowed us up in a deep darkness, there was only the sounds of people whimpering and moaning in disbelief. Me and Laquisha squeezed each other's hand. I still couldn't wrap my head around what I'd just fucking seen—this wasn't a *Godzilla* movie, this was my own naked eyes resting on the bombed shell of New York City. It somehow felt more shocking to see the city, the smoke, and the vanished towers now, through the windows of the bus, than it had been three days earlier, on TV, watching them fall. At last, the tunnel spat us out into Midtown's seven-a.m. cacophony. We pulled into a dark underground bay at the Port Authority Bus Terminal and everyone numbly gathered their stuff and climbed down off the bus onto an oil-stained patch of pavement, where the driver unloaded our luggage a bag at a time and handed it off to whoever came forward to claim it.

Laquisha found her bags, gave me a long, meaningful hug, said goodbye and that she hoped to see me soon, and hurried off toward the subway to catch a train uptown. The woman in the black coat grabbed a small suitcase and disappeared, too. I never learned if her son was found alive or dead, assuming he was found at all—I'd never even learned her first name. The Amish kids, the old Somali woman, the Canadian couple, the Long Island cop, they all grabbed their things from the driver and melted away. These days, on a thousand-mile bus trip like that, after all those interviews and brief but intense conversations, I would've gathered a slew of e-mail addresses and made a dozen new Facebook friends. But that was another time, before the souls we cross paths with could be collected like passport stamps, and I never saw or heard from any of those people again.

On the subway platform, headed to my aunt and uncle's place at the far end of Brooklyn, I reached into my pocket to give a dollar to a homeless guy playing "America the Beautiful" on a piccolo and a gust of wind from a passing Bronx-bound local snatched the scrap of paper with Laquisha's number from my hand and sucked it away into oblivion. I spent a half hour scouring the tracks as trains came and went, sure I'd eventually spot it, but it was gone, gone, gone. I lashed myself for my carelessness, and for the fact that I hadn't saved her number on my phone or at least asked her last name. Two days later, I even went to the Sbarro's in Times Square to look for her, but nobody who worked there seemed to know who I was talking about and they all treated me like a weirdo when I asked if I could leave a note for her anyway. It wasn't that I believed Laquisha was my soulmate exactly, but our friendship meant something to me, and it made me sad to imagine what she might make of the fact that I never called, if she might believe that our friendship had meant nothing to me, or was only temporary, when the truth is that Laquisha sticks with me and matters to me to this day.

I spent the next week and a half in New York, wandering the streets and interviewing people. I saw plenty of reporters and TV crews badgering folks in Union Square who were putting up flyers of their missing loved ones, and firemen sitting in front of their local fire stations with their heads in their hands, but I couldn't bring myself to do the same. Instead, I sought out stories from those who'd been less directly affected—a gyro vendor outside Madison Square Garden, two Dominican teenagers who met every afternoon in a park to play NFL Blitz on a Game Boy, an elderly Danish tourist who was on his first visit to the

U.S. and had landed in the city on September 10. I started each little interview by asking folks where they'd been when the towers had been struck, but the conversations quickly spilled over into the rest of their lives—where they were from, how they'd first come to New York, what they most wanted, what they were most afraid of. Basically, the disaster, and the fact that the city was crawling with so many reporters, gave me an excuse to accost anyone I chose to and ask for their life story.

Anyone who's ever gotten into photography for a minute knows that when you start taking a lot of pictures, you start seeing the world in a different way. Your awareness of your surroundings shifts and deepens, and even when you don't have your camera in your hands, you become constantly struck by the lyricism of passing visuals. It's the same way with audio gear. When you've got your headphones on all day and are always armed with a microphone, you grow more attuned to the infinite range of voices and accents, the inflections and cadences of speech, quick intakes of breath, the struggle to find the right word, the little barbed pause when someone's about to choke up. And after a while you don't need to be wearing headphones or recording someone for your conversation with them to have the same potency, and affect you on the same profound level.

I never pieced together any story about September 11 for *This American Life*, but I still have the tapes of all the interviews I did that week and a half, including one with my aunt and uncle in Coney Island, who've both died in the years since, and sometimes on long drives I'll listen to that one, and remember the hot air in the living room of their apartment and the damaged looks on their faces as they tried to make sense of what had happened, weeping for all the lives that were lost, and for the end of a certain time of peace. Other times I'll listen to the tapes of Laquisha dissing one late-nineties rapper, then lavishing praise on another and wondering what the future held in store for her, her baby sister, and all New Yorkers. I can almost remember the specific moments where I'd thought to myself, "Oh my God, wait till I get back to Chicago and play this part for Susannah," but of course by the time I'd made it back to Chicago two weeks later, Susannah had hooked up with a handsome writer named Todd Bell, and it wasn't long before they'd moved to Birmingham, Alabama, for teaching jobs, and eventually married and had kids, whose Olan Mills portraits I get to see from time to time in Picasa albums online.

The whole time I was in New York, I'd steered clear of the World Trade Center district—not because it was cordoned off and guarded by police and soldiers, but simply because it seemed too horrible to face in person, and I was afraid I'd only be in the way. My last night in town, though, at around two in the morning, I took my tape recorder and microphone, slipped past an unwatched barricade, and headed deep downtown on foot.

The streets were eerily calm, with no cars, no people, and no lights. I'd been in ghost towns out west, but the ghost *city*— where the only sounds were street signs creaking in the wind and rats pattering from one storm drain to the next—was chilling. Past Canal Street, dark empty skyscrapers towered like the grand remnants of an ancient civilization. I knew I was getting close to where the Twin Towers had stood from the singeing, metallic odor in the air, and the thousands of loose sheets of paper carpeting the streets and sidewalks—paper, apparently, had somehow survived the fall of the towers, while iron, stone, and concrete had been turned to dust.

I came around the corner of Church Street and Chambers, and the sight took my breath away—four short blocks south, the remains of the World Trades smoldered in a massive, smoking, tangled heap, glowing orange and red, like the last embers of an eighteen-story campfire. This was what, at the time, people called "the Mound" or "the Pile," and on all sides of it, hundreds of firemen scrambled around, shining zillion-watt spotlights, and aiming long, powerful hoses into the fray. The steaming wreckage was so mighty and oversized, it made the firefighters look like ants, their trucks and cranes like Lego toys. I sat on the hood of an abandoned taxicab layered in gray, powdery bits of rubble and took in the scene, in all its transfixing, surreal, and terrible splendor. This, I realized, as one hour hazily passed, and then another, was why I'd boarded the bus from Chicago—not to impress a girl, but to be there and see things with my own eyes, and to try to understand.

It was a waking dream. Every once in a while, a dozen firemen, rescue workers, or soldiers emerged from the tableau and trooped past me, their faces dark and haunted, and another dozen clattered from behind me, toward the blazing Mound, pulling on helmets and buckling gear to their belts, ready to start a fresh shift. Giant flatbed haulers carried rubble away, past me up Church Street, one after another, each rig straining under the weight of a single sixty-foot iron girder. Tears stung my eyes. I felt invisible; I felt made of air; I felt consumed by grief and marvel.

At some point I pulled my headphones on, and with my microphone pointed straight ahead, I could make out the sounds of the firemen's voices, shouting out to one another, maneuvering ladders and hoses and winches and ropes; I could even hear a sound I took to be the hiss and crackle of the dying blaze itself. Then, another sound flowed into my ears, but it was so faint and so odd that I took it at first to be my imagination—it was the sound of someone singing.

After a few minutes, I slid off my taxicab perch, and with the mic held out in front of me like a divining rod, I followed the strange, delirious voice, up Church Street, toward the action at Ground Zero. One block up, at Church and Warren, around the corner from a boarded-up pharmacy, two old black men in tattered coats and lumpy knit hats stood scratching their backs on a street pole, facing the Mound. The shorter one stared straight ahead, while the taller one, with a salt-and-pepper beard, had his head tilted to the side and his eyes closed, having just finished a song.

I made a motion with my microphone to indicate my question to the shorter of the two: Would it be all right if I recorded this? He nodded and waved me closer. I stepped right next to them, at arm's length, catching the hard scent of peppermint schnapps on their breath, mixed with the acrid burn of melted copper wire from smoke off the Mound. The taller man smiled, eyes still closed but aware of my presence, and lifted his voice again in song. I closed my eyes to listen in, and felt immediately overcome with emotion, ripped with sadness, fear, and hope. I believed in that moment, and still do, that if me and those two hobos could stand together on that four-a.m. street corner and love one another, then there was still hope for our world.

This, then, is the most miraculous, piercing, and devastating two minutes of tape I've ever recorded—the song that old dude sang with great, half-drunken, gravelly abandon, his voice smoky, textured, and resonant as any legendary bluesman, while the junk trucks continued to grind past in the background, ratcheting from first to second gear, laden with debris. The song? I think it's a Frank Sinatra song. It's called "New York, New York." I'm sure you know it.

TESSA

My cousin called the teams—me and him versus his roommate Bauer and Bauer's girlfriend, Tessa. This was down in the raw stink of a crumbling frat house basement on the Drexel University campus in West Philly. My cousin was a college junior; I was a high-school freshman, deposited with him for the weekend while my dad made sales calls in the area. I'd never played beer pong before, and had hardly ever tasted alcohol.

The game, as they explained it, was simple: two plastic cups of beer perched at either end of the table. You played with paddles and everything, like regular Ping-Pong, but if you plunked the ball against the other team's cup, both of them had to drink. Land the ball inside the cup, they had to down the whole beer. Win the game, they had to down two.

Within a half hour, we were all fucked up. Now, twenty years and a thousand drinking sessions later, I can recognize the types of drinkers each of us were. There was my cousin, the jolly, rambunctious sort of drinker who just wants to get everyone wasted, especially the shy, the officious, or the kid who's never been drunk before. That was me, the newbie who doesn't know how to measure his level of drunkenness and just keeps laughing and saying shit that doesn't make any sense, before eventually throwing up and passing out in an alleyway or on the bathroom floor. There was Bauer, the guy who turns wicked with drink, full of torn-up fury, whose only outlet is to pop someone in the eye or crack a pool cue over some poor sap's head. And then there was Tessa, the kind of beautiful girl who downs drinks in long pulls, who smiles sad smiles and plays with her jewelry and looks lost and big-eyed and at the end of the night targets a stranger to make out with to keep her seeping darkness at bay. These days I could take one glance into a basement like that and tell you how shit was about to go down. But I was fourteen then and I had no idea.

Bauer kept knocking over his own beers, which meant, according to house rules, that he had to drink a full cup each time as a penalty. He started shouting and swearing at us, at himself, and especially at Tessa. As me and my cousin won game after game, Bauer and Tessa got more and more drunk.

Then, for about ten minutes, they put on a surprising rally. A shot hit the net and dribbled over. Another nicked off the very end of the table, unreturnable. Before long they'd taken a seventeen-to-six lead. Whenever they hit our cup of beer and we had to drink, I took small sips, while my cousin guzzled. "You're not drunk enough!" he roared, with an affectionate whomp on my shoulders. He explained his theory that in all sports—pool, basketball, beer pong—there was a sweet spot of drunkenness necessary to maximize your skills. Too little drink and you were tentative, indecisive; too much drink and you were popping the cue ball off the table or airballing shots over the backboard. "Down this," he said, topping off a fresh cup from the keg on the floor. I glugged the whole thing down, and Tessa clapped and smiled and flashed her green eyes at me, her beauty both painful and electrifying.

Me and my cousin began an epic comeback. I found that Bauer couldn't handle the slightest bit of topspin. He howled at each point we scored and soon his face was pink. Tessa teased an impossible shot off the corner of the table to tie the game at nineteen, but Bauer slapped my next serve into the net and my cousin slammed home a drop shot to give us the win. While we celebrated with a series of emphatic high fives, Bauer and Tessa quietly drank two beers each. Bauer then mashed his empty cups against his face—one to his forehead, one to his jaw, and hauled Tessa close for a kiss on the neck. She spun away. Bauer fixed us with a mean look and said, "You fuckers are going down."

Finally, after we beat them once more, Bauer whipped his paddle across the table; it whizzed past my ear like a throwing star and took out a chunk of wall behind my head. He lifted the entire table, crashed it onto its side, and stormed away up the stairs. Tessa stared at the table forlornly, as though it were a dying dolphin, then looked up at me and my cousin with wet eyes. In just a couple of hours, I'd fallen powerfully in love with her. I'm pretty sure my cousin was in love with her, too, but he was dating a girl who managed a bar up in Allentown and he split right then to go crash at her place.

Dazed, supremely loaded, and too full of desire for Tessa to say a word to her, I found my way up to the room my cousin and Bauer shared on the third floor of the house and sank into a bed, staring at the walls. On each wall, my cousin and Bauer had painted a giant mural representing one of Philadelphia's four major sports teams—the Phillies, the Sixers, the Flyers, and the Eagles—complete with team colors and insignias and crudely crafted faces of a dozen of their favorite players. They loomed over me like doctors over a sick infant—Mike Schmidt, Randall Cunningham, Moses Malone.

The door opened. Tessa slipped in. She climbed into bed beside me and without a word pressed her lips to mine. Her breath was hot, salty, and strangely copper-like. For some reason, I pretended to be asleep, and then pretended to be waking from sleep. I kissed her back. My heart blammed like a tommy gun. I couldn't believe this was happening.

Tessa took hold of my hand and pressed it against her breast. Then she clutched my other hand—like it was a dead thing—and pushed it down her stomach and inside her jeans. "I don't have a condom," I squeaked, and she shushed me and pulled her jeans off in one deft move and tossed them into the darkness, knocking bottles off a dresser.

It was another minute or so before Bauer came crashing into the room and things turned ugly. First, though, I said to Tessa, "Wait, I just want to kiss you some more." It wasn't that I didn't want to have sex for the first time—I did, as badly as I'd ever wanted anything—but kissing her, just kissing her, felt so exquisite, so holy, so unimaginably thrilling, that I wanted to savor it for as long as possible. So we kissed for a few long moments, not like drunks tearing at each other, but with tenderness, longing, and real love.

A strange thing happened as we kissed—I began to replay our rounds of beer pong in my head, and suddenly all these deep truths of the game revealed themselves to me. I understood the shots I should have made, the times I'd held off the ball, waiting for my cousin to make a move when the move was mine to make, and even how I'd been balancing on my heels when I needed to shift more onto my toes. It's not that I wasn't present with Tessa, wildly in the moment with her—no, the opposite was true. I was so entirely in the moment that the whole night seemed to bleed together into one pulsing beat. Flashes from my past and from my future strobed through my mind. Everything made sense to me—where I'd been, the mistakes I'd made, and where I wanted to be and what I had to do to get there. Musical prodigies, genius mathematicians, and world-class athletes call this being in the zone. Maybe it's what Olympic Ping-Pong players feel in the heat of competition, closing in on the medal rounds, this sensation of profound understanding and insight, as close to nirvana as I've ever felt.

In the midst of this I felt my entire body jerked upward, like a beached whale in a chopper's sling, and then I was heaved face first into a wall (the Sixers wall, incidentally), Bauer's iron elbow pinned to my spine.

"What the fuck is going on right now?" he yelled with anguish and rage. He pulled my right arm behind my back, and my shoulder burned with pain, as though the socket might cave and let my limb loose. I opened my eyes and discovered that my face was pressed directly into the eerie portrait of Sixers point guard Maurice Cheeks. Before I could respond or even cry out, Bauer dumped me out of his room, into the stairwell, and slammed his door shut.

I faced the door; I could hear him shouting on the other side. Then, after a half minute, he settled down, and not long after I heard him and Tessa start fucking. Hollowed out, on the edge of tears, I wandered down the stairs. In the dark living room, a dozen of my cousin's housemates were passed out on sofas and across the floor like victims of an atomic blast, caught in SportsCenter's grim flicker. I grabbed a stray cushion, continued on down to the basement, and sat against a wall, sipping on the last third of a beer, lost as an old-timer at the end of the bar. At last I righted the Ping-Pong table, stretched out on top of it with the sofa cushion as a pillow, and fell fast asleep. At dawn, I slipped out of the house before anyone else was up, and a day later I was headed back to Michigan. On the train ride home I wrote Tessa a long love letter that I mailed to her at her parents' house in Glasgow, Delaware (the registrar's office gave me the address). I proposed that we run off together out west. I never heard back.

But it's funny the way one night can shape you. For example, I discovered that night that Ping-Pong tables are oddly comfortable to sleep on. I've slept on about thirty in the years since; I will always sleep on a Ping-Pong table if the choice is between a Ping-Pong table and the floor. Also, whenever I'm at the bar and I glance at a TV hanging from the rafters and happen to catch any Philadelphia sports highlights, I still get a strange, hot jolt—those murals in my cousin's bedroom the night I kissed Tessa, they're to credit and to blame. I'll even pass a dude on the street wearing a Phillies jersey and that room comes back to me, Mike Schmidt's bug-eyed face, the taste of Tessa's lips.

If I'd known that night, as I sat sipping the last third of a beer in the basement of my cousin's frat house, that I'd still be in love with Tessa twenty years later, that I'd be spending four nights a week at bars in cities like Mobile, Alabama, and Kansas City and Little Rock, falling in love with Tessas, dying to kiss them, would I have done anything differently? Maybe once a year I get to kiss a Tessa, the other eleven months and change I get tossed out of Bauer's room and sleep on Ping-Pong tables, but still, if it happens even once a year, all those trips to the bar are worth it. I'll never be the kind of drinker who drinks to get wild or drinks to get numb; I'll be the kind of drinker who drinks because that's what you do at a bar, and I'll hang out at bars because that's where you'll find Tessas.

Tessa, I still love you. Tessa, see what you've done?

THE STRONGEST MAN
IN THE WORLD

Once a year, maybe every year and a half, I go to visit my friend Byron Case at a sprawling, maximum-security state prison called Crossroads Correctional Center in the town of Cameron, Missouri. Picture me early this morning, driving up I-35 from Kansas City in a soft, warm rain, Byron's mom, Evelyn, in the passenger seat of my van, telling energetic stories, and in the back, my brother Peter, listening in and looking out the window. It's November, the week before Thanksgiving, and once we're through the suburbs, the rain-soaked malls and Best Buys and Outback Steakhouses slide away, and dense patches of woods, filled with black, wet trees, their branches shaken free of leaves, rise up on either side of the highway, beside vast empty fields of yellow wheat and dirt, and an occasional farmhouse or pair of sagging barns slumbering in the distance out on the rolling plains. Crows feasting on a roadkill deer halfway on the shoulder, halfway in the ditch, scatter as we rumble past, and I watch in my rearview mirror as they reconvene. Every time I make this drive, I feel the same heavy combination of emotions—excitement to see my friend, and an unshakable melancholy that another year has passed and Byron is still locked up. In my sadness, the world grows more vivid.

After an hour, Evelyn says, "Okay, it's this one," and we coast up an exit ramp, hang a left, then a right, and roll down Cameron's main commercial drag—a Wal-Mart, a four-screen movie theater, a bowling alley, two pawnshops, a shuttered appliance store, and a guy under a tarp selling tires in the lot of a long-forgotten Dairy Queen. At the end of the stretch, oddly close to town—where you might expect to find the high school instead—a series of low-slung tan brick buildings folds into sight. If it weren't for the high, chain-link fences and fearsome rolls of razor wire, you could mistake the prison for the campus of an aging, underfunded community college. The lot out front is so full that it's hard to find a parking space, a reminder of just how many locals the prison employs.

Inside the lobby, we fill Evelyn's clear change purse with quarters for the vending machines, leave our keys and wallets in a tiny coin locker, show our driver's licenses to an officer at the desk, and walk through a metal detector and on through two sets of security doors into a Plexiglas antechamber that looks out into the visiting room. Evelyn is buzzing; these visits with her son, she's told me, are the highlight of her week. She introduces me and Peter to some of the other folks in the waiting room—the parents, spouses, and young kids of other inmates at Crossroads. There's a compassionate, knowing kindness and friendliness to the small talk—whatever anguish you experience when your son or husband is locked up, it's nice to be around people who won't judge you and understand exactly what you're going through.

Even as she chats freely, Evelyn keeps one eye trained on the visiting room, and when she sees Byron walk in, she cries out with the giddy chirp of a teenage girl, "Here he is! Here's Byron!" She gives him a friendly, excited wave, and Byron breaks out in a smile and waves back. He's in his late twenties, pale-skinned with buzz-cut black hair, a wispy goatee, and the open, friendly look of a college kid working the help desk at Barnes &

Noble. He smooths out the folds in his gray prison scrubs, waiting for an officer to retrieve us from the waiting room. Once we're inside, he gives his mom a hug, then turns and wraps a strong hug on me. "It's great to see you, man!" he says with quiet vigor.

"It's great to see you, Byron!" We release. "You remember my brother Peter?"

"Of course I do," says Byron, and when he and Peter share a hug, that, for some reason, is when I start to get teary. "Well," says Byron, looking out across the room, "let's find a place to sit down. I believe we've got some catching up to do!"

Lincoln Cemetery, on the eastern edge of Kansas City, is best known as the burial place of jazz legend Charlie "Bird" Parker. It occupies a large swath of forest and open land on Truman Road just off I-435, opposite a stretch of gas stations, adult bookstores, and seedy motels. On October 23, 1997, around four a.m., a Kansas City cop on routine patrol was rolling a slow loop through the pitch-black graveyard when he saw a teenage girl lying on her back near the road. He figured she was either drunk or passed out, but when he climbed from his squad car and approached her, he found, to his horror, that she'd been shot in the face at close range. Blood had pooled in the grass under her head. She was cool to the touch, as though she'd been dead for hours, her eyes wide open. Her name was Anastasia Witbols-Feugen, an eighteen-year-old college freshman.

The next day, before police had a chance to question him, Anastasia's boyfriend, Justin Bruton, was found dead behind an abandoned warehouse fifty miles south of town; he'd turned a shotgun on himself. After some investigation, the cops told the local press that they believed it was a murder-suicide, though they lacked conclusive evidence, and soon the case faded from view.

Years later, though, an old friend of Anastasia's named Kelly

Moffett, who was being treated for an addiction to crack cocaine, came to the cops with a different story. She told them she'd witnessed the murder of her friend, and that the killer was not Justin, it was the guy who'd been her own boyfriend at the time—Justin's best friend, Byron Case. Kelly said Byron and Justin had felt that Anastasia was "annoying" and had decided to kill her, and that Byron had pulled the trigger. Byron was arrested and tried for the crime.

The prosecution had no murder weapon, no crime-scene DNA—in fact, no physical evidence of any kind. Their star witness had a fragile mental state and had spent time on the street strung out on drugs, and there was no one to corroborate her story. Any motive for Byron was murky at best. But the case went forward, and the prosecution found ways to sneak in mentions of Byron's "goth" lifestyle—the fact that he wore a black trench coat, and that he used antique autopsy pictures, pulled from the Internet, as screensavers on his computer. The Jackson County jurors—blue-collar, churchgoing, and conservative—appeared to be swayed by this testimony, according to the accounts I read. As for Kelly Moffett's reliability as a witness, the prosecution turned her past as a drug addict on its head—they suggested that she'd gone downhill only because she'd witnessed Anastasia's death and had been harboring a "horrible secret," though Byron contends that she'd been unstable and had experimented with drugs long before Anastasia was killed.

Byron was too poor to hire his own lawyer and was represented in court by a public defender named Horton Lance. While many public defenders are known for their seriousness and effectiveness, they're also notoriously underfunded and overworked. One of my close friends, a public defender in the Bronx, often complains of being stretched too thin, without adequate resources to research cases or the time to properly prepare for a trial, and worries that his most skilled colleagues burn out quickly, while the incompetent ones are rarely weeded out. Perhaps these factors explain some of the crucial mistakes Horton Lance made during Byron's defense, as revealed in the case's 1,290-page trial transcript.

Now, I'm no courtroom pro, but I've spent enough time around trial lawyers to know that although defendants are meant to be presumed innocent, with the burden of proof in the hands of the prosecution, things often don't play out that way. At Byron's trial, the prosecution offered a single, compelling, and vaguely plausible explanation for Anastasia's death, and made up for their lack of material evidence with convincing, emotional witnesses, especially Kelly Moffett. Horton Lance, on the other hand, failed to present any alternative scenarios for the defense. He said only that the cemetery was bordered by sketchy neighborhoods, the oblique implication being that Anastasia might have been the victim of a stranger's act of random violence. (Indeed, in the years before and since Anastasia's death, other random shootings have dotted that stretch of Truman Road close to the cemetery.) Lance never delved into the fact that Anastasia's boyfriend, Justin, had purchased firearms in the past, while Byron had never even held a gun in his life. And he did little to highlight the inconsistencies in Kelly's account or to reflect on what motivations she might have had for lying about Byron's involvement.

At one point, Kelly blurted out from the stand that she'd passed a lie detector test, which was highly misleading. First of all, polygraphs are rarely admissible in a courtroom because of their unreliability, and the truth was, she hadn't taken a polygraph, she'd taken an even less reliable voice stress test, and in that conversation she'd actually attested to Byron's innocence. Although the judge cautioned the jury to disregard Kelly's remark, the damage was done—in a case that depended largely on one person's word against another's, Kelly had gained the upper hand. Here, Horton Lance could have moved for a mistrial; he failed to do so. Byron, who'd proclaimed his innocence since day one, then testified on his own behalf, but when he took the stand, Lance had no cohesive plan for what to ask him, and Byron's sullen, disengaged testimony may only have marred the jury's perceptions of him.

The trial had been short, just three and a half days. After each side gave a closing statement, the jury deliberated for a couple of hours and came to a decision—Byron Case was guilty of murder, they said. His sentence: life in prison.

The magazine I run, *Found*, collects notes, letters, and pictures found on the ground and on the street by readers across the country and around the world. In the early days of the magazine, I used to personally open every found item we received, and often, if it was a particularly captivating or intriguing find, I'd write back to the person who'd mailed it in.

Byron Case was an early reader of the magazine, and he'd regularly send us to-do lists and love letters and other fascinating scraps he'd plucked off the floor of his favorite coffee shop in Westport, Kansas City's quaint hipster neighborhood, or had discovered in a used book, or come across in his old job as a front desk clerk at a motel. He always wrote short, funny letters to accompany his finds in distinct, carefully printed handwriting, and before long I found myself trading letters back and forth with him.

After a period where I hadn't heard from Byron for a couple of years, I sent him a copy of the latest issue of *Found*, which included a couple of finds he'd sent to me long before. Two weeks later, I got a note from his mom, Evelyn, explaining that Byron was in prison, the result of a wrongful conviction. She gave me his new address, and referred me to a website built by friends of his outlining the details of his case. I remember the shock of logging on and seeing that he'd been handed a life sentence. I spent all night poring through trial documents online, horrified that someone could be locked up on the basis of such flimsy evidence. Like all of life's massive strokes of misfortune—fatal car accidents, plane crashes, spinal injuries, testicular cancer, Lou Gehrig's disease, or losing both arms or both legs in an IED blast north of Mosul—it's never a surprise that these kinds of things happen, it's only a surprise that it's happened to someone you know. As dawn light filled my bedroom, I imagined Byron waking up in his bunk in prison, and having to register again, each morning, that this Kafkaesque nightmare was real.

The next night, I settled down again at my computer to research his case some more, when I came across another site, created by friends and family of Anastasia WitbolsFeugen, partly as a memorial for Anastasia, but mostly, it seemed, to refute the claims on Byron's site. This opposing site painted Byron as a coldhearted killer who was brilliant and sophisticated, full of dark menace and masterful cunning. For every question raised on Byron's site that seemed to point toward his innocence, Anastasia's memorial site had laid out a convincing rebuttal. Each site also had a guestbook page, and on these pages a furious feud had broken out between supporters of Byron and those who believed he'd been convicted justly. The same was true in the comments sections of the articles about Anastasia's death and Byron's trial and conviction on the websites of the *Kansas City Star* and the *Pitch*, a local alt-weekly. A short blurb about the case on the site of a community college's school paper would be followed by hundreds of comments, condemning the courts, the cops, the prosecutors, and Kelly Moffett—Byron's accuser—and, in immediate response, condemning Byron himself. Many of the commenters had resorted to back-and-forth name calling, but a lot of them also dug into the facts of the case right down to the most infinitesimal minutiae, arguing about evidence presented during trial, as well as evidence that was never presented. People who'd personally known Byron, Kelly, Anastasia, and her boyfriend, Justin Bruton, offered anecdotes attesting to either

Byron's guilt or innocence, and to the idea that Kelly had lied on the stand, or that she'd been telling the truth.

In the week that followed, I found myself talking about the case to anyone who would listen—and for as long as possible—until they'd leave the room to get away from me. At night, I lay awake, turning things over in my head, trying to pierce the knot of contradicting stories. The more and more I read, and the more anonymous, wild accusations I sifted through online, the further I felt from getting a sense for what had really happened to Anastasia that night. From a distance, the case was impenetrable. The only way I'd be able to sort it out in my own mind, I decided, was to reach out personally to those involved, and hear the story in their own words. For that sole selfish reason, pretty much, I decided to leap right in.

I e-mailed Evelyn, Byron's mom. The next day we spoke on the phone for two hours. She had a strong German accent, and explained that she'd come to the States at the age of twenty, just to explore for a few months, but had met Byron's dad, Dale, fallen in love, and remained in the country ever since, though she and Dale had eventually separated. She was friendly, gracious, smart, tough, and clear minded, with a mother's absolute (if predictable) faith in her son's innocence, but also a detailed grasp on the mistakes that had been made during the trial. At one point, she began to choke up. "If only I had more money," she said, her voice breaking. "We wouldn't have had to go with that—that crummy defense lawyer. I just figured it was all a big mistake and they'd get everything figured out and it would quickly be over with. Oh boy, was I wrong." She allowed a short laugh. "It's okay. We're gonna keep working till Byron is home." Evelyn seemed to have channeled the bulk of her grief over her son's predicament into an energetic, protracted campaign to fight for his freedom. She worked as a language tutor and a pet-sitter and sold vintage furniture and housewares she turned up at estate sales, and her limited income was funneled almost entirely into paying the lawyers who were working on Byron's appeals. When possible, she traveled the country to attend conferences for the Innocence Project and other wrongful-conviction groups, bending the ear of anyone who might be sympathetic to her son's plight.

Finally, she told me, "Look, the biggest expert on Byron's case is Byron. Why don't you come for a visit? You can talk to Byron himself."

A few weeks later, in early December, I was on a late-night DC-10 shuttle from Detroit, looking out the window as the twinkling lights of Kansas City came into view, surrounded by desolate prairie blackness. Was I making this trip as a journalist? A self-styled criminal investigator? A friend of Byron's? I wasn't really sure, but I felt nervous and excited, eager to penetrate the mystery.

At midnight, I wound my rental car through quiet neighborhood streets in Kansas City's deepest southeast corner, toward Evelyn's house—she'd offered to put me up while I was in town. The homes on her block were perched close together, tiny but well kept, with Christmas wreaths on the front doors and old, weather-beaten Fords and Pontiacs in the driveways. I pulled up in front of her house. It was a strange feeling, after my earlier correspondence with Byron, the recent calls with his mom, and a fanatical month of immersion into his case, to suddenly find myself walking up the front steps and ringing the bell. This, I knew, was the house that the cops had raided when they'd come to arrest Byron a couple of years before.

Evelyn greeted me warmly and helped me carry my bags inside, and we sat sipping hot chocolate at her kitchen table, and chatted for an hour. She was in her mid-fifties, with dyed blond streaks in her hair and a nose ring. Her bohemian vibe and affable intelligence reminded me of an old friend of mine's mom, who was an art professor from Stuttgart. Evelyn was excited by my visit—it wasn't often that someone from another part of the country took such an interest in Byron's situation, and the fact that I sometimes wrote for national magazines and appeared on public radio was appealing to her. The most important thing she could do, she felt, was to get word out about the details of her son's case. I was careful not to promise anything—for all I knew, Byron was guilty. I wanted to meet him before I offered to get seriously involved.

Evelyn brewed another round of hot chocolate, and asked about my work and my family, and if I had a girlfriend. There was a part of her that seemed to luxuriate in having a young man in her kitchen roughly the same age as her son, someone she could tease, scold, flatter, and fuss over. At one point, I heard a toilet flush in another part of the house. Evelyn saw my curious look and explained that it was her boyfriend, Napo. She called him into the room, and he sat with us for a few minutes—a kind, soft-spoken Ecuadorean in his forties who worked as a housepainter and played soccer on the weekends. "Byron is a dear friend to me," Napo said. "I visit him every week. I go there thinking, 'I will keep his spirits up,' but it's always him that keeps my spirits up. God has chosen him to walk a very unusual path. But I know He has a plan for Byron."

Evelyn said to me, "You must be beat. We've all got an early morning tomorrow. I like to head out around seven thirty so we can be the first in line when visiting hours start. Come on," she said. "I set you up in Byron's room."

She showed me into a small bedroom at the end of the hallway and said good night, and I slowly moved around the room, gazing at Byron's Victorian novels and punk rock CDs and all of his little knickknacks lining the shelves and windowsills. I imagined that at some point Evelyn had straightened up a bit, but that she'd otherwise left the room mostly untouched since the day of Byron's arrest, as though any day the world might right itself and Byron would come ambling through the front door.

I turned off the lights and got under the covers. Byron, I knew, had spent many nights in his bedroom during high school hanging out with his best friend, Justin, and their girlfriends, Kelly and Anastasia, devouring pizza and guzzling Mountain Dew, listening to Siouxsie and the Banshees records, watching Monty Python flicks, and bad-mouthing their narrow-minded teachers and classmates with other friends in AOL chat rooms. It was heartbreaking to picture them lounging here—on the bed, in the kneeling chair at Byron's desk, flopped on the giant bean-bag chair on the floor—caught up in their ordinary rebellious and playful teenage banter, and then to consider all of the chaos that followed: Anastasia in the cemetery grass, blood leaking from the holes in her face and the back of her head; Justin, sitting behind the abandoned warehouse south of town, shotgun in his lap, his head blown clear off; and Byron, in an orange Jackson County prison jumpsuit and ankle chains, being hauled away after his sentencing hearing. Beyond the bedroom door, I could make out the tones of Evelyn and Napo talking softly, teasing each other, as they brushed their teeth and headed to bed. I lay there for hours, listening to trees creak and sway in the wind, and staring into the darkness, exhausted but unable to sleep.

In the morning, we drove up to Cameron, Missouri, in my rental car, Evelyn keeping me company up front while Napo dozed in the back. In college, and again a few years after, I'd taught creative writing classes at prisons in Jackson, Michigan, and Lorton, Virginia, so when we arrived at Crossroads Correctional Center and went inside, the place already had a familiar feel—familiar lighting, even a familiar institutional odor. All U.S. prisons, I've come to believe, order the same sour buff-and-wax floor soap and the same bluish, buzzing fluorescent bulbs.

Evelyn knew each guard's name, and they acknowledged her with measured politeness, leading us through the security doors, past the Plexiglas waiting room and into the visiting room, where Byron stood in his prison grays, a smile on his face. He was a bit shorter than me, and stockier than I'd imagined—most of the pictures of him on the Web were from high school, so it made sense that he'd filled out a bit, especially after a couple of years working out in prison weight rooms. He had a wide face, friendly brown eyes, and the kind of thin, black mustache that had been making a comeback in hipster circles, though Byron told me later that he'd grown his not for style points, but on the advice of other inmates who'd told him it would help ward off unwanted sexual advances. "Thanks for coming so far to see me," Byron said, shaking my hand vigorously. He swept an arm through the air. "Hey, come on in, grab a seat. It's not much, but we call it home."

The visiting room had the size and feel of a grade-school cafeteria. Low wooden tables sat in three rows of ten, four plastic chairs clustered around each of them. A few vending machines in the corner offered plastic pop bottles and microwaveable snacks; nearby, a counter held a stack of games, including chess, checkers, Candy Land, and Sorry! Off to the side, a children's area was stocked with small toys and picture books, and in the back of the room, an amateurish yet oddly appealing mural of a mountain landscape had been painted across the back wall—by a prisoner, I assumed. This, I learned, was where visitors to Cross-roads could have their pictures taken with incarcerated friends and loved ones.

Byron, Evelyn, Napo, and I found a table in the middle of the room and took a seat. The stage was set for some initial awkwardness—after all, Byron and I had only exchanged a handful of letters, and my reasons for making such a long trip to be there weren't entirely clear, even to me. But from the moment we sat down, the two of us started talking like old friends. Byron took the lead, telling stories about his current cellmate, Donnie, who loved crossword puzzles but couldn't solve a single clue without Byron's help. At night, Byron said, while he read in the top bunk, Donnie would lie below, rattling off clues: "Okay, okay, come on, just one more. Twenty-three down. Minority whip. Six letters." Byron had tried steering him toward word-search puzzles, but Donnie was devoted to crosswords. "He doesn't really care if we get the answers right," Byron said. "He just likes seeing them all filled out."

I really hadn't had any idea what to expect, but still found myself surprised by Byron's relaxed charisma, sweetness, curiosity, and nerdy wit. Even after a couple of years in prison, he seemed, remarkably, to have not one trace of hardness in him. The prosecutors—and those who frequently posted on comment boards and Anastasia's memorial site and believed that the state had convicted the right man—had made him out to be a savage, remorseless killer, a sociopathic, cyberpunk freak. But in person, he was just a nice, smart, funny guy, who seemed no different from half the kids I'd gone to high school with—goth types and punk rockers whose entire wardrobes were still black a decade later, though they'd left most of their other macabre trappings behind, graduating from H. P. Lovecraft and Marilyn Manson to Harry Potter, trips to Burning Man, and NPR. Indeed, Byron told me that he was a fan of the public radio quiz show *Wait Wait . . . Don't Tell Me!* and seemed more impressed that I'd once had a beer with its host, Peter Sagal, than with anything else I could offer.

We talked about books—Byron was on a Dave Eggers and David Foster Wallace kick, and we wound through the things that we'd been amazed and annoyed by in *A Heartbreaking Work of Staggering Genius* and *Infinite Jest*. We exchanged lists of our favorite cult-classic movies, like *Strange Brew* and *Flash Gordon*. Byron told me he still had a soft spot for *Nosferatu* and other old-school, early twentieth-century horror flicks. There's certainly more to people than the books and music and movies they like, and I kept reminding myself that just because we had an appreciation for the same kinds of shit didn't mean that Byron couldn't have committed any crimes. But as the hours rolled by, it was hard to dismiss his essential kindness and goodness. Evelyn and Napo gave us room to chat by playing long games of gin, and I found myself talking on and on to Byron about all the creative projects I was working on, and the current fucked-up state of my love life. Byron listened patiently, asking questions about the specifics, and doling out spoonfuls of thoughtful, helpful advice. Even with his state-issued threads and the guards posted by the door, it was easy to forget that we were inside a maximum-security prison and not a college-town café. I felt as if he and I were no different, and that if I'd suffered a few strokes of miserable luck things could've just as easily been reversed, with him visiting me in prison instead.

Later, when I asked Byron about his dad, Dale, he told me that he'd died of AIDS a few years before, just two months after Anastasia and Justin's deaths. He told me the story of coming home one day from middle school to find his mom in tears, and how she'd explained to him that Dale had come out to her, and that they'd soon be separating. Still, even after the separation, he said, his mom and dad had remained close friends, and Byron had even formed an affectionate bond with his dad's longtime boyfriend. Byron reminisced about a weeklong camping trip he'd taken with his dad and his dad's boyfriend the summer before his dad died. "Someone had given my dad a bunch of fishing gear," Byron said. "But none of us had ever gone fishing before, and we had no idea how to use it. It was fucking hilarious. We were waist deep in this river, all our lines tangled, using Cheetos as bait. These old-timers were watching us, shaking their heads. It's about as happy as I remember being." His smile faded. "A couple months later, everything pretty much went to shit."

Gradually, the visiting room had filled up. I went to inspect the wares in the vending machines, and picked out a somewhat edible-looking burrito. While it cooked in the microwave, I took a look around, gazing at all of the other families gathered at neighboring tables, talking, laughing, playing Connect Four— the inmates in gray scrubs, their parents in sweatshirts and jeans, wives all dolled up, hair freshly curled, and here and there, little kids scrambling around at their feet. The older prisoners looked as friendly and docile as high-school math teachers, and the younger prisoners seemed soft and vulnerable, visibly nourished by the company of their family and friends. It was hard to fathom what crimes had landed them in one of the state's harsher prisons.

Crossroads, Byron told me, was not like prisons in the movies or on TV—rapes and assaults were rare, and he didn't feel like he was in constant danger. The worst part about it all was the end-less, mind-numbing boredom, stretching out for eternity. Prison was not hell, it was purgatory. Byron spent a lot of his time writing letters, essays, and short stories, and his job in the prison library gave him steady access to a stream of decent books, but there was no one around to talk to about them, or share his writing with, no one who could string together enough words to challenge him in Scrabble. Most of the inmates came from either inner-city St. Louis or tiny, rural farm towns, and though some were pleasant enough, Byron had little in common with any of them. For a while, he'd been lucky enough to share a cell with a kid named Pablo, also from Kansas City, who loved manga and indie rock, and had frequented a lot of the same spots in Westport that Byron had once hung out in; they even had some mutual friends and acquaintances on the outside. But after six months, Pablo completed his sentence and went back to Kansas City, where he'd enrolled in college and now did what he could to spread word about Byron's innocence. Pablo had begun to host a late-night college radio show, and in the wee hours he'd play Byron's favorite tunes. Once every great while, if the temperature and humidity and barometric pressure were just right, the station's trembling signal would carry across fifty miles of prairie to the tiny radio in Byron's cell, and he could hear traces of a song by Minor Threat or Joy Division, sweet as a pinch of sugar on the tongue.

Every time I looked up at the clock on the wall, another hour or hour and a half had passed. Before I knew it, it was almost five, and the guards were coming around to all the tables, telling us it was time to wrap things up. Me and Byron went to get our picture taken together in front of the mountain-range mural. A prisoner whose job this was snapped a Polaroid and handed it to me. As we waited for it to develop, Byron explained to me that he'd formerly had the job of visiting-room photographer, but had decided to quit since there was too much pressure from other inmates to try to smuggle in drugs and other contraband. The rest of the families were packing up games and saying their goodbyes. "Well," said Byron, "that went quick."

Can you really gauge someone deeply just by hanging out with them for eight hours? Probably not. I remembered a story my friend Alex had told me from her time working for a public-interest group in New Orleans fighting the death penalty. One day she'd gone to Angola, the famously bleak Louisiana prison, to interview a young inmate who'd already admitted to killing his girlfriend, their two young kids, plus three other random folks he'd encountered during a brutal weeklong spree. Her job was to learn about mitigating circumstances in his life—mental impairments, abuse he'd suffered as a kid—anything that might convince a jury to give him life in prison rather than consigning him to death row. The guy was utterly charming and winsome, Alex said; she even found him kind of cute. Of course, her attraction to him waned as he candidly laid out his gruesome crimes to her with stunning nonchalance, as though explaining the details of a bowl game played between two teams he had no rooting interest in.

Likable people, I know, can still be capable of horrendous things. And someone's state of mind in their mid- to late twenties may not be much of an indicator of what they were like at eighteen, Byron's age when Anastasia was killed. But over the years I've met and talked to a lot of people who were friends with Byron in high school; they now run organic farms in Florida, write code for websites in Philly, or work in the mayor's office in San Francisco. And every one of them says that Byron was the same then as he is now—a kind, creative soul with a wry sense of humor. He may have had his dark moments, but what teenager doesn't? On my first visit, me and Byron had barely scratched the surface talking about the details of his case, but even as I tried to resist it, I already had a belief in his innocence. Nice guys could still be killers, I told myself, and it was obviously in Byron' best interest to put on a show of kindness for anyone who could potentially help him, but I would've gladly bet my left nut that this guy, who tuned in every week to *Wait Wait . . . Don't Tell Me!* couldn't harm a fly, much less shoot a girl in the face.

"Come back and see me again sometime," Byron said, giving me a little half-hug. "You know where to find me." It was a strange, lacerating feeling to watch him trail out of the room with the other inmates and disappear, back to the patchy, frozen grass of the prison yard and the nothingness of his cell.

In the lobby, we gathered our keys and our wallets from the mini coin lockers, and Evelyn wiped the tears from her eyes, in a rush to get outside. Once we were in the car and I'd started the engine, she broke down and sobbed for a minute, while Napo put his arms around her from the backseat and tried to comfort her. "I never let him see me like this," she wailed, "but it hurts. It hurts every time."

She's right. I've been back to see Byron half a dozen times over the last few years, and the sinking, gut-shot ache in my stomach as I pull out of the prison parking lot at the end of my visit is always the same.

Once we'd left Cameron and made it back to the highway, Evelyn had pulled herself together. "I'm sorry," she said. She made a sad laughing sound. "Oh, you know what, that's just really hard. And I'm absolutely starving. Are you guys as starving as me? I'm starving. There's a Subway in Lathrop, about ten miles up. Do you want to stop? Do you guys want Subway?"

So, back to this morning. Imagine me, Peter, Byron, and Evelyn crossing the visiting room and taking our usual table near the back. The mountain-range mural has been painted over with flat yellow paint, though Byron's not sure why—who can guess at the arbitrary and sometimes hostile whims of the prison administration?

We start off with small talk. Me and Peter tell Byron some tales from our tour—the bar manager in Boise who tried to cheat us out of our cut of the door, until we took his favorite mouse pad hostage; the teenage sword-swallower we met in Charleston, West Virginia, and convinced to come along with us for a week as an opening act at our shows. I used to feel bad regaling Byron with stories of my adventures, but I finally came to understand how much he appreciates and even craves hearing them. He spends enough of his time suffering through the monotonous rhythms of life inside the prison walls, it's enjoyable—honestly thrilling, he says—to hear about our lives on the outside.

Byron asks for updates on my girlfriend situation, and what new movies, books, and music I can recommend. We talk about the stuff he's been writing and the stuff I've been writing. Peter mentions a couple of the new songs that he's been performing on tour, and Byron begs him to sing one for him. Peter laughs and shakes his head at first, but after a bit of wheedling persistence from Byron, Evelyn, and me, he closes his eyes, clears his throat a couple of times, and then, very softly, begins to sing. The pureness of his voice, even at low volume, is beautiful, and I notice that a few of the families at neighboring tables have dropped their conversations to listen in. The guard senses a change in the air and takes a few steps in our direction, but decides not to intervene. When Peter's done, everyone claps, and Byron says, "I'll tell you what, that's a song I'd put on every mix tape I ever made for a girl."

Finally, Byron starts to fill us in on the latest developments with his appeals. He's already filed for ineffective assistance of counsel, which was quickly denied. (No matter how poorly your lawyer might have performed, it's incredibly rare for incompetent representation to cause a case to be overturned, even in extreme instances.) Byron's appeals regarding procedural mistakes the judge may have made and other grounds have all been turned down, and his remaining hope now seems to ride on an appeal known as actual innocence—introducing new evidence (or a new way of looking at the evidence) which contradicts your guilt and shows that you were convicted in error. Recently, in letters back and forth, we've been digging into the details of his case, exploring every aspect of it to hunt for any pieces that don't fit. I'm no professional sleuth, but Byron tells me that sometimes the biggest breaks in the cases of other inmates who've been exonerated came from casual observers who were able to look at things freshly and have a flash insight.

Basically, there are two conflicting accounts of what happened the night that Anastasia was killed. The story that Byron and Kelly told police the day after Anastasia's body was found—and that Byron has never wavered from—is that they were driving around with their best friends just before dusk when Justin and Anastasia fell into one of their frequent spats—for months, Justin had wanted to end the relationship, and Anastasia, admittedly obsessed with Justin, hated him for it. As they argued at a stoplight on Truman Road, Anastasia hopped out of the car, slammed the passenger door shut, and stormed away, toward the gas stations and pawnshops that bordered Lincoln Cemetery.

Though he knew how sketchy the neighborhood was, Justin, who was driving, just shook his head, and when the light changed, he hit the gas, and the three of them continued on their way, figuring that Anastasia would find a pay phone and call her parents to come pick her up. This sort of thing had happened many times before. A couple of hours later, though, feeling bad that they'd ditched her, Justin called Anastasia's house to make sure she'd gotten home okay, and her parents said they hadn't heard from her. She was found—shot to death—by the patrol cop a few hours after midnight. The police talked to Byron and Kelly the next day, but were unable to track down Justin. Meanwhile, Justin had stopped at a gun store, bought a shotgun, and driven to DeSoto, Kansas, where he pulled off the road near an old warehouse, wandered around back, put the shotgun barrel in his mouth, and pulled the trigger.

A few years later, during a stint in drug rehab, Kelly mentioned to her counselor that she'd witnessed her friend Anastasia's murder. She said that Justin and Byron had always been fascinated with death, and, sick of Anastasia's antics, had decided to kill her. They'd brought Anastasia to the cemetery, Kelly said, and Justin had shot her. The alarmed counselor called in her parents, and then the police, and several times Kelly repeated her story, with one crucial new wrinkle. Now Kelly said that Byron had been the one with the gun. She said that at the last second, Justin had tried to intervene, but Byron had ignored him and blown Anastasia away. Certain aspects of Kelly's story were consistent with unreleased details of the crime scene, which intrigued the detectives, although other parts of her story—including the type of gun that was used, and where she said they'd gotten it—didn't make much sense. Kelly said that after the shooting, they'd dumped the murder weapon in an industrial area, and had concocted the story of Anastasia leaping out of the car and walking off, since that stretch of Truman Road was known to be shady, and they felt that the notion of a random killing in the vicinity would probably be believable. This was contradicted in court by an Amoco station mechanic who said that right before nightfall he'd seen a car stop at the light and a young woman jump out and stalk angrily away, toward the cemetery. Later, he'd even identified Anastasia from a set of photographs shown to him by the cops.

If Byron was innocent, why would Kelly have incriminated him, knowing how grave the consequences might be, and even putting herself in legal jeopardy for her role in covering up the crime? There are a few theories. After the deaths of Anastasia and Justin, Byron and Kelly had dated for another couple of years. But her emotional neediness, erratic behavior, and continued drug use became too much for Byron and at last he'd broken things off with her and made plans to move to St. Louis, four hours away. Friends of Byron's say that before he headed off, Kelly levied a threat: if he left her, there would be "hell to pay." Byron left. Six days later, Kelly was telling the police that Byron had killed Anastasia.

Accusing someone of murder may seem like an extreme way to exact revenge over a breakup, but it's worth considering what else Kelly stood to gain. For years, she'd been estranged from her family due to her drug problems—she was forbidden to even step into her parents' house. All that changed when she came forward with the story of witnessing Anastasia's murder. The idea that she'd been harboring a horrible secret—that she was a victim herself—immediately brought her back into their good graces. She had a tidy explanation now for her years of dishonesty, disloyalty, and substance abuse, and she was welcomed home to try to make a fresh start.

Was this part of her plan? If she made the whole thing up, I doubt it was that well thought out. It's easier for me to imagine Kelly making an impulsive claim to her rehab psychologist, not really aware of the entire chain of dominoes she was tipping into motion. At each step—repeating the story to her parents, to the sheriff's deputies, in her first meeting with them, again at her official deposition a couple of weeks later, and once more when she testified in court—she would've had a chance to turn back, but the more her tall tale snowballed, the harder it would've been to stop its progress. Sometimes, if you lie enough about something, you start to believe in the lie yourself. A month after Byron was arrested, Evelyn says, Kelly called her at three in the morning, frantic. "This is insane!" she told Evelyn. "I can't believe what they're doing to Byron!" Had she thought she could blame him for Anastasia's murder without a dire outcome? Her promise of "hell to pay" had been borne out beyond measure.

These days, with the emergence of complex new DNA tests, science has freed hundreds of people wrongfully convicted for robberies, rapes, and murders. Each case has become a vividly drawn lesson in shoddy police work, coerced confessions, prosecutorial overzealousness, and an overreliance on faulty or fraudulent eyewitness testimony. But Byron's challenge is uniquely steep. How do you overturn a conviction when there was no physical evidence of any kind to begin with? Kelly claimed that Byron had shot Anastasia right beside Justin's car, and the medical examiner later established that the bullet had come at point-blank range, yet a lab analysis discovered no traces of blood on the car or on Byron's clothes, nor in the trunk of the car, where Kelly said Byron had initially stashed the gun. A murder weapon was never found. Byron's hazy motives, as suggested by the prosecution team—that he was jealous of the time Justin spent with Anastasia, and that he wanted to see what it would feel like to kill someone—remain unprovable, but by the same token, they can't be disproved. Unless the real killer comes forward and confesses to the crime, the best hope has seemed to be for Kelly to recant her story.

After Byron received his life sentence, Evelyn began to pepper Kelly with postcards, simply listing how many days Byron had been locked up. She prayed that an appeal to Kelly's conscience would bring a change of heart. But that began to feel like a long shot, especially after hearing that Kelly had complained about the cards to a friend of Byron's, and said, "Whatever Byron gets, he deserves."

In court, the prosecutors stressed Kelly's reliability as a witness—freed of the burden of her horrible secret, they said, she'd finally broken free of the grip of substance abuse and was putting her life back together, completely sober. Evelyn never bought this whole narrative. Even before Anastasia was killed, Byron had told his mom that Kelly was struggling with alcohol, and that she sometimes used hard drugs. Kelly's demons, Evelyn felt, hadn't been loosed by witnessing a murder and concealing its details; by the same token she doubted that they'd been banished through providing phony testimony.

One day, posting handmade, photocopied "Free Byron Case" flyers in Westport, Evelyn got a tip from a goth kid at the Broadway Café, Byron's old hangout. Kelly, the kid told her, had started dating a guy in Lawrence, Kansas, who played calliope in an indie band called The Strongest Man in the World. If Evelyn wanted to confront Kelly, she realized, she could probably find her at one of the band's shows. Evelyn had been warned by a lawyer friend that stopping by Kelly's parents' house might constitute harassment, but approaching her in public seemed within bounds. A couple of weeks later, Evelyn and a friend made the hour-long drive to Lawrence, parked on Main Street, a few blocks from the Kansas University campus, and found the bar where Kelly's new boyfriend's band was playing.

Evelyn told me the story the next day over the phone. As she and her friend edged into a booth at the back of the bar, Evelyn said, she was twitching with nervousness, upset at herself for not formulating more of a plan for what she would say if she came face-to-face with Kelly. Evelyn and her friend had arrived three hours early, and they waited, eyes glued to the door, ordering round after round of Cokes, as the bands loaded in their instruments and gear and warmed up onstage. One opening band played, and then another, but Kelly still hadn't appeared, and Evelyn had the sinking feeling that she wasn't going to show. She'd sucked down so many soft drinks, she desperately needed to pee, though she was reluctant to abandon her post, with its view of the front door. Finally, during a break between bands, just before The Strongest Man in the World took the stage, Evelyn hurried into the bathroom. She peed and came out of the stall just as the bathroom door swung open and Kelly Moffett walked in, sipping a gigantic whiskey drink through a pair of black straws.

They stared at each other in stunned silence. Kelly was bulgingly pregnant. She lowered the drink in her hand, and Evelyn saw that her other hand held an empty shot glass. "What the *fuck* are you doing here?" Kelly sputtered at last.

"Oh, Kelly," said Evelyn, shredded by a wave of emotion. "All I want is the truth. That's all anybody wants."

Kelly turned pale and ashen.

Evelyn went on, aching inside but fighting to keep her voice strong and clear. "My son's not supposed to be in prison, is he? Remember, you're not just punishing him, you're punishing his mom. His friends. We all need him back." She could hear her voice cracking, and feel herself beginning to break apart. Her eyes burned with tears. "Nobody's going to hold anything against you," she said, "but it's time to do the right thing and end all of this."

Kelly met her gaze, eyes flashing fiercely. Finally, she cried, "Everything just got all fucked up! Nothing was supposed to turn out this way!" She smashed the empty shot glass against the granite lip of the sink and it fell in shattered pieces to the floor. "Ouch, fuck!" Kelly said. She inspected her hand. Blood began to well up from her sliced palm.

"Oh no, are you all right?" asked Evelyn. Without a response, Kelly turned and crashed out the door. Evelyn gave chase, but right at that moment the band blasted into their first number and the crowd surged toward the stage, carrying Evelyn along with them, giving Kelly a chance to separate herself. Evelyn glimpsed Kelly heading toward the front door, but by the time she made it out to the street, Kelly had disappeared.

Granted, this is only Evelyn's version of the story, and it's possible that Kelly would describe the episode differently. But over the years, as I've continued to get to know Evelyn, I've found myself impressed, time and again, by her awareness and intelligence, and inspired by her ability to deal with a situation that's clearly so painful with such openhearted honesty, optimism, and grace. She's always struck me as entirely credible.

In the months that followed, Evelyn made other trips to see The Strongest Man in the World play at other clubs in Lawrence and at clubs in other towns, but never saw Kelly again, and eventually, one night, learned that Kelly and the guy in the band had broken up. She called me when she got home to pass on this latest bit, and, as always, managed to find levity even in a dark moment. "That guy better watch out," she said. "I hope Kelly doesn't find a murder to pin on him. And at least I got to see The Strongest Man play again tonight," she went on. "I've actually become a real fan. I love their music. I know all their songs now. They've got great lyrics. You know how they got their name?"

"How?"

"It's from Ibsen. Byron told me. He knew the quote. 'The strongest man in the world is he who walks alone.'"

Not long after, Kelly was arrested and convicted on a domestic assault charge and sentenced to six months in a Kansas prison. I'd come to learn that even when a witness recants testimony, it rarely does much to clear someone who's already serving time. The initial statement someone gives to the cops is what stands. Kelly's story had already mutated several times over the years, and though her drug problems and state of mental disarray had been downplayed during the trial, her continued path of self-destruction would likely be used to discredit her if she tried to change her story once more.

In fact, there was one other piece of evidence presented during Byron's trial that was probably more damning than Kelly's testimony. After Kelly told the cops that Byron was the one who'd killed Anastasia, they asked her to call him to try to elicit some admission of guilt, while they sat beside her and recorded both ends of the conversation. But as her drug problems had worsened, Byron had grown tired of her calls, badgering him about their failed relationship, begging to borrow money, or even asking if she could come over to take a shower during stretches when she'd been living on the streets. By the time he'd moved to St. Louis, he'd made a practice of avoiding her calls entirely; his roommate would tell her she had the wrong number. With the cops at hand, Kelly made a bunch of attempts to get Byron on the phone, but could never make contact. Ultimately, all they had was her word against his. The investigation stalled.

Eight months later, without the detectives there to assist her, Kelly called Byron in the middle of the night, her tape recorder running. He was back from St. Louis, living with his mom again, and sick with the flu. In court a year later, the transcript of their conversation that night was likely the critical piece of evidence that led to Byron's conviction. The recorder hadn't been set up properly, so while Kelly's voice is clear on the tape and easy to understand, Byron's voice is muffled and at times impossible to make out.

In the transcript of the call, Kelly says, "Seriously, why'd you have to kill Anastasia? What was the whole fucking big deal? Could you explain that to me? Because I don't get it. She's dead for no reason. Justin's dead for no reason. It's all fucked up. I mean, if you could seriously explain to me as to why you actually felt the need to kill her, then that would really help me feel better about the whole fucking thing. I mean, seriously, was there any reason to all of this?"

Byron's response: "We shouldn't talk about this."

"Now the cops are around, asking me questions," Kelly continues. "I really need to understand. Just tell me. Why'd you have to kill her?"

Byron says nothing. Then he begins to coach her on how to speak to the police: "If they're asking you questions, just say 'I don't know,' or 'I don't remember.'" At the end of the conversation, Byron tells Kelly he'll talk with her more once they can meet up in person. They make plans to rendezvous in a park the next day and hang up—the whole call lasts less than four minutes.

Kelly skipped the meeting, though. She'd already shared the tape with the cops. At first, there was some concern about the legal merits of a recording that had been made in an uncontrolled setting, without police assistance. But when Kelly tried calling Byron again, with officers present, she failed to mention Anastasia or the murder, which made the recording virtually useless. After a few more attempts went nowhere, police reviewed her initial call and felt they had what they needed to make an arrest. Days later, twelve deputies stormed Evelyn's house and took Byron into custody.

During his trial, the prosecutors played the tape for the jury, and handed each juror a transcript so they could make out Byron's words in places where the recorder had failed to pick up his voice. If you were innocent, the prosecutors said to the jury, and someone called and asked why you'd killed someone, wouldn't you say, "You're crazy! I don't know what you're talking about!" Why would Byron instruct Kelly to obfuscate the truth? Why not just tell her to be honest and tell the cops everything that had happened? Though Byron had never explicitly said he'd shot Anastasia, they argued, his vague answers, his efforts to convince Kelly not to cooperate with the authorities, and his general lack of response to some of her most pointed questions could be seen, in combination, as a tacit admission of guilt. In their brief three-hour deliberations, the jury asked to hear the tape again, and to study the transcripts of the call, and then they emerged and convicted Byron of Anastasia's murder.

I'll be honest. Though I'd never heard the actual tape, I'd read the transcript of that conversation dozens of times, and had long struggled to reconcile my belief in Byron's innocence with some of the things he says during that phone call. It just looks bad, there's no way around it. I'd often explained it away to myself this way: Byron had a terrible flu, he was sick of Kelly calling him in the middle of the night saying crazy things, and just wanted to get off the phone with her as quickly as possible. "We shouldn't talk about this" doesn't necessarily mean "We shouldn't talk about this because, yeah, I'm the one who killed Anastasia and we need to keep it hush-hush"—it could also mean "We shouldn't talk about the death of our friend, because you're bat-shit crazy and I don't know what the hell you're talking about."

Still, my own doubts lingered. Though I could talk about any other aspect of the case with Byron, I never asked him to explain the taped call of him and Kelly. Sometimes I wondered if maybe he was truly guilty. I'd let my doubts recast everything I knew about the case in a new light, and even though I trusted him and loved him as a friend and felt I knew him deeply, it was possible to imagine the story that Kelly had told on the stand as the truth. And if Byron was guilty, what of my friendship with him? Somehow, for me, the question of his guilt or innocence was secondary. I'd glimpsed his kind and compassionate qualities, his suffering, his gentle humanity, and had also shared much of myself with him over the years, and even if he'd done what some believed he'd done, that didn't mean he wasn't deserving of my love and friendship. In a sense, though I held on to a belief in his innocence, I'd already forgiven him for the things he might have done. Of course, I recognized that this was easier for me to do since I'd never known Anastasia. If she'd been my daughter, sister, cousin, or niece, and I believed Byron was the killer, I knew forgiveness might have been out of the question.

Recently, though, new revelations came to light about Byron's taped phone call with Kelly. A guy from Long Beach, California, named John Allen got in touch with me; he'd been researching Byron's case, he said, and writing a book about it, and had discovered some of my online postings about Byron. Could we meet?

A couple of months later, I found myself walking down basement steps into a Polish restaurant called the HMS Bounty on Wilshire Boulevard, just west of downtown L.A. It was two in the afternoon and the place was completely empty, except for one table in the back. John Allen got up to greet me. He was in his sixties, gray haired and hefty, a retired engineer, with a kind, confident air. He introduced me to his wife, Lynn—friendly, gracious, and seated in a wheelchair—and his niece, Lauren, who was in her early thirties and incredibly, mind-meltingly hot, in a tight black sweater, with long black hair and a mischievous glint in her eye. Throughout our lunch, Lauren kept smiling at me and holding my gaze, making me drunk and dizzy.

John gave me some background. A few years before, he'd been a juror in a child molestation case. The rest of the jury had been in a rush to convict, but John, guided by a scientist's finely tuned skepticism, felt that the prosecution's case was full of holes, and that they'd failed to prove guilt beyond a reasonable doubt. His resistance to go with the flow eventually resulted in a hung jury, and during a retrial new evidence was introduced which pointed toward the defendant's innocence, and the man walked free. John was relieved at the outcome, but bewildered and dismayed by the lack of inquisitiveness shown by his fellow jurors. They seemed to take everything that the police and prosecution said at face value and discount the words of the accused. How many trials had been resolved unjustly, he wondered, by juries that had no skeptical voice to rein them in?

When he'd first begun to research Byron Case's situation, John said, he thought Byron might very well have been guilty. The transcript of Byron's phone call with Kelly was just too weird to ignore. But as he combed through each detail of the case, with help from Lynn and Lauren, tiny inconsistencies, one after another, began to appear: Kelly said Byron had shot Anastasia at a distance of five to eight feet, but the autopsy revealed that she'd been fired at point-blank. Kelly said that the murder weapon was a shotgun; Anastasia's wounds suggested a handgun. Then one day John managed to track down the original recording of Byron and Kelly's phone call, and used some free audio software he'd downloaded to enhance the sound of Byron's voice. What John discovered was shocking—the transcript was riddled with inaccuracies and omissions that seemed intentionally misleading. In fact, in every instance the faulty transcript worked to Byron's disadvantage. At moments when Kelly had asked Byron certain questions, the transcript merely said, "NO RESPONSE," when actually Byron was responding for as long as thirty seconds at a time, though his words were subaudible and couldn't be made out. According to the transcript, Byron had told Kelly, "We shouldn't talk about this." Actually, he'd said, "We *should* talk about this." John was fuming. "The prosecutors couldn't have hoped for a better tape. Since no one can hear much of what Byron is saying, they were able to just make up whatever they wanted, call it a 'transcript,' and pass it out to the jury. The jury listened to the tape, sure, but what they were really using as evidence was the transcript, as authored by the prosecution, and corroborated by Kelly herself. The whole thing's a fiction!"

Down in that homey Polish restaurant's cool basement, I felt a thrilling surge of hopefulness and relief, not just because John's discovery held real glimmers of promise for Byron, but also because he'd managed to douse my own lingering suspicions about Byron's guilt. It was all I could do, at the end of the meal, as we said our goodbyes, not to give Lauren a powerful, celebratory kiss on the lips.

It's small, ragged bands of passionate believers like John Allen, Lynn, and Lauren, or Reuben "the Hurricane" Carter's trio of kindly Canadians, who often help the wrongfully convicted find their way to freedom. But will John's discovery of the flawed transcripts one day lead to Byron's exoneration? It's hard to know. No matter what, it's going to be a long climb.

If Byron didn't kill Anastasia, who did?

In the visiting room this morning, while Peter and Evelyn play cards, me and Byron discuss that question. Byron says, "Well, I'm uniquely qualified to know that *I* didn't do it, which helps me focus on the other possibilities. But it's been ten years and I still can't say I've solved it."

In the months after Anastasia was killed, gossip about her death ran rampant through her old high school and Kansas City's goth scene. Some said it had been a game of Russian roulette. Others said the killer was a rival girl from a nearby town, jealous of Justin's affections for Anastasia. Meanwhile, the police kept poking around the neighborhoods surrounding Lincoln Cemetery, with the idea that a stranger might've committed the crime. Long-haul truckers, vagabonds, and drifters had long been attracted to that stretch of Truman Road just off I-435 by its adult bookstores and cheap motels, and a large sex shop called Erotic City, four blocks down from the entrance to the cemetery. It wasn't uncommon to see guys panhandling or selling drugs at a gas station, or prostitutes walking the street, even in broad daylight. Perhaps Anastasia had wandered into Lincoln Cemetery, investigators imagined, trailed by some bad fucking dude. This, of course, was the failed line of defense that Horton Lance had tried to pursue in court.

A couple of years after Anastasia's death, a businessman was biking home along Truman Road from his office downtown when he was shot and killed in a parking lot. No one had spotted the gunmen; he'd apparently been fired upon from a line of bushes fifty yards away. Eventually, the police turned up his assassins—a pair of young locals in their late teens and early twenties. They hadn't even known the guy on the bike. All they said by way of explanation was that the guy looked like a chump.

Killings by strangers are rare but not unheard of. A few months after Byron's trial, John Muhammad and Lee Malvo—the so-called Beltway snipers—shot and killed fourteen people in their cross-country spree. Could a stranger have killed Anastasia? Byron tells me he thinks it's possible, but considers the odds remote. "Yeah, I suppose it could've been some creep from the neighborhood," he says, "or someone just passing through town. They could've been long gone before her body was even found."

But the evidence, Byron points out, suggests that Anastasia knew the person who shot her. Though her purse was missing, there'd been no sign of a struggle or any attempt at a sexual assault. She'd been shot in the face, point-blank, staring into the eyes of the person who shot her, with no effort made, it seemed, to flee or defend herself.

"What about Anastasia's dad?" I ask Byron. "Robert Witbols-Feugen." I tell him I've heard that over the years WitbolsFeugen has shown signs of aberrant behavior. In a police interview, his ex-wife, Betsy Owens—Anastasia's mom—reported that he'd regularly beaten her, sometimes so badly she'd ended up in the emergency room, and that he'd left welts on Anastasia as well. After Anastasia's death, when police had tentatively called it a murder-suicide and moved on, WitbolsFeugen harangued them to continue their investigation. In fact, his harassment grew so intense—he sent a hundred and fifty messages to the lead investigator's personal e-mail account in the span of a few months—that the investigator sent him an official request asking him to back off. To me, all of this seemed like the natural (if overbearing) response of an angry and grieving man whose daughter had been killed and felt the full story of her death hadn't been uncovered. But even after Byron's conviction, WitbolsFeugen's campaign of harassment toward police and public officials continued. His constant presence at public board meetings, often bearing handmade protest signs, spooked county clerks and councilmen; some quit their posts, fearing for their safety. He was eventually arrested at a meeting after disturbing the peace and assaulting a cop. There's something weird enough in his obsessive tendencies, I tell Byron, that I've wondered if I should feel suspicious.

Byron mulls over his response. "You know, there's something not right about Bob WitbolsFeugen. And it didn't start with Anastasia's death. He was always a scary guy, and I know sometimes she was scared of going home. That's why she loved Justin so much, she felt safe with him. But no matter how much I try to make the pieces fit, I can't really believe that he could've done it, that the guy could've killed his own daughter. He may be a bit off—maybe a lot off—but I believe he loved Stasia with all of his heart. The guy was just broken when she died, unhinged." Byron looks at me. "You know, the pressure he put on the cops to make an arrest is probably a part of why I'm here today. But as much hatred as I feel toward him at times, I mostly just feel sadness for what he's been through, losing a daughter. I guess I just can't imagine him killing her. It had to be somebody else."

In the end, there may be a more obvious answer. John Allen, after a year of intense research, believes that Anastasia was killed by Justin Bruton as part of a suicide pact he'd made with her. "It's Occam's razor," he told me during our lunch in L.A. "The simplest explanation is generally the correct one." He laid out his case for me: At the time of her death, Anastasia was clearly suicidal; as John had come to learn, she had recently tried to slash her own wrists. When that failed, she asked her dad for sharper razor blades. The week of her death, she'd asked her mom to help her get pills so that she could kill herself. She even left a suicide note of sorts on Justin's computer, a journal entry that said, among other things, "I never wanted to feel life." Justin, too, was suicidal, and had attempted suicide at least once before. The night before Anastasia was killed, he'd gone to a gun show, and it was there, presumably, that he'd picked up the handgun he'd used to shoot her inside Lincoln Cemetery.

But if Justin and Anastasia had vowed to off themselves together, I asked John, why the lag time between her death and his? John's not sure. But he knows that hours after Anastasia's body was discovered, Justin walked into a gun store, bought a shotgun, and was eventually found in the countryside, an hour away, having taken his own life. After a long, emotionally draining, on-again, off-again relationship filled with two years of vicious squabbles, the troubled teenagers were dead, both at the hands of Justin, John Allen believes, just as the cops had suspected for years.

I share John's take with Byron and he drops his head. "I've always understood why other people would think it was Justin," Byron says. "But he was my best friend. My *best friend*. I knew him better than anybody. And I'm telling you, for the longest time I couldn't imagine that he could've been capable of hurting her, of hurting anyone. I simply didn't believe he could've done it. I gave it real thought, plenty of times over the years, and in the end I always ruled it out completely." He lifts his head to look at me, welling up with emotion, his voice going soft. "But you know," he says, "there's nothing else that makes sense. I still can't accept it myself, I can't say, 'Justin did it,' but if that's what other people believe, I can't try and argue with them."

There's something incredibly moving about Byron's loyalty to Justin and the faith he still clings to in his friend, even though it may have been Justin's actions that have doomed him to a decade— and counting—in prison. While I know it's neither here nor there, I tell Byron about a dream I've often had of Justin writing a suicide note in which he admits he's killed Anastasia, and hiding the note in a book on his shelf. In my dreams, I explain to Byron, I'm always clawing apart thousands of books—a whole library full—searching for Justin's confession.

Byron looks at me, unsure, it seems, how to respond. "That's nice," he says at last, drily. "I guess that would be helpful. Let me know if you find it." He rubs his cheeks, looking from me to Peter and Evelyn, who by now have been drawn into our discussion.

"We may never know exactly what happened to Anastasia," Byron goes on, wearily. "All I know is that I didn't do it. But some way or another, I really believe one day the truth will come out, and everyone will see that I've been innocent all along." He flashes a strange, sad smile, and looks around the room at the other inmates huddled around neighboring tables with their own families, the guards at the front of the room, killing time themselves, the giant classroom clock hanging above the door, and the yellow wall where the painted mountain range used to be. He slumps back in his chair, and spreads his arms wide. "For now, though, I'm here."

Evelyn cries softly in the backseat of my van all the way to Lathrop, where we always stop for Subway. It's the saddest sound in the world, but I know there's nothing I can say to relieve her heartbreak, though I try. Byron's sentence has become a sentence for her, too. She's told me that she longs to move home to Germany, but would never leave the area while Byron's still locked up. She's his anchor, and her weekly visits are what keep Byron going strong. Yes, he's got other friends and loved ones on the outside, but I can't help but wonder, in dark moments, how he'd fare if Evelyn ever got too old or sick to visit him at Crossroads, or if she passed away. It hurts to imagine just how alone he'd be.

We grab subs and punch it south, driving in silence straight to our show at the Record Bar in Kansas City. Peter hauls his guitar and sound equipment inside, and while Evelyn helps me set up a table with our *Found* books and T-shirts and CDs, my brother plays the Bon Jovi song "Wanted Dead or Alive" to the empty room to warm up his voice. God, I think, what a beautiful fucking song. I head back to the van to put my stack of found notes in order and get some drinking done.

An hour later I head in, more bent than usual. The place is packed. Evelyn's at a table in front with Napo, Byron's old cellmate Pablo, and ten other friends of hers and Byron's. I pick up a couple more drinks at the bar, get up on the microphone, and do what I do. Each found note and letter I read to the crowd feels doubly piercing, and when it's Peter's turn to perform, he seems to sing with more emotion than ever. Throughout the show, I'm on the edge of tears.

Before we're finished, I find myself making a half-drunken impromptu speech about the injustice of Byron's fate and pleading with the crowd to check out his website and spread the word. I pull my hat off my head and get it going around the room, collecting money toward Byron's legal expenses.

Afterwards, Evelyn gives me a hug, and tells me she loves me, and I tell her I love her, too. We say goodbye. Me and Peter pack everything up and square up with the club owner, and I head around the corner to another bar to hang out with two girls who work at the local public radio station while Peter crashes out in our makeshift bed in the back of the van.

At the bar, the girls ask me more about Byron, and I try to impress them by telling them about my visit with him earlier in the day—having a friend in prison serving a life sentence, I imagine, makes me appear more edgy and hard-core than I really am. For half an hour, I keep downing drinks, ranting on and on about Byron's situation, explaining everything in explicit detail. The girls listen raptly, asking questions here and there, moved, it seems, by my devotion to him. Finally, one steps out to smoke a cigarette, and I quickly fuck everything up with the other. I try to kiss her, and she drops her chin and turns away, and I end up kissing her glasses instead. "I've got a boyfriend," she says. "Sorry. You should've gone for Celeste. She's single. Hold on, I'll be right back." She joins her friend out on the sidewalk in front of the bar, and when they come back in, they say they've got to go, they've got an early start at work the next morning.

"Okay," I tell them. "Scram. I'll get the tab."

"Thanks. We'll see you next time you come through town."

I head for the van, crank her up, pound a bottle of water, half of another, snap the radio on, and head for the highway. It's a long haul to Nebraska, and we've got another show the next night. Recently, on the road, I've been tuning in to the *BBC News Hour*'s coverage of the war in Afghanistan. I wonder, with so many young Americans dying cruel deaths overseas, will anyone care about one kid rotting away in prison who's very likely (but not blatantly) innocent?

All of a sudden, on the edge of town, I see a sign for the Truman Road exit. I pull off the highway, and at the end of the long ramp find myself stopped at a traffic light—the same light, I realize, where Anastasia leapt out of Justin's car that night after their fight, twelve years and one month ago. Across the way is the Amoco station where the mechanic worked who'd seen her storm away, toward Lincoln Cemetery. I hang a right and cruise past a row of eerie, run-down motels. Misshapen men in groups of two and three peer back at me from each parking lot. A few blocks down, on the left, I spot a high stone arch over a tiny dirt drive leading up into the graveyard where Anastasia was killed. All these visits to Kansas City, and I've never come to check the place out. My heart accelerates into a cantering beat. I'm spooked but drawn in.

The gravel road winds its way through the cemetery, and somewhere halfway around the loop, I pull over, kill the engine, and climb outside. It's intensely dark and quiet. The sky has

rained itself out, but in the trees above me, raindrops gently pat-
ter from leaf to leaf. I pad my way twenty feet from the road, find
a seat in the damp grass between a pair of headstones, and lie
back, curled in my coat, staring up into the darkness.

This could be the spot where Anastasia was found, or maybe
it was another part of the cemetery close by, it doesn't really
matter. I feel plagued by the mystery of what happened to her
that night, ripped up, torn asunder. I mean, it's the fucking future already. Technology won. There are few mysteries left in
the world—we know who's calling our phone when it rings; we
know how to sew a soldier's leg back on, or Skype with someone
in Mozambique, or play with remote-controlled cars on Mars; if
I want to, I can text ChaCha and find out how fucking poison-
arrow frogs make their fucking poison. Why can't someone tell
me with absolute certainty what happened to Anastasia?

I find myself a little choked up, not for Byron, not for Evelyn,
nor for Justin's family, or Robert WitbolsFeugen, but for Anastasia herself. She was shot while facing her attacker. She had to
know what was coming. Did she hear the sound of it? Did she
see the flash of light at the tip of the muzzle? I know what Anastasia's voice sounds like from the brief, haunting audio clips that
her family has posted on her memorial site, and as terrible and
disturbing as it is, I can't help but imagine the sound of her letting out a cry as her killer stepped close. Even if she'd entered a
suicide pact with Justin, in the moment before he pulled the
trigger, it seems to me, she might have wished for him to call it
all off. I think of Justin, or whoever killed her, and how dam-
aged they must have been to have done what they'd done, their
cold amazement in the moment after. It's all too much. I'm shredded, squeezed, incensed, and I feel like screaming from anger
and sorrow. In the trees above me, owls hoot in the night.

A figure steps toward me in the darkness, a shadow in the
shadows, accompanied by the sounds of sticks breaking under its
feet, and I sit bolt upright and start scrambling backwards, heart

clanging, my breath caught in my throat. "Who's there?" I say sharply, jarred by the fear in my own voice.

"Dude, what the fuck." As soon as I hear him speak, I realize right away it's only Peter, and sag back on my elbows in relief. "What the hell's wrong with you?" he asks. "Don't you remember, we've got a radio thing? We're supposed to be in Omaha by noon."

"Yeah, I know. I just wanted to make a little stop." I grab hold of a tree trunk, pull myself to my feet, and slap the wet grass and leaves from my pants. My emotional reverie has quickly flared out, and I know it's time to move on. "Think you can drive for a while?" I ask Peter.

"I guess. Give me the keys."

I settle into the bed in the back of the van and watch out the window as we roll down Truman Road, back onto the interstate, and join the quiet stream of traffic headed west. It starts to rain again. All I can see are dark wet forests, punctuated by the occasional flash of a green highway sign, or the zillion-watt glare of a passing billboard. We could be anywhere in America. After a few minutes, I close my eyes and fall into a dreamless sleep. By the time I wake up, hours later, at some cold gas station, the sky's already getting light, though the sun's not up yet, and we've left Missouri behind.

AIN'T THAT AMERICA?

I was introduced to Anna, the British girl, one April a few years ago at a crowded, upscale bar in West Hollywood called the Village Idiot. She was a friend of a friend, which earned me the chance to chat her up without any of the awkwardness of macking on a stranger. As our conversation blossomed, I could hardly believe my luck—with her wide blue eyes, delicate nose, and genuine, radiant smile, she was easily the most beautiful girl in the room, and though she was only twenty-five, she was also probably the most accomplished. I realized, as I asked her questions about her day and she laughed and talked on in her cheery British accent, that this was the girl my friend had been marveling about and telling me he wanted to introduce me to. She'd published her first novel at nineteen, directed two prize-winning documentaries in her early twenties, and was regarded back home as one of England's finest young creative talents. She'd come to L.A. for a two-year screenwriting program, and was set to return to London in a few weeks to finish her biography of former prime minister Tony Blair—who was a family friend—and then begin shooting her first narrative feature.

A part of me was amazed that in this bar, surrounded by a sea of gorgeous, dapper, successful men, she'd locked in with me, the small-town dude in grubby maroon pants and a Rasheed Wallace jersey, just visiting from Michigan. I had no statuettes on my desk, no house in the hills. In fact, I'd slept the last three weeks in a battered recliner on the back porch of a friend's house near Pico and La Brea, and had been spending my days shooting hoops alone at the park and my nights putting together a zine made of trash found on the street. But she was cool like that—she didn't seem to notice a single one of those tanned Hollywood heroes, the actors, agents, directors, and producers. And I suppose that when I drink I've got the gift of gab, and that can go a long way. It did that night, at least. Before we left the Village Idiot, me in my rented pickup, her with the friend of mine who'd delivered her to me (God bless you, Sam Hansen), she'd agreed to go on a date with me—an ambitious date, really—an overnight trip to Joshua Tree.

All clean-shaven, spic-and-span, I picked her up at her apartment in Los Feliz the next Friday around two in the afternoon, and we barreled east on I-10 toward Palm Springs, telling long, funny, intricate stories to each other. Anna's generous laugh and persistent curiosity made me feel like the most interesting guy in the world. And her stories fascinated me—rivalries at school; travels in Laos; family sadnesses; Labour Party political imbroglios—all told with a mix of intelligence, thoughtfulness, and compassion, but not without a certain edge. The sweet, expressive timbre of her voice, along with the endearing accent, diction, and casual Britishisms, made for an intoxicating brew.

"I love the way you say the word 'literally,'" I told her. *"Littrilly."*

She fumed, playfully defensive. "And how is one supposed to say it?"

"Lit-er-ull-lee."

"Lit-trilly," she said, and started to laugh. "Damn you, I littrilly can't say it right!"

Focused on the road, I allowed myself only an occasional

sideways glance, and instead let myself fall into the delightful swoops and swirls of her words. It was like falling in love with a stranger over the phone, except she was right there beside me, in a giant pickup zooming for the desert. This was it! At long last I'd found a soulmate, a kindred spirit, and each new, unsurpassable level of happiness I experienced was surpassed twelve minutes later, as one of us came to the end of a merry, strange, or melancholy tale and we sat in connected silence for a moment, only to be blown past once more eleven minutes later, when the next story had reached its finish. We swung off the interstate onto Highway 62, steep and winding, and ascended into the high desert, through the town of Joshua Tree, as the sun loped along, low in the sky, and radio signals faded. Soon we reached Twenty-nine Palms, where Anna marveled at the glut of gun stores, tattoo parlors, and barber shops (Stud Cuts, Stud Cuts #2, and Stud Cuts #3) which serviced the local Marine base, and I pointed out each trippy desert mural splashed on the sides of abandoned buildings.

I can't say it was the most well-planned move, zipping past the boutique hotel where I'd booked us a bungalow and heading straight for the National Park, but I didn't feel like playing the percentages and bunting my way onto base, I felt like swinging for the fences. I knew where I wanted to be at sunset, and that was with Anna atop a giant hunk of rock called Ryan Mountain, my favorite spot in the park. We drove through miles of red, dusty terrain and pulled into an empty lot by the roadside trailhead; it was late in the day and any other visitors had long since cleared out. I warned Anna that to reach the peak meant a tough ninety-minute climb. Some girls might've been put off by the prospect of such a hike; Anna pranced ahead like a gazelle, noting the subtle shades of beige, green, and purple in the desert rocks and vegetation, while I huffed and puffed a few steps behind her. Along the trail, she told me the story of her parents' odd courtship, and how a month after their wedding her mom had fled for another man, but then, a year later, had come back home to her dad, without a hiccup in their marriage, remarkably, or any lingering resentments. I shared my own family history, telling stories I'd never told before, maybe because no one had ever asked. Our conversation felt like one continuous spool of lustrous yarn that stretched from the bar the weekend before to the cab of my rental F-150 to the desert mountain switchbacks.

When we finally reached the top, close to dusk, we both fell into stunned silence at the majestic three-sixty view—the desert floor, far below, rippling gently for miles and miles, distant mountain ranges on three sides, bathed in golden light, and to the south, like a wide, flat gem, the Salton Sea. It was an eagle's perspective, and the periodic gusts of wind combined with our great height made it feel like we were actually flying. I cracked open two minibottles of white wine I'd carried up the hill in the pouch of my hoodie, and wordlessly we clanked to our good fortune, the glories of nature, and the kickass turns of luck life doles out once in a while if you let it, and are open to adventure. Then I pulled Anna close, and right before we kissed her eyes flashed as they met mine, and then I closed my eyes and we kissed long and hard, and I'll tell you, from what I've heard old-timers say, a moment like that you hold close on dark days, a moment like that you take with you to the grave. Overhead, one by one, the stars marched in.

No one falls out of love in this story. Nothing sours. Not exactly. That night, back in our elegant hut on the grounds of the Twenty-nine Palms Inn, I drank so much, in celebration, that I spilled open my mind and let Anna rake through the contents like a kid with a sack of Lego blocks. I told her my every wish and dream, the plots, beat by beat, of all the movies I wanted to one day make, and the details of shit I'd witnessed as a kid that had mystified me or made me sad. She embraced it all with good humor and kindness, listening with an intensity that felt almost inconceivably generous. (She may have been drunk, too.) We had a pillow fight. We made out. We tickled each other. I played her songs by a white Phoenix rapper I'd seen perform in an empty club and had become obsessed with; she sang me ridiculous tunes that she claimed all British kids learn at summer camp. In a way, Anna's looks and exotic speech reminded me of June Gudmundsdottir, the character played by Greta Scacchi in the Robert Altman movie *The Player*, who'd defined sexiness for me throughout college. But when I told her that she took offense. "I've seen that movie," she protested. "She shacks up with the guy who killed her boyfriend!" We stepped outside to peek at the stars. The alcohol, combined with my wild, swooning emotions, made me feel like I was flipping on 'shrooms, and the constellations pranced and swayed in a shimmering fresco. "How can the desert be so cold?" asked Anna, tugging me back inside.

In my backpack, I had a recent issue of *The Believer*, which contained a sheet of temporary tattoos—a Winnebago, a battle-axe wedged into a heart, a pair of spooning otters, a finely detailed portrait of the Chinese dissident artist Ai Weiwei. Anna and I didn't make love that night—I feared that if we did it would seem to her like that was the sole reason I'd lured her to the desert—but perhaps with equal intimacy, we peeled the tattoos loose one at a time from their cellophane sheet in the magazine and licked them and affixed them to each other's bodies in the softly lit bedroom, and at last, around five a.m., fell asleep, all but naked in each other's arms.

The next afternoon, once our hangovers had subsided a bit and we could move again, we piled our things into the Ford pickup and started the drive back toward the city—Anna had to meet with two fellow students who were working with her on a group project due in a couple of days. We'd spent the morning sick, sweating out the booze, but there was something romantic and tender involved; it was like our whole lives had flattened and compressed, and we'd become an old, ailing couple, taking care of each other. We'd pounded Advils, joked around a bit, still drunk, kind of, admiring each other's tattoos, and then dozed with our arms draped here and there and our hands joined. Around three I snuck out and brought back some French toast and waffles from a diner down the road, which we ate in bed, like a honeymoon couple, before packing up to head for L.A.

The afternoon sun was scorching, and we closed up the windows and pumped the AC. I decided to take the scenic route and cut through the National Park to I-10 because it didn't add too many miles and I'd never been down that road before. It felt like driving on an alien planet: we cruised through strange fields of enormous boulders, across plains of twisted red rock, as bizarre, towering cacti that looked stitched together from giant pipe cleaners waved their tentacles at us from the shoulder. Anna kept marveling at how human-like the ubiquitous Joshua trees seemed to be, each one uniquely expressive, its lower limbs extended like a pair of arms, and its third limb, up high, a craned neck, with a head and face screwed on top. We laughed, ascribing them separate human emotions and stories. "That one's pissed off because you didn't clean your room," Anna said. "She's sending you to bed without dinner!"

"You're right!" I cried. "Wait, check out that one with the broken branch. He's begging his bookie for another week to come up with the money."

"And there's the bookie!" Anna said, pointing down the road. "He's calling his enforcer to come finish the job."

This merriment continued for forty-five minutes. At the far end of the park, we stopped to refill water bottles at a rest area, and then lapsed into silence as we passed the gate at the south entrance and coasted down a long steep hill, where a stream of cars, pickups, and big rigs came into sight, hurtling west along

I-10. Somehow the sight of the interstate broke the spell of the past twenty-four hours, and I was struck by a wave of sadness and anxiety, worried that our return to civilization might cause Anna's affections to taper off. No matter how perfect things go the first night you spend with someone, in those early stages everything is still fragile and precarious, and you never know what surprises lie around the bend. I stole a glance at her: arms crossed, brow furrowed, like something in her had shifted, although her neck and shoulders were still swathed in temporary tattoos, a reminder of the previous night's adventures. Behind her, the sun settled toward the horizon and the sky filled with a red glow.

"You know," she began, very quietly, "this is as much fun as I've had since I've been in the States. It's like, we get on so well, it's easy to imagine if you were my boyfriend or something, how things could be, but I'm going home in a few weeks, and how would it really work to be with someone and live on separate continents? I don't think it could work."

Whatever her concerns about distance, her words thrilled me and filled me with glee. I'd been too cautious to say anything of the sort or expect too much from one night in the desert, no matter how magical (though this might also have been the first time I'd been invited to enter a relationship and then booted out of it in the same line of thought). I wasn't too crushed—any obstacles before us, it seemed, could surely be hurdled. As we rolled down the entrance ramp onto I-10, caught speed, and merged with the flow of traffic, we began to parse the possibilities. Would she be willing to stay on in the U.S.—if not Ann Arbor, maybe L.A. or New York? Not possible, she said. She had to get back to London to finish her book on Tony Blair. After that, she had other projects already in the pipeline with friends in the U.K. Besides, she said, she'd spent the past two years in the States, far from her friends and family, and she was ready to be home.

So the other option was for me to head to England. "Would you ever consider that?" Anna asked. On the one hand, it seemed crazy to uproot myself and move across the globe for a girl I'd spent one night with; on the other hand, Anna was completely dazzling, and I could picture us leading a life of unbounded happiness and fulfillment—writing books together at her family's country place in Devon; traveling to exotic corners of the world to shoot documentaries; raising kind, grounded, cosmopolitan children—and it seemed crazy not to. Before I had a chance to respond, though, I felt the truck suddenly drained of its power.

I jammed my foot on the gas pedal, once, twice, and again, to no avail. A quick glance at the gauges, which apparently I'd been blind to, told me all I needed to know: we were out of gas, beyond empty. The engine hadn't so much thrown its hands up and quit as submitted to an instant, powerful slumber. A trucker in the semi behind us laid on his horn, and I hit the blinkers and guided us off the highway onto the wide shoulder, where we slowly drifted to a stop.

"What's wrong?" said Anna. Without AC, the desert heat quickly began to flood the cab of our pickup.

"Out of gas," I said with embarrassment.

I'd always prided myself on being a masterful marathon driver, but I did have the tendency, from time to time, to run a tank dry and find myself stranded. The ramp where we'd gotten on the interstate was only a mile or two back, but it was in the middle of nowhere, and I was sure I hadn't seen any gas stations. I looked at my phone—no service out here; I couldn't call for roadside assistance. There was only one thing to do, the same thing I'd done the other half dozen times I'd found myself in this sort of predicament: hitch a ride. It couldn't be that far to the next exit, I figured, where I could fill a gas can and catch a ride back. But with dusk moving in, and headlights popping on in the opposite lanes, I knew my window of opportunity was closing fast. It's not so hard, most of the time, to catch a ride in daylight hours; after dark, it's next to impossible. No sense dillydallying. "Look," I said to Anna, "I am *so* sorry. I'm a total idiot. Just hang tight, and I'll be right back." I jumped down from the truck, faced the oncoming traffic, and stuck out my thumb.

The very first vehicle to pass us was an old black van with dark tinted windows. Its brake lights flashed red, and I watched it swerve onto the shoulder, fishtail a bit on a patch of wind-blown gravel, and come to a stop about a hundred yards ahead. I took off, jogging after it, and watched two figures emerge from the passenger side and head toward me. We met in the middle, halfway between my truck and their van, a small, wiry man in his forties, nose and cheeks brushed red by the sun, wearing a black T-shirt and a desert-camo baseball cap that said *It's Miller Time!* and his shy-looking son, shirtless, maybe fourteen years old, with dark, stringy hair and the first wisps of a mustache, only an inch or two shorter than his dad.

"What's the story?" the man shouted, over the howl of passing semis, a touch of beer on his breath.

"Ran out of gas. Can I get a ride?"

He gave me a quick once-over, taking note, it seemed, of the temporary tattoos clustered around my neck from my chin down, cholo-style, disappearing into the collar of my shirt. "It's a ways to the next town," he said. Then he pointed at my neck, with a degree of suspicion. "Who's that?"

"Which one?" I had no idea which tattoos had ended up where.

"Funny-looking guy with the beard. That your dad or some-thin'?"

"Oh, that's got to be Ai Weiwei. He's this Chinese artist and political activist. Always under threat of being locked up by the state because of his views."

He gave me a look. "A rebel, huh? I like that."

I nodded, not sure if he meant Ai Weiwei or me. Cars went shrieking past, just a few feet away from us. It's strange how safe it feels to be inside one, rocketing along at eighty-five or ninety miles an hour, and how dangerous it feels to be on the shoulder, changing a flat tire, or hoping a stranger will give you a lift, as traffic whips by.

"Any weapons on ya?" the guy asked. "Pistol? Knife?"

"Nope. Nothing." I patted myself at the hips: *See? I'm not packin'.*

He glanced at his son, rubbed his chin, smiled for the first time, and said, "Well, come on then, let's hit it," and hurried back toward the van, his son at his heels. I turned quickly, waved my hand, and flashed Anna a thumbs-up, though from that distance I didn't know if she could see me, and then whirled after Miller Time and his boy. When we reached the van, the dad hopped in up front, riding shotgun, and the boy popped open the side doors and climbed in. The back of the van, I could see, had been stripped of its seats, and from the darkness, a pack of kids crowded across the floor gaped at me blankly, like a family of raccoons peering from inside a storm drain. Loud country music twanged over the radio. Behind the wheel, a robust middle-aged blond woman sang along. She craned her head around. "You coming or what?" she shouted.

"Danny, give the man a hand and help him up," said Miller Time.

His son and another boy reached out their hands and hauled me in, and before they'd even closed the doors, I heard the wheels spinning in the gravel and catching hold. I lost my balance and pitched to the floor at the back of the van, and as we shot off westbound, Miller Time cackled with glee, slapped the dashboard, and hollered, "That's right, boys, the Black Stallion rides again! Giddyap! Giddyap! *C'mon, git!*"

Gradually my eyes adjusted to the darkness. There were five boys in the back with me—Danny and a red-haired friend of his, lying with their legs out, propped on their elbows, passing a handheld video game back and forth and fiddling with their cell phones; two younger boys, eight or nine years old, sitting cross-legged, sipping red straws from Burger King soda cups, watching me with wide eyes; and one giant, oversized boy with buzz-cut hair who looked between all of them in age, eleven or twelve, but was by far the largest of the bunch, hunched closest to the front, facing me, gazing with fierce concentration at a small plastic toy held inches from his face.

"What you got there?" I called out to him, over the country song's rock-and-roll ruckus.

He made no response, but one of the younger kids leaned toward me and hollered, "It's a game. You got to get all the marbles in the right place to win. Can't nobody do it, though!"

I nodded and sat back. I was wedged between Danny and his friend and a stack of a dozen hard, black plastic cases, long and flat, the kind that might house electric guitars. "Your dad a musician?" I asked Danny, but he was playing his video game and didn't seem to hear me, and the two younger kids stared at me without a response.

I looked out the back windows. Darkness had fallen, and all I could see was the glare of headlights behind us, red taillights in the eastbound lanes. I wondered how Anna was faring, stuck in the hot cab of our pickup. It occurred to me that I should've pulled farther onto the shoulder—each passing truck, I was sure, was rocking the whole vehicle. I checked my phone to see if I had service yet, and saw that my battery had all but drained itself, searching for a signal.

Up front, Miller Time turned his head and shouted, "All right, you boys ready for some more of this?" Danny winced and shook his head with an embarrassed smile, but the two youngest boys faced forward with looks of delight. I had no idea what to expect.

Miller Time rolled down his window, and as the hot, singed

desert air whipped inside the van, he took off his hat, leaned his head outside, and stood, so that his whole upper body was flapping in the breeze, silhouetted against the sky's dark-red, post-sunset glow. We pulled up alongside the cab of an eighteen-wheeler in the right lane, and he shouted, "Hey there, look at my titties!" and lifted his shirt, showing off his lean, hairless chest. He pumped a fist, asking the trucker to tug on his horn, and when the trucker responded with two short, bellowing blasts, he gave a wild, victorious whoop and dropped back into his seat, laughing so hard his whole body shook. "That was a good one," he called back to us. "Come on, let's do another!"

Some truckers honked their horn; others didn't. But it was undeniably hilarious, the surprised, amused looks on the truckers' faces, and the joy that Miller Time seemed to take from springing himself on them. I wished Anna was with me to see it. The woman piloting our van—Miller Time's wife? girlfriend?— played gamely along, speeding to catch up to each semi and then falling in right alongside them until he flashed them his chest, before she pounded the gas and we zoomed away. "I wanna try," said the youngest kid, steadying himself on his feet and working his way up front.

"You crazy?" shouted Miller Time with a laugh. "You'd fly right out the window!"

Finally, he sat back, rolled his window up, popped his cap back on, and turned his attention to the radio dial. The country station was fading, and he switched it to a metal station and began singing along to a metal tune he didn't seem to actually know, shouting nonsense lyrics and thrashing his head. Danny and his friend exchanged bemused, worried glances. When the song ended, he found a hip-hop station and started rapping along, making up the words, and waving his hands in the air. This, apparently, was what it took to finally win over Danny and his friend. They broke out in big, goofy smiles and laughed out loud. All the while, the oversized kid with the buzz cut never took his eyes off his marble puzzle, sullen as a swan in winter.

I appreciated the guy's good-natured clowning, but it felt like we were passing a number of exits without getting off the highway. Granted, they'd all looked completely barren, not a gas station in sight, but every mile we drove west was another mile I'd have to hitch back, and I was getting worried about leaving Anna alone for so long in the middle of nowhere. I felt eager to resume the conversation with her about our joint future, which felt, each moment, to be slipping further away.

"Where you guys headed?" I called out to Danny, over the thumping beat.

"Home," he said.

"Where's that?"

"Downey."

This, I knew, was a blue-collar suburb of L.A., though I couldn't have pointed it out on a map. "Where you coming from?"

"Oh, just out in the desert," he said.

"Hiking?"

"Nah. Shootin'."

"Yeah? What do you hunt out here?"

"Nah! Shootin'!"

He gestured toward the black cases I was leaning against. "Wanna see?" Without waiting for my response, he crawled around me and popped the lid on one. Inside was an enormous black machine gun, maybe the biggest gun I'd ever seen, like something out of *Die Hard*. "Pretty sweet, right?"

"Yeah. Wow." I felt stupid for having imagined that they were all musical instruments.

"It's my dad's. He was in the Marines," he said, by way of explanation. "Now he's a fireman." He shifted the cases around, lifting each lid to reveal an astounding, frightening array of automatic weapons, one after another. Growing up in Michigan, I'd seen my share of hunting rifles and shotguns, but never this kind of Desert Storm arsenal. "Hey," he said, "let me show you mine." All of a sudden the music went silent and his dad's voice boomed from the front.

"Danny, what the hell are you doing? Don't mess with those while we're driving, you know better than that!" Chastised, Danny hustled back to his seat on the floor next to his friend. "You see that?" Miller Time said to his girl, incredulous, speaking loud enough for all of us to hear. She shrugged, and after a moment, the music came back on.

Danny's friend, the red-haired kid, eyed me and said, "Hey, were you in prison?"

"Me?" I said. "No. Maybe a night or two in jail." If my neck tattoos made me seem like that much of a badass, I thought, I'd have to get the actual ink done. "What made you think that?" I asked.

"Danny told me," he said. He held up his phone, and grinned. "We've been texting."

"You guys have service?" I pulled out my phone but it was still out of range.

"Yeah, I thought that's what you told my dad," explained Danny. "When we picked you up. You said you were locked up. Or just got out or something."

I understood the confusion. "Oh, no, I was talking about Ai Weiwei. This guy." I tapped my neck, and explained how the Chinese authorities had often harassed him for his political muckraking.

"That your friend?" asked the red-haired kid.

"Well, I don't know him personally. But I admire his work, I suppose."

"My dad's in prison," the kid said. "But Danny's dad takes me shootin'."

"Hey, hang on a minute," I said. After half an hour on the road, we'd finally reached civilization, signs for fast-food joints and a truck stop cropping up along the shoulder, and it looked like at last my phone had reception. I tried dialing Anna, doubting she'd even have service, but her phone started to ring, rather than going straight to voice mail, and I felt hopeful that I might get through. Then the ringing stopped and the line went quiet.

"Anna!" I said. "Are you there? Can you hear me? You doing all right?" But as I waited for a response, my phone made a *bloop* and cut out, powering down on its own, out of juice. "Damn," I said. I could've asked Danny or his friend to use their phone, if I'd known Anna's number by heart.

"Your wife's stuck back there, huh?" said Danny.

"Yeah," I said, and experimented with the words: "My wife." It gave me a little charge, like touching a nine-volt battery to the tongue.

Some old, melancholy country song filled the van, and we coasted into the right-hand lane, approaching an exit. I realized that there was only one thing to do, and that was to say *fuck it*, take a chance, roll the dice, and move with Anna to London. We could even get separate places at first, so that we could date for a while like normal people, before moving in with each other. It would be hard to leave all my friends and family in Michigan behind, but after years and years of fighting to find the perfect girl, why give up on something just because it required sacrifice? If things didn't work out, I could always come home again, and if they did work out, well, maybe one day I'd be able to convince Anna that we should move back to the U.S. It was thrilling beyond measure and at the same time a little bit heartbreaking to imagine myself, a few weeks later, getting dropped off by my dad at the airport in Detroit, hugging him goodbye, and telling him, "All right then, I'll see you when I see you."

Our van curved off at the Indio exit, slow-rolled a stop sign, and swung into the lot of a Roadside 76 station. I hopped out, offering my profuse thanks.

"It's nothing," said Miller Time. "We never leave a man

behind in the desert. Hey, you want anything from Jack in the Box?"

"No thanks, I'm good. But seriously, you guys, thanks again."

I closed the side doors behind me, and Miller Time, his woman, all five boys, and their Nakatomi Plaza–worthy stash of weapons rolled away in the van. Over the roar of the exhaust and the music's receding din, I could hear Miller Time whooping it up, "Giddyap! Giddyap! *C'mon, git!*" And then they were gone, as quickly as they'd appeared.

"We don't have gas cans here," the ancient counter clerk told me, inside the Roadside 76 station, a half minute later. "You can try the Texaco, it's a couple miles down the road."

Fuck. That meant a lengthy walk, or else begging one ride to the next gas station, then another back the other direction, toward the spot where Anna was staked out waiting for me, twenty-five or thirty miles east. But an old woman who'd overheard the conversation said she thought she had a spare gas can in her trunk, and returned a minute later with an antique-looking one, healthy sized, painted green and made out of metal, sporting a John Deere logo. "You sure?" I asked her. I'd seen these go for fifty bucks at estate sales.

"Tell you what," she said. "When you're done with it, just drop it back here. Henry'll get it to me. Right, Henry?"

The old clerk nodded. "Okay, Darlene." I thanked her and she went on her way.

Outside I pumped three gallons in, and then started explaining my situation to anyone who pulled in for a fill-up, asking if they were headed east. But my luck had run dry: each of them edged cautiously away from me, as though I was one of those hustlers with complicated appeals for help you'll come across in shady neighborhoods outside of baseball stadiums or floating around Greyhound stations late at night. They all seemed to be locals, with destinations close by, or at least claimed that was the case after taking stock of all the tattoos on my neck and my arms. The best bet, I guessed, was to cross the highway and work the entrance ramp for I-10 with my thumb out. I knew it could be a long wait. Few people stopped for hitchhikers at night; fewer still would want my old gas can spewing fumes inside their car. As I cast about for other motorists to accost, I saw, to my great astonishment and relief, that the Black Stallion had returned: the same black van that had stopped for me before was clattering back into the lot, its horn honking, *Shave-and-a-haircut, two bits.* Miller Time had his window rolled down, and he slapped the side of his door as they pulled up next to me. "Come on, Tumbleweed!" he called. "Hop in!"

He laughed, as his woman steered us over a bridge and down the eastbound entrance ramp for the interstate. "What'd ya think?" he said. "We was gonna leave you for the coyotes?" He hooted and hawed, his enjoyment of the joke nearly equal to my surprise and gratitude at the sheer depth of their generosity. I tried to tell him how much I appreciated them coming back for me and he cut me off. "Nah, we just had to get some food for the little guys and some drinks for me. Here, ya want one?" He passed me a tallboy of Budweiser, which somehow seemed funny to me, with his *Miller Time* ball cap and all. "I told you," he went on. "We don't leave *no one* behind. *Especially* out here in the desert."

"Well, can I at least offer you a few bucks for gas?"

He waved his hand, slightly offended. "Just have a drink with me."

I propped the gas can in the door well, far from the weapons cases and ammunition, settled into my spot way in the back, and we wound our way east along I-10 the way we'd come. The wild atmosphere of our westbound ride had been replaced with the quiet, focused intensity of mealtime. No one said a word; everyone was devouring their burgers and chicken sandwiches from Jack in the Box. Even the oversized kid with the buzz cut had given up on his marble game for the time being and double-fisted a burger and a chocolate shake. The radio was pumped up high, some classic rock and oldies station. I looked out the window at distant lights across the desert plains, nursing my Budweiser as the miles slid by.

Fifteen, twenty minutes later, all the boys had finished their food, crumpled up their bags, and, giggling, tossed them up front at Miller Time, who wearily chucked the first couple back our way, and then ignored the rest. "Now, here's a tune," he said, cranking up the volume so loud that the speakers were crackling. It was John Cougar Mellencamp singing:

Oh, ain't that America? You and me . . .
Ain't that America? Somethin' to see . . .

This, from what I knew of it, was one of those songs, like Bruce Springsteen's "Born in the U.S.A.," that had been written as a eulogy for the dying American Dream but had been so widely misinterpreted as an anthem of patriotism and working-class pride that its original intent had been usurped in the popular imagination. And, actually, when you really thought about it, the artists were wrong and the popular imagination was right, for how could you listen to Mellencamp sing the chorus and not feel stirred by a love for America, whatever its shortcomings might be? As the song went on, Miller Time lifted his voice to sing along, his can of Bud held aloft and swaying, like a candle at an arena rock show, and when the chorus returned he shouted, "Everybody now!" to press the boys in back—and me, too, I guess—to join in.

I'd actually once been to the old, sagging farmhouse in Brownstown, Indiana, where Mellencamp had recorded this tune "Pink Houses," down in the Dagobah-like bogs and hollows near the Kentucky border, and I found myself thinking about the strange, dilapidated beauty of that part of the country.

The song continued, swelling into its next verse, and I couldn't help but think of the beauty and sadness of a lot of the places I'd been and a lot of the roads I'd traveled, a montage of Americana imagery with a personal bent. As corny as it might sound, I felt moved by the song in a way I never had been the other eight thousand times I'd heard it, maybe because before the past hour and a half, I'd never really considered leaving the country for good, and you can't truly appreciate something until it's slipped from your grasp, or is about to.

And if I stopped to think about it, how could I really leave home and abandon my country? Here, apparently, bighearted Marines in vans packed full of machine guns traipsed the land, rescuing stranded travelers. Try finding that in England. But it was more than that: some of my best friends were transplants from places like India, Senegal, and Sweden, and as grateful as they were for the (mostly) kind ways they'd been treated in the United States and the opportunities that had come their way, they were also honest about their divided hearts, that weird gnawing ache of living in an adopted home that even with its blessings can never truly feel like home. Could I give up my home for Anna? She was an angel, brilliant, cool as fuck, and it killed me to think of throwing in the towel on something magnificent before it even had a chance to really start, but maybe, in spite of everything I'd believed—or had wanted to believe—about my own impulsive sense of adventure, I wasn't ready to cash in my dollars for pounds and move across the pond for a chance at love. Maybe I'd hang around the U.S. a bit longer and see what else came my way. Maybe, as a couple of friends had told me, I didn't want to find love in the first place, because if I'd wanted to find it, they believed, I would've found it already. Maybe they were right, and that precious, terrible longing I felt every time I saw a girl who could be "the one" was an end in itself, and all I truly craved. As the last verse played, I chugged the rest of my Bud and buoyantly joined in, belting out the final chorus with Miller Time, his lady friend, and four out of the five boys, all of us singing with great feeling:

> *Oh, ain't that America? For you and me . . .*
> *Ain't that America? Somethin' to see, baby . . .*
> *Ain't that America, home of the free!*
> *Yeah, little pink houses for you and me.*

The song ended and Miller Time shut off the radio, passed another Budweiser back to me, and announced that he was taking a nap. He reclined his seat and planted his cap over his face. I cracked the beer and sat looking out the windows. Our communal sing-along high began to fade, and the night grew steadily cool and mournful. By now, we were just a few miles from where I'd left Anna in the truck. I often wished that I could split myself a hundred ways and live a hundred separate lives—one part of me might have whisked off to London to try and build a life together with Anna, while another part of me might have jumped ship, rolled along with Miller Time and his brood and built a life for myself in Downey, and still another part of me could keep on the same directionless path I'd been treading. But in the end, I supposed, we only had one life to lead, and the roads not taken would always outnumber and outshine the roads we ended up taking, day by day, without plan.

"There it is!" cried the youngest boy, who'd been gazing out the window with me. "That's your truck, right?"

Indeed, there it was, my pickup, abandoned on the distant shoulder, hazards still blinking, flashing in the lights of passing traffic, as trucks veered into the far lane to avoid coming too near. A quarter mile up the road, Miller Time's girlfriend spotted a gravel turnaround in the median and eased off the pavement into the dirt, kicking up pebbles and a cloud of dust behind us. She waited for a break in traffic, then spun into the westbound lanes, and pulled up right behind our pickup. Anna, in the cab, turned to look at us, her face ghostlike in the van's head-lights.

Miller Time came hazily awake. "We home?" He sat up a little. "Oh yeah, Tumbleweed."

I worked my way forward, opened the side door, and began to fumble through some kind of meaningful goodbye to every-body, but right at that moment, the big pudgy kid with the buzz cut, who hadn't said a single word the entire time I'd been with them, jerked his head up and shouted, "You guys, you guys, look, I did it! No way, *look*!" And balancing it with extreme care, he held his puzzle high to show off his hard-earned victory, every marble in its place, while the boys and even Miller Time himself marveled in amazement and gave him his props. The kid had stolen the thunder from any grand pronouncements I might have had, but that was okay, because what was there for me to really say but thanks and God bless?

I grabbed the gas can, stepped down from the van, shut the doors, and headed for the pickup, where I paused to empty all three gallons of gas into its thirsty tank. Finally, I rested the can in the bed of the truck. Anna reached over to unlock the driver's-side door, and I climbed inside. "You're back," she said with a smile, having already forgiven me, it seemed, for being such a dumbass and forgetting to fuel up. It was a joy to see her, though her beauty felt doubly painful, now that I'd put to rest, for the most part, any dreams of us living out our lives together.

"Yeah," I said. "Sorry that took so long." I watched in the side mirror as the Black Stallion edged back onto the highway and gently passed by, with nary a "Git!" nor a "Giddyap!"

"It's okay," Anna said. "I had my book with me. And I saw the most unbelievable sunset. Did you see it? Right over the road."

"I missed it, I guess."

"Oh, it was gorgeous. It was one of a kind. Spectacular, really."

"You know what that means," I said, as I started the engine, and, once traffic lulled, guided us back onto the freeway asphalt.

"It means, if we hadn't run out of gas, we could've driven off together into the sunset. Literally."

She laughed. *"Lit-trilly."*

"Yeah. Lit-er-ull-lee."

We fell quiet for a moment. "Well, I'll tell you what," she said. "There'll be other sunsets. There'll be another sunset tomorrow." But she seemed withdrawn, and her words felt coded. Was she saying we'd have other chances to watch the sun set together, or had she, in my absence, surrendered on our future as well—and by "other sunsets," did she mean other people for us to fall in love with?

"It won't be like this sunset," I said. "The one I missed out on. It'll be different. Inferior, maybe."

"There's a million sunsets out there," Anna said urgently. "Each one is magical." And with that, she slipped her seat belt off, slid across the seat, took my hand, and gave me a wondrous kiss on the cheek.

It wasn't all it could have been, perhaps, but in that moment, it was enough. I smiled and put my arm around her, floated over to the fast lane, and hit the gas, and we hightailed it for the coast, the desert at our backs, the city ahead. For a little while longer, at least, it was just the two of us and the road.

SHOUTS

This book wouldn't exist if it weren't for the openhearted generosity of the fellow drifters and wanderers who've crossed my path over the years and shared their stories with me, and the kind, alluring females I got all crazy about who tolerated my company for a moment or two. To all the dear friends, loved ones, and passersby depicted in these pages—under their real names or otherwise—I offer my heartfelt, enthusiastic thanks.

I have enormous gratitude for the many people who have made my travels so rich—had a drink with me, given me a place to sleep, or introduced me to adventure. Thank you! Your kindness means more than you know. Much love to my brother Peter, my longtime road partner, and the other brave souls who've joined us in the van—Brande Wix, Sarah Locke, David Meiklejohn, Andrew Cohn, Brett Loudermilk, Devon Sproule, Benoît Meulewaeter, Megan McDowell, Esther Rose, Javan Makhmali, Shawna Jo Lee, and Alex Gross, plus our tour partners Chandra and Leigh Watson, Nick Prueher and Joe Pickett, Eli Horowitz and John Brandon, and that stone-cold pimp Frank Warren. And giant thanks to my wise, loving, and inspiring parents, my incredibly kick-ass housemates, and the amazing communities in Ann Arbor and L.A. who always make coming home such a delight.

I learned how to write from Judith Dewoskin, Warren Hecht, Ken Mikolowski, Sara Corbett, Eileen Pollack, and Charlie Baxter—thank you for your hard work, generous spirit, and encouragement. Thanks to storytelling gurus Ira Glass, Julie Snyder, and Alex Blumberg; to the magazine editors I've been lucky enough to work with: Andy Ward, Mark Kirby, John Hodgman, Kevin Awakuni, Shaina Feinberg, Heidi Julavits, Andrew Snee, Tim McKee, Sy Safransky, Carlin Flora, Mike Dawson, Dave Swanson, Juliet Litman, Rafe Bartholomew, Jay Kang, Dan Fierman, and Lorin Stein; and serious props to some brilliant writers who have shown me great kindness: Dave Eggers, Miranda July, Jim Carroll, Jonathan Ames, Susan Orlean, Carrie Brownstein, Sarah Vowell, Elizabeth Gilbert, Aimee Bender, David Sedaris, Bill Simmons, Chuck Klosterman, and Tom Robbins.

For the gale-force inspiration, thank you to my brother Mike, Devin Friedman, Josh Bearman, Mike Kozura, Daniel "D Shot" Garvatt, Vaughn "Count Mack" Taormina, Luke "Classified" Boyd, Randy "Biggz" Ingram, "Mic Dangerous" DiBella, A-Side Worldwide, the Jenkers, the Del Rio Six, the Medora Hornets, Seth Bernard, Willis Earl Beal, Rae Spoon, Danny Schmidt, Kelli Shay Hicks, Will Sheff, Bob Ritchie, Carson Mell, Tim McIlrath, Joe Principe, Brandon Barnes, Zach Blair, the Gaskets, Frank and Muriel Salzman, Jeff Kass, Mark Borchardt, Allison Anders, Lynn Shelton, Dan Tice, Liam Murphy, the Sanford-Durant Family, the Brodsky Family, Mimi, Grandma Bobbie Mitchell, Deep Spring Center sangha, Elks Lodge #322, Alley Bar, Amanda Patten, Dean Bakopoulos, Rachel Dengiz, Brandon Baugh, Jason Orfanon, Brooke Bailey, Dan Zatkovich, Jalen Rose, Will Bynum, Anna Stothard, Chuck D, Tim Haldeman, Richard Frey, Hakim Selby, Byron Case, and all the other champions who keep me flying high. Thanks to the *Found* magazine team for their selfless service: James Molenda, Al McWilliams, Jason Bitner, and all the finders and friends who've made the *Found* family so meaningful. Thanks to T. Williams Samuels,

Sr., and Booker Noe for getting me into trouble. And thanks to A. J. Wilhelm for bailing me out of it too many times to count.

For their clutch assistance during the writing of this book, I want to thank the lovely Zoe Ruiz and the equally lovely Dani Davis. Much respect to Robb Bindler, Matthew McConaughey, and John Mellencamp for their kindness; also, to legal badass Sam Bayard. John Allen offered generous, invaluable assistance with my research for "The Strongest Man in the World." I encourage anyone who's curious to learn more about Byron Case's situation to read John's incredibly engaging and detailed book, *The Skeptical Juror and the Trial of Byron Case*, and to check out the website FreeByronCase.com.

At Farrar, Straus and Giroux, I've been blessed with a team of talented, dedicated, bighearted heroes: Emily Bell, whose ideas and constant support have been an immeasurable boost; Steve Weil, for being so damn down and going way beyond the call of duty; Mareike Grover, Ed Cohen, Rodrigo Corral, Spenser Lee, and Abby Kagan for their devoted contributions; and all the other kings and queens on West 18th Street. I have unlimited adoration for the folks who work so hard to make books the best they can be, and to get them into readers' hands. Thank you!

Three last crucial shouts to the three people who willed this book to life: my editor and friend, Sean McDonald, for his vision, humor, and perceptive insight, and a belief in me so dogged it's sometimes led me to shed a tear; my baller agent, Jud Laghi, who's been a lead blocker and trusted friend these past ten years; and the incomparable, exquisite Mary Margaret Box, whose love and friendship is an absolute blessing, proving that even the most idiotic of idiots can be cured.

Finally, my biggest thanks are reserved for you, dear reader, for hopping in and going for a ride with me. I wrote this book for you. Hope to see you on the road.

PEACE—DAVY